INTRODUCTORY LANGUAGE ESSAYS

Introductory
Language Essays

Edited by

DUDLEY BAILEY

UNIVERSITY OF NEBRASKA

NEW YORK
W · W · NORTON & COMPANY · INC ·

PRINTED IN THE UNITED STATES OF AMERICA
FOR THE PUBLISHERS BY THE VAIL-BALLOU PRESS, INC.

2 3 4 5 6 7 8 9 0

Contents

v

Preface

This is a digest of many books to make yet one more. And, to echo Samuel Johnson, it may seem like bread in a besieged city, where everybody gets a mouthful but nobody gets a meal. Certainly this is neither a comprehensive nor a systematic text. Though it touches on a number of the aspects of the study of modern English, it does not pretend to cover all of that remarkably rich and diffuse study; no one volume could hope to do so. Though much of it is concerned with the grammars of modern English, it does not pretend to be a systematic grammar of the language or a critique of the various grammars we have. It is based upon the assumption that the study of one's own language is a legitimate and basic study, as much an end in itself as any other study in the curriculum of the schools and not merely a means to good citizenship, more exact communication, or a higher salary. Yet this book is not meant to be the ultimate textbook at all. On the contrary, it is meant as an introduction. It may seem an odd introduction, at first glance; but I think it is an introduction in the oldest and best sense of that word—for it is designed to lead into a rewarding and fascinating study.

Most students inherit an all but universal ignorance of their own language and a consequent fear of it. Americans stand in uneasy awe of the "linguist," who speaks a language they do not comprehend and which they privately suspect. Americans also have an uneasy contempt for the "English teacher," before whom they protest that they must "watch their language"—and would, no doubt, if they knew how to go about it—but whom they honor rather less than teachers of other subject matters. Americans are almost unbearably voluble in situations which require only the vocabulary and linguistic patterns of childhood; they are almost unbelievably dumb in situations which require a mature command of the language they are supposed to speak. In short, Americans are linguistic adolescents. And their attitudes and behavior toward language everywhere show signs of adolescence—willful resistance, braggart pretense, mock humility, painful insecurity.

This text is designed as a partial antidote for this condition. And the essays in it are ordered with this condition in mind. The first essays presuppose no knowledge beyond what the average college freshman may be expected to have. As the text preceeds, more difficult concepts are introduced. By the time the student has studied the final essays, he should be able to read books on our language with reasonable confidence and understanding.

This text may be useful for advanced students preparing to teach English or to take graduate work; but it was designed for freshman English courses in which emphasis is placed upon the language as a subject matter worthy of serious study. It may strike some as too difficult for such students; but our experience at the University of Nebraska over the past five years has been that freshman students are capable of very demanding work and, more significantly, that their response to meaty assignments has been uniformly rewarding to themselves and their teachers alike. The limitation upon the subject matter of the essays is motivated in part by the desire to provide an adjunct textbook which will insure, by its limitations, some uniformity in multiple-sectioned courses and yet allow various instructors some elbowroom.

Two principal criteria underlie the selection of essays: readability and the depth of content. Unhappily, they are not always found together. The notion that a knowledge of one's language is certain to make for good writing reflects an attractive idealism, but a naive one; for some of our most knowledgeable linguists write abominably, and some of our most fetching writers on language are not entirely dependable. I have had to pick and choose, and I have not always been content with my choice. I have neither sought to correct "errors" nor presumed to rewrite opaque passages, hoping rather to give some notion of the range of writing about our language in small scope. Editorial changes in the essays have seldom gone beyond the deletion of cross-references and the addition of bracketed section numbers. The numbers have been inserted to expedite the student's study and reference to the text in class discussions, and are referred to in the summaries and notes at the ends of the essays.

In terms of the intended audience, the selections range from that of John Moore, meant for the general reading public, to that of Leonard Bloomfield, meant for reasonably advanced students of language; other selections fall between these extremes. None of the essays is easy in the sense that the daily newspaper is easy. Each presents facts and ideas which may be new and in some cases difficult. As Samuel Taylor Coleridge remarked of some of his essays, these selections will demand attention everywhere and in some places thought as well. The short summaries and notes for some of the essays are intended to direct and simplify note-taking and to explain some of the difficulties in the reading. But beyond them I have not invaded the proper domain of the instructor. Twenty years of teaching and a number of years of supervising large multiple-sectioned courses have taught me that instructors know much better than writers of textbooks how to conduct their classes.

Though these essays are not easy, students need not be foolishly fearful nor unrealistically humble. After all, even the least well-prepared have some understanding of their language. They know that it is not the only language in the world, that it is both spoken and written (and hence heard and read), and that the spoken and written versions of the language are different. They realize that the language of Shakespeare's time differs from the language of today—indeed, they realize that a sizable portion of our vocabulary did not exist a century ago (*automobile, airplane, nylon, penicillin, thermonuclear, cold war,* to cite but a few obvious examples)—and if they have read even one play of Shakespeare, they also know that part of the vocabulary of the seventeenth century is no longer part of our vocabulary. They may very well suspect that there are very different views toward language and that none of them is necessarily "wrong." Many will feel in agreement with the sentiments of a neighboring lawyer, who years ago replied, when I told him I taught English at the university, "What sort of English? I had never heard before and have never heard since the sort I was taught in school!" Such students should derive some aid and comfort from this introduction to the study of their language. For it runs counter to the "school" view of language which has dominated American education for a century and a half.

That "school" view of language study traces back to English grammars of the 1760s and especially to the *Short Introduction to English Grammar* of Bishop Robert Lowth, 1762. Bishop Lowth, reflecting views which were widely held in his day—and held surprisingly widely today, for that matter—thought that a study of language should be prescriptive, logical, and corrective in nature, and that English should be modeled upon Latin. That is, he thought the schools should prescribe what our language ought to be (we should say "had rather," not "would rather"; "have sung," not "have sang"; "I shall go," not "I will go"). Moreover, he thought we should speak "logically," and hence he argued that such a sentence as "I never hurt nobody," containing two negatives, really must mean "I hurt somebody." This view of language study centered upon "correction" of misspellings, of wrong forms, of awkward or inelegant expressions. And throughout, Latin was taken as a sort of ideal language toward which English *ought* to move.

Despite Bishop Lowth and his very formidable array of successors, Latin and English are very different sorts of languages. Language is not always logical; and English, like any other language that is not dead, changes as it will, despite the "rules" of grammarians. Long and vigorous application of the "school" view of the language has not only failed to "correct" the language but has frustrated and hobbled students instead. It is little wonder that we live in a world of linguistic adolescents.

The view of this book is quite different. It assumes that the proper study of language is descriptive, flexible, and coherent. In other words, we must take our language as it is, not as some self-appointed linguistic dictator thinks it ought to be; and we must realize that a living language changes from time to time, from place to place (Nebraska English and Georgia English are not identical), and from situation to situation (the language of the poolroom is not exactly the language of the Sunday school). Facing the facts of a variable language, we must strive for as sensible a description of it as the facts permit, if we are to say that we "understand" the sort of language we use.

Now, this view is often regarded as an attitude that "anything goes" or "whatever is, is right." It is nothing of the sort. No modern linguist speaks or writes like a thug or an ignoramus; none proposes that college students should speak and write like five-year-olds or bums. The linguist simply realizes that different sorts of English do exist. And he holds that, while poolroom English may be suitable for poolrooms, Sunday-school English for Sunday schools, legal English for legal briefs, and very formal English for a formal wedding invitation—still none of these is exactly suitable for the college classroom, or for courting a girl-friend. In short, the question of standards, of "good English," is not a question of moral right and wrong but rather a question of suitability to the occasion. The mark of an educated person is his ability to shift linguistic gears. The lawyer who always talks like a lawyer, the football coach who always talks like a football coach, the preacher who always talks like a preacher, the sorority girl who always talks like a sorority girl, and the professor who always talks like a professor are equally distressing individuals. We laugh at them all, and with good reason. Linguistically, they haven't grown up.

If one is to grow up linguistically, he must work at it. The permanent teeth appear, the body lengthens and fills out, the voice changes, the hair grays, whether we work at it or not. But our command of language does not come automatically. Admission to college does not bring with it linguistic respectability—and neither does graduation, as the lawyer, coach, and professor we laughed at above demonstrate. Neither, alas, can the study of language assure us of the mastery of our tongue. But unless we somehow gain an understanding of our language and develop an interest in exploiting its marvelously wide range of expression, linguistic immaturity is a dead certainty.

Good English of this sort, like a wife worth having, will come to one only if sought and sought diligently; and it will remain by him, a stay and comfort and source of great joy, only if continuously courted.

DUDLEY BAILEY

Acknowledgments

I owe thanks for encouragement and advice to my colleagues at the University of Nebraska, and especially to Gene B. Hardy, Paul A. Olson, and G. Thomas Fairclough. Harris Ward Wilson, of the University of Illinois, read the manuscript with care and offered many helpful suggestions. Mrs. Butler Shaffer gave generous assistance in the preparation of materials. The staff of the Otto G. Richter Library of the University of Miami extended me every courtesy, and I am particularly grateful to Archie McNeal, Robert Morgan, and George Rosner.

A fellowship from the Woods Charitable Fund allowed me freedom to gather and edit these materials.

My wife and sons and Dr. and Mrs. Virgil Barker of Miami managed to make work on the book a continuous pleasure.

D. B.

PART ONE   Some First Considerations

Language

H. A. GLEASON, JR.

Henry Allan Gleason, Jr., has taught linguistics at Hartford Semi-
nary since 1947. His Introduction to Descriptive Linguistics,
from which this selection is taken, has been widely used in ad-
vanced courses, but he deals with some of the basic questions in
language study with ease and lucidity.

[1]   As you listen to an unfamiliar language you get the impression of a torrent of disorganized noises carrying no sense
whatever. To the native speaker it is quite otherwise. He pays
little attention to the sounds, but concerns himself instead with
some situation which lies behind the act of speech and is, for him,
somehow reflected in it. Both you and he have failed to grasp the
nature of the phenomenon. Neither the casual observer nor the
usual native speaker can give any real information about a language. To be sure, some people, Americans perhaps more than
most others, have decided notions about language. But the ideas
held and discussed come far short of giving a complete picture of
the language and sometimes have very little relationship to the
facts. Even people with considerable education are often wholly
unable to answer certain quite simple questions about their language. For most people language is primarily a tool to be used,
rather than a subject for close and critical attention.

It is probably well that it is so. Yet there are important human problems into which language enters intimately and on which it exerts such a profound influence that an understanding of its mechanism would contribute materially to their solutions. Moreover, every phase of human activity is worthy of study. Thus, for practical reasons, as well as to satisfy man's innate curiosity, language deserves careful and intelligent study.

[2]   Language has so many interrelationships with various aspects of human life that it can be studied from numerous points of view. All are valid and useful, as well as interesting in themselves. Linguistics is the science which attempts to understand language from the point of view of its internal structure. It is not, of course, isolated and wholly autonomous, but it does have a clearly and sharply delimited field of inquiry, and has developed its own highly effective and quite characteristic method. It must draw upon such sciences as physical acoustics, communications theory, human physiology, psychology, and anthropology for certain basic concepts and necessary data. In return, linguistics makes its own essential contributions to these disciplines. But however closely it may be related to other sciences, it is clearly separate by reason of its own primary concern with the structure of language.

[3]   What then is this structure? Language operates with two kinds of material. One of these is sound. Almost any sort of noise that the human vocal apparatus can produce is used in some way in some language. The other is ideas, social situations, meanings— English lacks any really acceptable term to cover the whole range —the facts or fantasies about man's existence, the things man reacts to and tries to convey to his fellows. These two, insofar as they concern linguists, may conveniently be labeled *expression* and *content.*

The foreigner who hears merely a jumble of sounds has not really heard the language, not even the part of it which we have called *expression.* All that he has heard is sounds, the material which language uses to carry its message. This is not the domain of the linguist, but that of the physicist. The latter can analyze the stream of speech as sound and learn many things about it. His findings have both theoretical and practical importance; the designs of telephones, radios, and much other electronic equipment depends in an essential way upon such findings. They also contribute basic data to linguistics, and to numerous other sciences, including psychology and physiology, as well as to physics itself.

The linguist is concerned with sound as the medium by which information is conveyed. To serve in this way, speech must be something quite different from the jumble of sound apparent to the foreigner. It is, in fact, an organized system or structure, and it is this structure that lies within the subject field of linguistics. The linguist analyzes speech as an orderly sequence of specific kinds of sounds and of sequences of sounds. It is orderly in terms of a very complex set of patterns which repeatedly recur and which are at least partially predictable. These patterns form the structure of **expression,** one major component of language in the sense that the linguist uses the term.

The native speaker has his attention focused on something else, the subject of the discourse. This may be a situation which is being described, some ideas which are being presented, or some social formula which is being repeated. None of these things are language, any more than are the sounds which convey speech. The subject of the discourse stands on the opposite side and in much the same relationship to speech as do the sounds. The speaker comprehends what he is talking about in terms of an organizing structure. This structure causes him to select certain features for description and determines the ways in which he will interrelate them. It also cuts the situation up into portions in a characteristic way. These selected features, like the sounds mentioned above, also form patterns which recur, and which are at least partially predictable. These recurrent patterns are the structure of **content,** a second major component of language as the linguist treats it.

Finally, these two structures are intimately related and interacting. Parts of the structure of expression are associated in definite ways with parts of the structure of content. The relations between these two complex structures are themselves quite complex. In every language they are different from what is found in every other language. The differences may be profound and extensive, or they may be relatively slight. But in every instance, the two structures are intricate and their relationships quite characteristic.

[4]   The native speaker uses this complex apparatus easily and without conscious thought of the process. It seems to him simple and natural. But to a speaker of another of the world's three thousand languages it may present quite a different picture. It may give an impression of being cumbersome, illogical, or even ridiculous. Actually, of course, the strange language is merely different.

A true picture of language can only be had by seeing languages more objectively. Such a view will emphasize the immense complexity, the arbitrariness, and the high degree of adequacy for their purposes—features which are shared by all languages in spite of their divergencies.

[5]   The dual structure of language can best be made clear by an example. The more technical description which will follow later in this book will afford more refined examples, but the following will indicate something of the possibilities without involving complicated terminology or technical concepts.

Consider a rainbow or a spectrum from a prism. There is a continuous gradation of color from one end to the other. That is, at any point there is only a small difference in the colors immediately adjacent at either side. Yet an American describing it will list the hues as *red, orange, yellow, green, blue, purple,* or something of the kind. The continuous gradation of color which exists in nature is represented in language by a series of discrete categories. This is an instance of structuring of content. There is nothing inherent either in the spectrum or the human perception of it which would compel its division in this way. The specific method of division is part of the structure of English.

By contrast, speakers of other languages classify colors in much different ways. In the accompanying diagram, a rough indication is given of the way in which the spectral colors are divided by speakers of English, Shona (a language of Rhodesia), and Bassa (a language of Liberia).

ENGLISH

purple	blue	green	yel-low	orange	red

SHONA

cips*ʷ*uka	citema	cicena	cips*ʷ*uka

BASSA

hui	zīza

The Shona speaker divides the spectrum into three major portions. *Cips*ʷ*uka* occurs twice, but only because the red and purple ends, which he classifies as similar, are separated in the diagram. Interestingly enough, *citema* also includes black, and *cicena* white. In addition to these three terms, there are, of course, a large number of terms for more specific colors. These terms are comparable to English *crimson, scarlet, vermilion,* which are all varieties of *red*. The convention of dividing the spectrum into three parts instead of into six does not indicate any difference in visual ability to perceive colors, but only a difference in the way they are classified or structured by the language.

The Bassa speaker divides the spectrum in a radically different way: into only two major categories. In Bassa there are numerous terms for specific colors, but only these two for general classes of colors. It is easy for an American to conclude that the English division into six major colors is superior. For some purposes it probably is. But for others it may present real difficulties. Botanists have discovered that it does not allow sufficient generalization for discussion of flower colors. Yellows, oranges, and many reds are found to constitute one series. Blues, purples, and purplish reds constitute another. These two exhibit fundamental differences that must be treated as basic to any botanical description. In order to state the facts succinctly it has been necessary to coin two new and more general color terms, *xanthic* and *cyanic,* for these two groups. A Bassa-speaking botanist would be under no such necessity. He would find *zīza* and *hui* quite adequate for the purpose, since they happen to divide the spectrum in approximately the way necessary for this purpose.

[6] Now for a simple statement of structure in the expression part of language: The sounds used by English are grouped into consonants and vowels (and some other categories). These are organized into syllables in a quite definite and systematic way. Each syllable must have one and only one vowel sound. It may have one or more consonants before the vowel, and one or more after the vowel. There are quite intricate restrictions on the sequences that may occur. Of all the mathematically possible combinations of English sounds, only a small portion are admitted as complying with the patterns of English structure. Not all of these are actually used, though the unused ones stand ready in case they should ever be needed. Perhaps some day a word like *ving* may appear in response to a new need. *Shmoo* was drawn out of this stock of unused possibilities only a few years ago. But *ngvi* would

be most unlikely: it simply is not available as a potential English word, though it contains only English sounds.

Six of these permissible sequences of sounds are somehow associated with the six portions into which English language-habits structure the spectrum. These are the familiar *red, orange, yellow, green, blue, purple*. This association of expression and content is merely conventional. There is no reason why six others could not be used, or why these six could not be associated with different parts of the spectrum. No reason, that is, except that this is the English-language way of doing it, and these are conventions to which we must adhere reasonably closely if we are to be understood. Sometime in the past history of the language, these conventions became established and have persisted with only gradual changes since. In their ultimate origins, all such conventions are the results of more or less accidental choices. It is largely fortuitous that the spectrum came to be so divided, that the specific words were attached to the colors so distinguished, or, indeed, that the sounds from which they were formed were so organized that these words were possible. These irrational facts, with many others like them, constitute the English language. Each language is a similarly arbitrary system.

[7] The three major components of language, as far as language lies within the scope of linguistics, are the structure of expression, the structure of content, and vocabulary. The latter comprises all the specific relations between expression and content—in the familiar terminology, words and their meanings.

Vocabulary comes and goes. It is the least stable and even the least characteristic of the three components of language. That portion of the vocabulary which changes most freely is sometimes referred to as "slang." But even staid and dignified words are constantly being created and continually passing out of active use, to be preserved only in literature which is dated by their very presence. While certain types of words are more transient than others, none are absolutely immortal. Even the most familiar and commonly used words, which might be expected to be most stable, have a mortality rate of about twenty percent in a thousand years.

Moreover, in the life history of an individual speaker the birth and death of words is very much more frequent than in the language community as a whole. Every normal person probably learns at least three words every day, over a thousand a year, and forgets old ones at an appreciable but lower rate. This figure must be a minimum, because most people have total vocabularies which could only be reached through even more rapid acquisition of vocabulary during at least part of their life.

We have no comparable method by which the rate of change of content structure can be estimated. The learning of new vocabulary, particularly technical terms associated with the learning of new concepts, does of course imply certain minor changes. But it is quite evident that change rarely touches the most basic features in any given language. With regard to the structure of expression the facts are clearer. Few, unless they learn a second language, will add, subtract, or change any of their basic sound patterns after they reach adolescence. Grammatical constructions may increase, but at a rate much slower than the increase of vocabulary. Vocabulary is indeed the transient feature of language.

[8] In learning a second language, you will find that vocabulary is comparatively easy, in spite of the fact that it is vocabulary that students fear most. The harder part is mastering new structures in both content and expression. You may have to free yourself from the bondage of thinking of everything as either singular or plural. Perhaps the new language will organize content into singular, dual, and plural (here meaning "three or more"). Or perhaps the new language will not give routine consideration to the matter. English speakers can never make a statement without saying something about the number of every object mentioned. This is compulsory, whether it is relevant or not. In Chinese, objects are noted as singular or plural only when the speaker judges the information to be relevant. The Chinese experience suggests that it actually seldom is, for that language operates with only occasional references to number.

You will have to make similar changes in habits of thought and of description of situations in many other instances. You may, for example, have to learn to think of every action as either completed or incomplete, and to disregard the time of the action unless it has special relevance. The reorganization of thinking and perception may extend much deeper than such changes. In some languages, situations are not analyzed, as they are in English, in terms of an actor and an action. Instead the fundamental cleavage runs in a different direction and cannot be easily stated in English. Some of these divergencies between languages have been described by

Benjamin L. Whorf. His formulation has been widely debated and perhaps is not at present susceptible to rigorous testing. Yet the papers are very suggestive and can be read with profit by every student of linguistics or languages.

You will also have to reorganize your habits of making and hearing sounds. You will have to discriminate between sounds that you have learned to consider the same. You will find that others, in clear contrast in English, function as one, and you will have to learn to respond to them as to one sound. Patterns which seem impossible will have to become facile, and you will have to learn to avoid some English patterns that seem to be second nature.

The most difficult thing of all, however, is that these profound changes will have to become completely automatic. You will have to learn to use them without effort or conscious attention. In this learning process constant disciplined practice is essential. Special ability may be helpful, but probably much less so than is popularly supposed. An understanding of the basic principles of language structure—that is, the results of modern linguistic research —while not indispensable, can contribute in many ways.

[9]   As we listen to a person speaking our native language we hear not only what is said, but also certain things about the speaker. If he is an acquaintance, we recognize him. If not, we identify him as male or female and perhaps obtain some idea of his age, his education, and his social background. A person's voice serves at least two functions in communication. One is linguistic, in that it serves as the vehicle of the expression system of language. The other is non-linguistic, in that it carries information of a quite different sort about the speaker.

This distinction is made, at least roughly, even by the unsophisticated. If we are told to *repeat* exactly what another says, we will duplicate (provided our memory serves us adequately) every feature which is included in the language expression system. We can do that, if it is our own language, even without understanding the content. In repeating we will make no effort to reproduce anything beyond the linguistically pertinent features. If, however, we are asked to *mimic* another, we attempt to reproduce not only the linguistic features, but every discernible characteristic. Few can mimic with any degree of success, whereas every normal native speaker can, perhaps with a little practice, repeat exactly up to the limit imposed by his memory span.

[10]   The most basic elements in the expression system are the **phonemes.** These are the sound features which are common to all speakers of a given speech form and which are exactly reproduced in repetition. In any language, there is a definite and usually small number of phonemes. In English there are forty-six. * * * Out of this limited inventory of units, the whole expression system is built up. In many respects the phonemes are analogous to the elements of chemistry, ninety-odd in number, out of which all substances are constructed.

The phoneme is one of those basic concepts, such as may be found in all sciences, which defy exact definition. Yet some sort of working characterization is necessary before we go on. The following is hardly adequate beyond a first introduction to the subject, but will make it possible to proceed with the analysis and enumeration of the phonemes of English. * * *

With this in mind, we may define a phoneme as a minimum feature of the expression system of a spoken language by which one thing that may be said is distinguished from any other thing which might have been said. Thus, if two utterances are different in such a way that they suggest to the hearer different contents, it must be because there are differences in the expressions. The difference may be small or extensive. The smallest difference which can differentiate utterances with different contents is a difference of a single phoneme. * * *

[11]   There are two things about phonemes that must be explicitly pointed out. * * *

Phonemes are part of the system of one specific language. The phonemes of different languages are different, frequently incommensurable. It is for this reason that a foreigner hears only a jumble which he cannot repeat. The sounds of the unfamiliar language do not fit into his phonemic system, and so he can comprehend no order in a simple utterance. If anything which is said about the phonemes of one language happens to apply to those of another, we must regard it as fortuitous.

Phonemes are features of the spoken language. Written language has its own basic unit, the *grapheme.* * * * If, of necessity, written words are cited as illustrations, it must be constantly borne in mind that the written form is not, and cannot be, an illustration of a phoneme. Instead, it is the spoken form which the written form is expected to elicit which illustrates the phoneme under discussion. This inevitably introduces a major difficulty into the presentation. The illustrative words have been selected with the intention that they should be as generally as possible pronounced by all Americans in the same way. Undoubtedly this principle of selection fails in some instances because of dialect and individual peculiarities of the writer and the reader. Such instances will not vitiate the argument. For some Americans other examples might be needed, but examples can be found which will lead to the same results.

[12]   The thinking that most Americans do about language is almost exclusively concerned with written English. A written language is, of course, a valid and important object of linguistic investigation. It can, however, easily mislead the unwary. Most of the misunderstandings which Americans have about language arise from a failure to keep clearly in mind the nature and limitations of a written language.

A written language is typically a reflection, independent in only limited ways, of spoken language. As a picture of actual speech, it is inevitably imperfect and incomplete. To understand the structure of a written language one must constantly resort either to comparison with the spoken language or to conjecture. Unfortunately, recourse has been too largely to the latter. Moreover, conjecture has been based not so much upon an intimate knowledge of the ways of languages in general (the results of descriptive linguistics) as to a priori considerations of supposed logic, to metaphysics, and to simple prejudice. While logic and metaphysics are important disciplines and can make significant contributions to an understanding of language, the customary manner of applying them has redounded neither to their credit nor to the elucidation of language structure. Linguistics must start with thorough investigation of spoken language before it proceeds to study written language. This is true of languages with long histories of written literature, such as English, no less than those of isolated tribes which have never known of the possibility of writing.

[13]   The second basic unit in the expression system is the **morpheme**. * * * For the present, * * * let us characterize a morpheme as follows: It is the unit on the expression side of language which enters into relationship with the content side. A morpheme is typically composed of one to several phonemes. The morpheme

differs fundamentally from the phoneme, which has no such relationship with content. That is, phonemes have no meanings; morphemes have meanings.

The simpler words of English are morphemes. Other words consist of two or more morphemes. Like the phonemes, the morphemes enter into combinations in accordance with definite and intricate patterns. The expression structure is merely the sum of the patterns of arrangement of these two basic units.

[14] Using the phoneme and the morpheme as their basic units, linguists have been able to build a comprehensive theory of the expression side of language, and to make detailed and comprehensive statements about the expression systems of specific languages. This is what is ordinarily called **descriptive linguistics.** It is the basic branch of linguistic science. Others are **historical linguistics,** dealing with the changes of languages in time, and **comparative linguistics,** dealing with the relationships between languages of common origin. Descriptive linguistics is conventionally divided into two parts. **Phonology** deals with the phonemes and sequences of phonemes. **Grammar** deals with the morphemes and their combinations.

In some respects linguistics has developed more precise and rigorous methods and attained more definitive results than any other science dealing with human behavior. Linguists have been favored with the most obviously structured material with which to work, so this attainment is by no means due to any scientific superiority of linguists over other social scientists. It is also the direct result of the discovery of the phoneme, a discovery which allows the data to be described in terms of a small set of discrete units. Within a given language, a given sound is either a certain phoneme or it is not; there can be no intergradation. This fact eliminates from linguistics a large measure of the vagueness and lack of precision characteristic of most studies of human behavior. It would be presumptuous to claim that this advantage has been thoroughly exploited by linguists, but it is certainly fair to say that in some places, linguistics has achieved an appreciable measure of scientific rigor and has the foundations for further development in this regard.

The chief evidence for the high order of development of linguistics as a science lies in the reproducibility of its results. If two linguists work independently on the same language, they will come out with very similar statements. There may be differences. Some of these differences will be predictable. Very seldom will any of the differences be deep-seated. Usually it will be quite possible to harmonize the two statements and show that by simple restatements one result can be converted into the other. That is, the two results will have differed largely in inconsequential ways, often only in external form.

[15]   The content side of linguistics has developed much less rapidly and to a very much less impressive extent than the study of expression. Indeed, it cannot as yet justifiably be called a science. Undoubtedly this has been a source of frustration in linguistics as a whole. One of the greatest shortcomings of descriptive work with the expression aspect of language has been a lack of understanding of the relationships between expression and content, and the inability to use the analysis of content in attacking related problems in expression. Here is the great frontier in linguistic knowledge on which we may look for progress in the next decades.

There have been three reasons for this neglect of the content side. First, linguists have been late in comprehending the real significance of the two-sided nature of language. Their attention has been diverted from this basic problem by the great advances being made within the analysis of expression.

Second, there has been no way to gain access to the content structure except through the expression structure. This requires an inferential method which has not appealed to linguists busy with building a highly rigorous method for the handling of more directly observed data. Content has therefore had an inferior status in the eyes of linguists.

Third, the content, apart from its structure, has not been amenable to any unified study. The substance of content is, of course, the whole of human experience. Thousands of scientists have labored, each in some one of numerous disciplines, in elucidating this mass of material. But there is no one approach which can comprehend the whole and so serve as a starting point for comparison of the different structures which can be imposed upon it: Only isolated portions of the content system can as yet be studied as structure imposed on a measurable continuum of experience. The examples of structuring of color concepts discussed above suggest the possibilities and make the lack of further opportunities for comparison the more tantalizing.

[16] In contrast, the expression plane starts with much simpler materials. The sounds producible by the human voice can be studied comprehensively by several approaches. Two of these have reached the degree of precision which makes them useful to linguistics: **articulary phonetics,** a branch of human physiology, and **acoustic phonetics,** a branch of physics. * * * It is hard to imagine the scientific study of the expression aspect of speech attaining anywhere near the present degree of development without the aid of phonetics. The structure can be systematically described only because the underlying sounds can be accurately described and measured.

The study of content structure must proceed, at present, without equivalent source of order in the totality of its primary data. Because of this it is relatively poorly developed. It is equally as important as the expression plane, yet it will be necessary to give it much less attention in this book. What little can be said is often semi-scientific at best. We do not even have a clear idea of the basic unit or units, and hence no basis for the high degree of precision which characterizes the study of language expression.

SUMMARY

[1–2] Language, quite properly, is something used and not studied by most people; but its study is important and interesting. Linguistics attempts to understand language from the point of view of its internal structure.

[3] The structure of language deals with two materials: the patterns of sound (expression) and the patterns of meaning (content).

[4–6] Differences in languages illustrate these features.

[7–8] The vocabulary of a language contains specific relations between expression and content; it is the least stable component of a language. Other features are more basic and more difficult to learn.

[9] Not all features of the spoken language are of linguistic importance.

[10–12] The basic elements of sound in any language are called phonemes. Phonemes are peculiar to a given language as spoken and must not be confused with the letters of the written language, which is an incomplete reflection of the spoken language.

[13] The second basic elements of a language's expression are called morphemes, or the smallest units of meaning.

[14–16] The branches of linguistics on the expression side of language have made great progress; those on the content side, for a number of reasons, have made little progress.

NOTES

Professor Gleason, in this introductory chapter, is facing up to an old and necessary problem of language study. A language concerns a complicated set of actual conditions: Mr. *A*, having an idea, tries to express the idea in words. Mr. *A* makes sounds. Mr. *B*, hearing the sounds, interprets those sounds into meanings. Now, a language has to do with all of this, and a student of language must approach it from some point along the line of these happenings. In the past, linguists attempted to begin with the ideas and concerned themselves with how ideas are expressed by a given language. Today, linguists begin with the sounds as heard and attempt to work toward what those sounds are interpreted as meaning. If you think about the problem, you may see good reason to start where Professor Gleason—and most American linguists—prefers to start. (Certainly, if you mean to study a new language, for which no grammars and dictionaries have yet been written, you have little choice in the matter. The sounds are all you have to work with.)

A few terms may need a word of explanation. Phoneme and morpheme are words manufactured by linguists rather systematically. *Phon-* (as in *telephone*) means "sound"; *morph-* (as in *metamorphosis*) means "form or shape." The *-eme* attached to them means "a unit of." Hence a phoneme is a "unit of sound"; a morpheme is a "unit of form." *Phonemics* is the study of a language's meaningful sounds; *morphemics* is the study of a language's meaningful forms.

A linguist discovers the phonemes in a language by what he calls "minimal pairs"—that is, two bits of the spoken language which differ in only one sound element. Thus *pin* and *pan*, as spoken, differ only in the sound element between the *p* sound and the *n* sound, which are alike in the two words. Again, the verb *decoy* and the noun *decoy* differ only in the comparative stress of the two syllables (de-COY and DE-coy). Again, the phrases *gray train* and *great rain* differ in the point of pause and the way the *t* is pronounced. By this method, Professor Gleason isolates forty-six English phonemes in all.

The morphemes are the smallest units of form—that is, the sounds or groups of sound in our language which have meaning to us. Some morphemes are said to be "free" or to have meaning all by themselves: thus such words as *boy, play, old*. Other morphemes are said to be "bound" or to have meaning only when attached to other morphemes: thus the *-s* in *boys,* the *-ed* in *played,* the *-er* in *older.*

The Conservative and Alterative Forces in Language

William Dwight Whitney was Salisbury Professor of Sanskrit and Comparative Philology at Yale from 1854 until his death in 1894. In this essay, using English as an example, he suggests that two general forces have influenced all languages: the force to change and the force to remain the same.

* * * The individual learns his language, obtaining the spoken signs of which it is made up by imitation from the lips of others, and shaping his conceptions in accordance with them. It is thus that every existing language is maintained in life; if this process of tradition, by teaching and learning, were to cease in any tongue upon earth, that tongue would at once become extinct.

But this is only one side of the life of language. If it were all, then each spoken dialect would remain the same from age to age. In virtue of it, each does, in fact, remain nearly the same; this is what maintains the prevailing identity of speech so long as the identity of the speaking community is maintained—aside from those great revolutions in their circumstances which now and then lead whole communities to adopt the speech of another people. This, then, is the grand conservative force in the history of language; if there were no disturbing and counteracting forces to interfere with its workings, every generation to the end of time would speak as its predecessors had done.

Such, however, as every one knows, is very far from being the case. All living language is in a condition of constant growth and change. It matters not to what part of the world we may go: if we can find for any existing speech a record of its predecessor at some time distant from it in the past, we shall perceive that the two are

---

Chapter III from *The Life and Growth of Language* (New York, 1901).

different—and more or less different, mainly in proportion to the distance of time that separates them. It is so with the Romanic tongues of southern Europe, as compared with their common progenitor the Latin; so with the modern dialects of India, as compared with the recorded forms of speech intermediate between them and the Sanskrit, or with the Sanskrit itself; and not less with the English of our day, as compared with that of other days. An English speaker even of only a century ago would find not a little in our every-day speech which he would understand with difficulty or not at all; if we were to hear Shakespeare read aloud a scene from one of his own works, it would be in no small part unintelligible (by reason, especially, of the great difference between his pronunciation and ours); Chaucer's English (500 years ago) we master by dint of good solid application, and with considerable help from a glossary; and King Alfred's English (1000 years ago), which we call Anglo-Saxon, is not easier to us than German. All this, in spite of the fact that no one has gone about of set purpose to alter English speech, in any generation among the thirty or forty that have lived between us and Alfred, any more than in our own. Here, then, is another side of the life of language for us to deal with, and to explain, if we can. Life, here as elsewhere, appears to involve growth and change as an essential element; and the remarkable analogies which exist between the birth and growth and decay and extinction of a language and those of an organized being, or of a species, have been often enough noticed and dwelt upon: some have even inferred from them that language is an organism, and leads an organic life, governed by laws with which men cannot interfere.

Plainly, however, we should be overhasty in resorting to such an explanation until after mature inquiry and deliberation. There is no *prima facie* impossibility that language, if an institution of human device, and propagated by tradition, should change. Human institutions in general go down from generation to generation by a process of transmission like that of language, and they are all modified as they go. On the one hand, tradition is by its very nature imperfect and inaccurate. No one has ever yet been able to prevent what passes from mouth to ear from getting altered on the way. The child always commits blunders, of every kind, in his earlier attempts at speaking: if careful and well trained, he learns later to correct them; but he is often careless and untrained. And all through the life-long process of learning one's "mother-tongue," one is liable to apprehend wrongly and to reproduce inexactly. On the other hand, although the child in his first stage of learning is more than satisfied to take what is set before him and use it as he best can, because his mental development is far short of that which it represents, and its acquisition is urging him on at his best rate of progress, the case does not always continue thus with him: by and by his mind has grown up, perhaps, to the full measure of that which his speech represents, and begins to exhibit its native and surplus force; it chafes against the imposed framework of current expression; it modifies a little its inherited instrument, in order to adapt this better to its own purposes. So, to have recourse to an obvious analogy, one may, by diligent study under instructors, have reached in some single department—as of natural science, mathematics, philosophy—the furthest limits of his predecessors' knowledge, and found them too strait for him; he adds new facts, draws new distinctions, establishes new relations, which the subsisting technical language of the department is incompetent to express; and there arises thus an absolute need of new expression, which must in some way or other be met; and it is met. Every language must prove itself able to signify what is in the minds of its speakers to express; if unequal to that, it would have to abdicate its office; it would no longer answer the purposes of a language. The sum of what all the individual speakers contribute to the common store of thought and knowledge by original work has to be worked into the "inner form" of their language along with and by means of some alteration in its outer form.

Here, then, at any rate, are two obvious forces, having their roots in human action, and constantly operating toward the change of language; and it remains to be seen whether there are any others, of a different character. Let us, then, proceed to examine the changes which actually go on in language, and which by their sum and combined effect constitute its growth, and see what they will say as to the force that brings them about.

[2]   And it will be well to begin with a concrete example, a specimen of altered speech, which shall serve as a source of illustration, and as groundwork for a classification of the kinds of linguistic change. The Frenchman would find his best example in a parallel between a phrase of ancient Latin and its correspondent in modern French, with intermediate forms from the older French;

the German could trace a passage backward through the Middle to the Old High-German, with hints of a yet remoter antiquity derived from the Gothic; to the English speaker, nothing else is so available as a specimen of the oldest English, or Anglo-Saxon, of a thousand years ago. Let us look, then, at a verse from the Anglo-Saxon gospels, and compare it with its modern counterpart:

> Se Hælend fôr on reste-dæg ofer æceras; sôthlîce his leorning-cnihtas hyngrede, and hî ongunnon pluccian thâ ear and etan.

No ordinary English reader, certainly, would understand this, or discover that it is the equivalent of the following sentence of our modern version:—

> Jesus went on the sabbath day through the corn; and his disciples were a hungered, and began to pluck the ears of corn and to eat. (*Matthew* xii. 1.)

And yet, by translating it as literally as we can, we shall find that almost every element in it is still good English, only disguised by changes of form and of meaning. Thus:—

> The Healing [one] fared on rest-day over [the] acres; soothly, his learning-knights [it] hungered, and they began [to] pluck the ears and eat.

Thus although, from one point of view, *and* and *his* are the only words in the Anglo-Saxon passage which are the same also in the English—and not even those really, since their former pronunciation was somewhat different from their present—from another point of view everything is English excepting *se,* "the," and *hî,* "they"—and even those, virtually; since they are cases of inflection of the definite article and third personal pronoun, of which other cases (as *the, that, they,* and *he, his, him*) are still in good use with us. Both the discordance and the accordance are complete, according to the way in which we look at them. We will proceed to examine the passage a little in detail, in order to understand better the relations between the older and the newer form.

[3]   In the first place, their pronunciation is even more different than is indicated by the written text. There are at least two sounds in the Anglo-Saxon which are unknown in our present speech: namely, the *h* of *cnihtas,* which was nearly or quite the same with the *ch* of the corresponding German word *knecht,* and the *y* of *hyngrede,* which was the German *ü* and French *u,* an *u*

(*oo*)-sound with an *i*(*ee*)-sound intimately combined with it. On the other hand, there are sounds in the English which were unknown to the Anglo-Saxon. Our so-called "short *o*," of *on*, was no ancient sound; nor was the "short *u*" of *begun, pluck*, which had then the vowel-sound of *book* and *full*; nor was the "short *i*" of *his*, which was more like the French and German short *i*, not markedly different in quality from the true long *i*, our so-called "long *e*," or *ee*-sound. All these are examples of the manifold changes of English pronunciation during the thousand years since Alfred—changes which have altered the whole aspect of our orthoëpy and orthography. And others of them are illustrated in the passage: for instance, our *knight* and *eat* show protractions of the short vowels of *cniht* and *etan*, each typical of a whole class of cases; and the lengthened *i* has been changed into a diphthong, which we call "long *i*" simply because it has taken the place of our former long *i* (*ee*); while we call the real long *i* of *eat* by the false name of "long *e*" for the same reason.

[4]   Again, we may observe in the forms of many words the effects of a tendency toward abbreviation. *Reste* and *hyngrede* have lost with us their final *e*, which in Anglo-Saxon, as now in German and Italian, made an additional syllable. *Ongunnon, pluccian*, and *etan* have lost both vowel and consonant of a final syllable; and these syllables were the distinctive endings, in the first word of the plural verbal inflection (*ongan*, "I or he began," but *ongunnon*, "we or they began"), in the other two of the infinitive. In *æceras*, 'acres,' and *cnihtas*, 'knights,' though we have saved the final *s* of the plural ending, it no longer makes an additional syllable. And in *sôthlíce*, 'soothly' (i.e., "truly, verily"), there is a yet more marked abbreviation, to which we shall presently return.

On the other hand, *ear*, "ears," and *fôr*, "fared," have been extended in modern time by the addition of other pronounced elements. It was the rule in Anglo-Saxon that a neuter noun of one syllable, if of long quantity, had no (nom. or accus.) plural ending. With us, every noun, of whatever gender or quantity (save a few exceptions, of which we need take no account here), takes *s* as its plural sign. As for *fôr*, the Anglo-Saxons conjugated *faran*, "fare," as they did *dragan*, "draw," and said *fôr*, "fared," like *drôh*, "drew" (compare the corresponding German *fahren fuhr* and *tragen trug*)—that is to say, *faran* was to them a verb of the "irregular," or "old," or "strong" conjugation. But for a long time there has existed in English speech a tendency to work over such verbs, abandoning their irregularly varying inflection, and reducing them to accordance with the more numerous class of the "regularly" inflected, like *love, loved;* and *fare* is one of the many that have undergone this change. The process is quite analogous with that which has turned *ear* into *ears:* that is to say, a prevailing analogy has been extended to include cases formerly treated as exceptional.

In connection with *ear* comes to light another very striking difference between the ancient and modern English: The Anglo-Saxon had grammatical gender, like the Greek and Latin and German; it regarded *ear* as neuter, but *æcer* and *dæg* as masculine, and, for instance, *tunge,* "tongue," and *dæd,* "deed," as feminine; to us, who have abolished grammatical gender in favor of natural sex, all are alike neuter.

[5] We turn now to consider a few points relative to the meaning of the words used. In *fôr* we find a marked difference of sense as well as of form. It is part of an old Germanic verb meaning "go," and is traceable even back into the earliest Indo-European, as the root *par,* "pass" (Skt. *pârayâmi,* Gr. περάω, Lat. *ex-per-ior*); now it is quite obsolete in any such sense as this, and rather unusual even in that of "getting on," "making progress": "it *fared* ill with him." Again, *æcer* meant in Anglo-Saxon a 'cultivated field,' as does the German *acker* to the present day; and here, again, we have its very ancient correlatives in Sanskrit *ajra,* Greek ἀγρός, Latin *ager;* the restriction of the word to signify a field of certain fixed dimensions, taken as a unit of measure for fields in general, is something quite peculiar and recent. It is analogous with the like treatment of *rod* and *foot* and *grain,* and so on, except that in these cases we have saved the old meaning while adding the new.

Among the striking peculiarities of the Anglo-Saxon passage is its use of the words *Hælend,* "healing one," *reste-dæg,* "rest-day," and *leorning-cnihtas,* "learning-knights" (i.e., "youths under instruction"), in the sense respectively of "Savior," "sabbath," and "disciples." Though all composed of genuine old Germanic materials, they were nevertheless recent additions to the language. The introduction of Christianity had created a necessity for them. For the new idea of the Christian Creator and Father, the old word *god,* ennobled and inspired with a new meaning, answered English purposes well enough. But there was no current name applicable to the conception of one who saved men from their sins, making them whole or *hale;* and so the present participle of the verb *hǽlan,* "make hale, *heal,*" was chosen to represent σωτήρ, and specialized into a proper name, a title for the one Savior. It is the same word which, in German, is still current as *Heiland. Reste-dæg,* as name for the sabbath, needs no word of explanation or comment. As for *leorning-cnihtas,* rendering *discipuli* and μαθηταί, its most striking characteristic, apart from its rather lumbering awkwardness, is the peculiar meaning which it implies in *cniht,* "knight." Between our *knight,* a word of high chivalric signifi-cance, and the German *knecht,* "servant, menial," is a long dis-tance: both show a deviation, the one in an upward and the other in a downward direction, from the indifferent "youth, fellow," which lies at the bottom of the use of the word in our Anglo-Saxon compound.

But a not less noteworthy point in the history of these words is that in our later usage they have all become superseded by other terms, of foreign origin. The Anglo-Saxon did not, like our English, resort freely to foreign stores of expression for the supply of new needs. It was easier than to accept the new institutions of Christi-anity than new names for them. We have wonderfully changed all that * * * and in place of the three new Saxon names we have put other yet newer ones: two Latin-French, *disciple* and *savior,* and one Hebrew, *sabbath.* The substitution exemplifies a capital trait in English language-history.

[6]   Our attention being thus directed to the introduction of new elements into Anglo-Saxon, we will note another case or two of the same kind of linguistic change in another department. *Sôthlíce* is an adverb, answering to our "truly." We recognize in the first part of it our *sooth,* a word now almost obsolete—quite so, as far as ordinary use is concerned. Its second part, *líce,* is our *ly.* But it is also a case-form (instrumental) of an adjective *líc,* our *like,* which was appended to the noun *sôth,* "truth," forming a compound adjective (or adjectival derivative) equivalent to *truth-like,* and completely analogous to *truthful,* from *truth* and *full.* Our adverbial ending *ly,* then, by which most of our adverbs are made, and which to us is only a suffix, is really the product of alteration of a case-form of a compounded adjective, a word originally independent. Instead of using, like the modern German, the base or crude-form of an adjective as adverb—that is to say, in

the formal grammatical charcter of adaptedness to qualify a verb or adjective rather than a substantive—we have wrought out for that purpose a special form, of which the history of development may be followed step by step to its origin, and which is exclusively the property of our language among its kindred Germanic dialects.

A second case is brought before us in *hyngrede.* Its preterit ending *de* is not, like the adverbial *ly,* exclusively English; it is rather, like the adjective *lîc,* a common Germanic possession. Without dwelling here at length upon its history, we will only observe that it is, like *lîce,* traced back to an independent word, the preterit *did,* which was in remote Germanic time added to some verbal derivative, or other part of speech, to form a new style of past tense, when the yet older processes of preterit formation had become no longer manageable.

There are also changes of construction in our passage which ought not to pass without a moment's notice. The word *leorning-cnihtas* is object, not subject, of *hyngrede;* and the construction is that peculiar one in which the impersonal verb, without expressed subject, takes before it as object the person affected by the action or feeling it signifies. This is still a familiar mode of expression in German, where one freely says *mich hungerte,* "me hungered," for "I hungered"; and even we have a trace of it, in the obsolescent *methinks,* German *mich dünkt*—that is, "it seems to me." Again, the infinitives *pluccian* and *etan,* being by origin verbal nouns and having properly the construction of nouns, are directly dependent, as objects, on the transitive verb *ongunnon.* We make the same construction with some verbs: so, *he will pluck, he must eat, see him pluck, let him eat;* and even after *began* shortened to *'gan* it is allowed; but in the vast majority of cases we require the preposition *to* as "infinitive sign," saying "began *to* pluck and *to* eat." This preposition was not unknown in Anglo-Saxon; but it was used only where the connection pretty manifestly favored the insertion of such a connective; and the infinitive after it had a peculiar form: thus, *gôd to etanne,* "good unto eating," and so "good to eat." The *to* which at the period of our specimen-passage was a real word of relation has now become the stereotyped sign of a certain verbal form; it has no more independent value than the ending *an* of *pluccian* and *etan*—which, indeed, it in a manner replaces; though not, like -*ly* and -*d,* combined with the word to which it belongs, its office is analogous with theirs.

We will notice but one thing more in the passage: the almost oblivion into which *sôth,* our *sooth,* has fallen. Only a small part of the great body of English-speakers know that there is such a word; and no one but a poet, or an imitator of archaic style, ever uses it. We have put in place of it *true* and *truth,* which of old were more restricted to the expression of faithfulness, trustworthiness.

[7]   The brief sentence selected, we see, illustrates a very considerable variety of linguistic changes; in fact, there is hardly a possible mode of change which is not more or less distinctly brought to light by it. Such are, in general, the ways in which a language comes to be at a later period different from what it has been at an earlier. They are matters of individual detail; each item, or each class of accordant items, has its own time and occasion, and analogies, and secondary causes, and consequences; it is their sum and collective effect which make up the growth of language. If we are to understand how language grows, we must take them up and examine them in their individuality. This, then, is the subject which is now for some time to occupy us: an inquiry into the modes of linguistic change, and their causes, nearer and remoter.

We have already rudely made one classification of these linguistic changes, founded on the various purpose which they subserve: namely, into such as make new expressions, being produced for the designation of conceptions before undesignated; and such as merely alter the form of old expression; or, into additions and alterations. It will, however, suit our purpose better to make a more external division, one depending upon the kind of change rather than upon its object. In carrying this out, it will be practicable to take everywhere sufficient notice of the object also.

We may distinguish, then:—

I. Alterations of the old material of language; change of the words which are still retained as the substance of expression; and this of two kinds or subclasses: (1) change in uttered form; (2) change in content or signification; the two, as we shall see, occurring either independently or in conjunction.

II. Losses of the old material of language, disappearance of what has been in use; and this also of two kinds: (1) loss of complete words; (2) loss of grammatical forms and distinctions.

III. Production of new material; additions to the old stock of a language, in the way of new words or new forms; external expansion of the resources of expression.

This classification is obviously exhaustive; there can be no change in any language which will not fall under one or other of the three classes here laid down.

NOTES

It may help you to have a rough idea of the sound of the passage of Old English which Professor Whitney cited in [2]. The following rough guide may suffice for you to sound out the passage:

VOWELS

Pronounce *a* like the *a* in *father*
Pronounce *e* like the *ey* in *obey*
Pronounce *i* like the *i* in *machine*
Pronounce *o* like the *o* in *home*
Pronounce *u* like the *u* in *put*
Pronounce *æ* like the *a* in *bat*

CONSONANTS

For the most part, as modern English consonants, but

Pronounce *g* in *dæg* like the *y* in *yet;* g after *n* as in *finger*
Pronounce *f* between vowels as *v* in *over*
Pronounce *c* always as the *k* in *kill* (except in *sothlice,* where it is like the *ch* in *church*)
Pronounce *s* always as the *s* in *silly;* pronounce *th* always as the *th* in *thin*
Pronounce the *h* in *cnihtas* like the *ch* in German *ich*
Pronounce the *y* like the German umlauted *ü* (say EE and round your lips, as you would to say OO)

Above all, remember to say all the sounds represented; there were no "silent" letters in Old English; every letter was sounded.

PART TWO Wells of Words

From Greece and Rome

*John Cecil Moore is an English journalist and author and fellow
of the Royal Society of Literature. In the past thirty years he has
written numerous books on widely different subjects. The book
from which this selection is taken,* You English Words, *is a collection of essays displaying the admiration and affection for language of a working writer.*

[1] Of course it is only a smattering of words that we have taken
over lock, stock and barrel from a foreign language. For the most
part our words came deviously, making their way by winding
paths through the minds of generations of men, even burrowing
like moles through the dark subconsciousness. Fancied like-
nesses, farfetched associations, ancient prejudices have acted upon
them. Superstitions, misapprehensions, old fables, mythologies,
taboos, the jests of simpletons and the vaulting imagination of
poets have all played a part in shaping them. During their labyrinthine journeys in time and space they have often changed their
form, spelling, pronunciation and, especially, their sense. A very
good example is the word "treacle," of which the origin is to be
sought in the Greek *therion,* meaning a wild beast. The association is so unexpected that it would probably have stuck in my
mind without the fortuitous mnemonic of the Lyle's Golden
Syrup tin, familiar at the school tea-table, which carried a picture
of a lion's carcass with bees flying out of it, and a caption from the

Chapter 9 from *You English Words* by John Moore. Copyright © 1961 by
John Moore, Published by J. B. Lippincott Company and in Canada by Wm.
Collins Sons & Co. Ltd.

Book of Judges: "Out of the strong came forth sweetness." This of course has nothing whatever to do with the derivation of "treacle"; but it ensured that I should never forget the curious connexion with wild beasts.

Now *therion,* by an extension of its meaning, came to signify "any dangerous or savage thing"; and since poisonous serpents were within this category a word was coined, *theriake,* for "an antidote against snake-bite." This became *triacula* in Low Latin and *triacle* in Old French; and in due course the word arrived in English as "treacle" but with the meaning: "A medicinal compound used against bites and poisons." Such a salve, which the apothecaries in their grand way called an alexipharmic, generally consisted of aromatic and soothing herbs like rue, garlic, germander and valerian, all of which incidentally are still known as Poor Man's Treacle or Countryman's Treacle in parts of the English countryside.

To make a good salve, it was necessary to bind together, with some harmless sticky stuff, the bruised or fine-chopped leaves. What better stuff for the purpose than thick black molasses? And so you see by what devious processes the Greek wild beast becomes at last the treacle which was mixed with dollops of brimstone for Smike and his companions at Dotheboys Hall.

Turning over the pages of an etymological dictionary, you begin to realise how much our language, whether homely or highfaluting, owes to Greece and Rome. The plumber is so called because in his trade he uses *plumbum,* lead; the carpenter was originally *artifex carpentarius,* a maker of wagons; and we have dentist from *dens,* vet from *veterinarius* ("pertaining to cattle"), artist from *ars* and his easel from *asellus,* a little ass, which seems extraordinary until you compare it with our English expression "clothes horse." If we say we don't care a jot we are using as a metaphor the Greek "i," *iota,* which is the smallest Greek letter. "Asparagus" is simply the Greek word for a sprout or shoot. "Asbestos" is Greek for inextinguishable. *Hupokritēs* meant an actor on the stage; and so a hypocrite is a person who pretends to beliefs and feelings which are not his own. *Aegis* was the dreaded shield of Zeus, made for him by Hephaestus. We treat the Cloud-Gatherer with little respect when we speak of a fête being held under the aegis of the Women's Institute. *Agonia* meant a contest, primarily in athletics. You have only to look at a photograph of anybody winning the 100 yards to understand how it came in its English version to have the sense of "agony."

[2]   Hundreds of our useful words,[1] and some of our most splendid ones, are taken direct from Greek. Labyrinthine, pandemonium and phantasmagoria are three beauties. "Labyrinth" may in fact belong to a still older language, out of Asia Minor or perhaps ancient Egypt; it is an appropriately mysterious word. "Pandemonium" (first used by Milton) has the awesome literal meaning of "the abode of all the demons." "Phantasmagoria" seems to have been invented by an enterprising showman in 1802 in order to advertise an exhibition of optical illusions produced by the magic lantern. Nowadays, however, it generally means "a series of drifting phantoms" such as you might see in a dream or a fever.

We have great Greek words for most of our physical diseases and for all our psychological troubles, not forgetting cremnophobia, "fear of falling from cliffs," and hagiophobia, "excessive dread of holy persons or things." If you are a fancier of rare and extraordinary words, here is a prolific hunting-ground. Another lies in the direction of ancient magic, where high-sounding Greek combinations were used to inspire awe and create an atmosphere of mystery. "Alectoromancy," for instance, meant "divination by a cock picking up grains." There are scores of these "mancy" words, interesting by reason of the glimpse they give us of the extravagances of the seers. Divination was even performed by dropping melted wax into water (ceromancy), by mirrors (catoptromancy), by salt (halomancy) and by mice (myomancy). I have no idea what experiments or observations were involved in myomancy, and I should like to know more about this long-forgotten chapter in the relationship of mice and men.

All the -ologies are named in Greek, e.g. palaeontology, the study of ancient things, and so are most of the ancient things themselves, such as the dinosaur, "the terrible lizard," and the pterodactyl, "the feather-fingered creature." Greek also provides us with a useful if peculiar vocabulary denoting the rarer kinks, vagaries and idiosyncrasies of the human race, such as a craze for setting things on fire, pyromania; the printing or painting of filthy pictures, rhyparography; fish-worship, ichthyolatry; love of

1. For example: orchestra, dogma, cinema, phenomenon, enigma (something "spoken darkly" or in riddles), museum, clinic, pylon, acrobat, phase, and philander.

corpses, necrophilism; the belief that one has turned oneself into a wolf, lycanthropy; and the contemplation of the navel for the purpose of attaining philosophic calm, omphaloskepsis! There is even a word expressive of the healthy male appreciation of a good-looking feminine bottom: callipygian; which Sir Thomas Browne explains as referring to "women largely composed behind." [2] Fashions change; and nowadays we should be more likely to describe such women as steatopygous,[3] fat-rumped. As somebody punned in Latin, *Ars est celare arsem!*

Because Greek is such a handy language for new-word-making, the professors have naturally played their little games with it. For instance, H. L. Mencken being asked by a striptease-girl to suggest a more dignified term for her profession put forward "ecdysiast," from Greek *ecdysis,* a shedding or throwing-off, as a snake sheds its outer skin. I am told that this word is now current among the more high-minded stripteasers in the United States; indeed according to Mr. Ivor Brown a Society of Ecdysiasts, Parade and Specialty Dancers has been formed to protect them against persecution and to defend their rights.[4]

I do not know whether "ioblepharous" can be said to exist in English; I heard it used by a don, by no means "remote and ineffectual," but observant of women's make-up, to describe a "violet-lidded" girl. The Greeks used to paint the eyelids of their female statues blue; and the adjective was *ioblepharos.*

"Triskaidekaphobia" must have been another scholar's fanciful formation; it is alleged to mean "fear of Friday the thirteenth," and would seem to be genuinely useful, for there is no way of describing that superstition more briefly. Seven syllables, however, have proved too many for the layman's tongue; and the word remains a donnish jest, as does "floccipaucinihilipilification," the longest word in the *O.E.D.,*[5] which is made up of several Latin

2. *Pseudodoxia Epidemica.*

3. Anthropologists apply this word technically to describe an abnormality found in the women of Hottentot Bushmen, especially a tribe called the Bongos.

4. *Say the Word.*

5. Thomas Love Peacock used a longer one in *Headlong Hall*—osseocarnisanguineoviscericartilaginonervomedullary, thus describing in 51 letters the structure of the human body. A Dr. Strother beat him by one letter with a word indicating the composition of the spa waters at Bristol: aequeosalinocalcalinosetaceoaluminosocupreovitriolic. Perhaps the longest word used in ordinary speech was Mr. Gladstone's antidisestablishmentarianism.

words meaning "at little" or "at nothing." The whole conglomeration therefore signifies "the action or habit of estimating as worthless." No doubt there are many more such ingenious inventions, which learned men in lighter moments juggle with as gravely as sealions balancing sticks upon their noses. Long may they continue to do so, those Dons of Might such as Belloc wrote of,

> Who shout and bang and roar and bawl
> The Absolute across the hall,
> Or sail in amply billowing gown
> Enormous through the Sacred Town,
> Bearing from College to their homes
> Deep cargoes of gigantic tomes:
> Dons admirable! Dons of Might!
> Uprising on my inward sight
> Compact of ancient tales, and port
> And sleep—and learning of a sort . . .[6]

Apart from such jokes as triskaidekaphobia, the joining-together of Greek elements has provided scores of words which we could hardly do without—chrysanthemum (gold + flower), cosmopolitan (world + citizen), phosphorous (light + bearer), panorama (all + view), heliotrope (sun + turning), chlorophyll (light green + leaf), pachyderm (thick + skin), xenophilism (foreigner + liking), logorrhoea (word + flow), photography (light + writing), telephone (far-off voice), helicopter (spiral + wing). Even your thermometer is named in Greek (heat-measurer); and the mercury inside it is so-called after the swift God who bore Zeus' messages and wore the wings upon his heels. And when you ask for the cereal at breakfast you are paying your respects to Ceres, the goddess of corn.

[3]   We have taken a lot of words from mythology, naturally enough; and we have made some strange uses of them. During the late war, when suddenly at dusk the air became filled with a sad discordant mooing, it occurred to me that we could hardly have chosen a more inept name for the instruments which were making the noise.

"The name of those fabulous animals (pagan, I regret to say) who used to sing in the water has quite escaped me." Mr. George Chuzzlewit suggested "Swans." "No," said Mr. Pecksniff. "Not swans. Very like swans, too. Thank you." The nephew . . . propounded "Oysters." "No,"

6. *Lines to a Don.*

said Mr. Pecksniff . . . "nor oysters. But by no means unlike oysters; a very excellent idea; thank you, my dear sir, very much. Wait! Sirens! Dear me! Sirens, of course." [7]

Odysseus made his men put wax in their ears, and bind him tightly to the mast, when they rowed past the Sirens' isle; so he alone of men was able to listen to the singing and yet survive; for the voice of a Siren (a creature part woman, part bird) was so sweet that sailors, unable to resist it, were lured ashore to their doom. But our wartime sirens played a tune such as the old cow died of; they had a blood-chilling effect upon some people, whose hearts, as they put it, "missed a beat" whenever they heard them. Before long London learned to shrug its shoulders at them in its own fatalistic way; and in the midst of their cacophony, on New Year's Eve, 1940, I heard a Cockney singing to a well-known hymn-tune:

> Sireens, sireens, sireens,
> Always bloody well sireens . . .

The long "e" was no innovation. Kipling wrote during the First World War of

> Five maned trawlers with their sireens blowing
> Heading the whole review.
> "Sweep completed in the fairway.
> No more mines remain.
> 'Sent back Unity, Claribel, Assyrian, Stormcock
> and Golden Gain." [8]

Mr. Pecksniff no doubt would have called a sylph a fabulous animal. Mr. Crummles saw the likeness of one in the unrivalled Miss Petowker of the Theatre Royal, Drury Lane. "She's the only sylph *I* ever saw, who could stand upon one leg, and play the tambourine on her other knee, *like* a sylph." [9] Today the word is most often used in the sense of "a successful product of slimming." Indeed nowadays we treat these airy spirits of the woodland and the waters with scant respect. Fishermen deceive trout with tiny hanks of draggled feathers which they call nymphs; and outside the company of anglers the word is more likely to be heard in the form of "nymphet," meaning an adolescent wanton, such as Lolita.

7. Dickens: *Martin Chuzzlewit.*
8. *Mine Sweepers.*
9. *Nicholas Nickleby.*

Mr. Nabokov did not, however, invent "nymphet." Drummond of
Hawthornden used it for a little nymph, and so did Michael Dray-
ton in *Poly-Olbion:*

> Of the nymphets sporting there
> In Wyrrall, and in Delamere.

"Nymphomania" was invented about 1800 for "morbid and uncon-
trollable sexual desire" on the part of a woman. Once a purely
medical term, it is now become a catty-cocktail-party word, used
by envious women to describe others more ardent or acquiescent
than themselves. Nympholepsy is a very different kind of frenzy,
which only poets can really understand. The word comes from the
idea that a man who beholds a nymph falls into a kind of hopeless
rapture; hence it implies the desire of the unattainable, and the
despair that goes therewith.

"Volcano" from Vulcan whose fiery forge lay in the heart of the
mountains; "martial" and the month of March from Mars the God
of War; "erotic" from Eros,—and also that booksellers' word for
dirty books,—I read an advertisement the other day, "WANTED,
Any high-class Erotica"; "fauna" from the woodland God Faunus
and "flora" from his sister; "jovial" from Jove whom we also swear
by: through these and many other words the Gods of Greece and
Rome speak to us still. "Hermaphrodite" comes from the name of
that unfortunate son of Hermes and Aphrodite who went for a
swim in a fountain and found himself merging into the nymph
Salmacis who lived there, so that the two bodies became one.
Sailors use the word figuratively—"hermaphrodite brig" [10]—and
Kipling called his Royal Marine "a kind of giddy Harumfrodite."
As for Aphrodite herself:

> Clothed round with the world's desire as with
>   raiment, and fair as the foam,
> And fleeter than kindled fire, and a goddess,
>   and mother of Rome—

she who

> Came flushed from the full-flushed wave, and
>   imperial, her foot on the sea.
> And the wonderful waters knew her, the winds
>   and the viewless ways,

10. Square-rigged forward, schooner-rigged aft.

> And the roses grew rosier, and bluer the sea-blue
>   stream of the bays— [11]

I must say it seems to me that we do dishonour to the language, and demonstrate a streak of shabbiness in ourselves, when we take the Goddess' name in vain for the contemptible pills and potions and powdered beetles which grubby backstreet chemists sell: and describe these fraudulent philtres as—the Goddess forgive us—aphrodisiacs!

We make partial amends for this affront if it is true that the word April is named after Aphro (a pet-form of Aphrodite) because it is the love-month, at any rate in Mediterranean lands. Even here, where the wind blows so chilly in the spring, we have a saying that when the little leaves on the elms are the size of a mouse's ears, then is the time for love; and the opening elm-leaves are just so big when the cuckoo comes. April is a lovely word, and it dances in our poetry—Aprille with his shoures sote, proud-pied April, and best of all:

> He came all so still
>   Where His mother was,
> As dew in April
>   That falleth on the grass.[12]

Of all the words the Gods have given us, the strangest is surely "panic." I think it is a terrifying word. It comes from *to panikon deima*, "fear caused by Pan," and an important part of the meaning is that the fear is *groundless*. Unexplained noises heard by night in the mountains; or deep in the woodlands, a tiny sigh on the windless air, a scuffle among dead leaves where neither bird nor beast was to be seen,—these were the sounds attributed to Pan, and the irrational terror caused by them is named after him. We use the word loosely nowadays; one even hears of panic on the Stock Exchange. But true panic is a very different thing; it is fear of something universal and protean, which inhabits the darkness, the air, the trees, the sky, the earth herself. We use some long Greek names for it, such as claustrophobia if it happens in an enclosed space, and agoraphobia if it happens in the open, and for the sake of completeness phobophobia which is simply fear of being afraid; but whatever we call it, this is the same ancient

---

11. Swinburne: *Hymn to Proserpine.*
12. *Sing of a Maiden.*

"panic" the Greeks knew. I have experienced it twice in my life. The first time was at nightfall in a wilderness. All about me there fell an unnatural silence; and suddenly this very silence grew loud, and began to shriek at me. I knew then what the author of Deuteronomy meant by a "howling wilderness"; I cowered in the face of its howling and I should have fled but there was nowhere to flee to; I should have hid but there was not a tree nor a hole in the ground to give me refuge.

The second time was during the war. I was told to do a weather flight, which involved going very high, and as I was at that time normally a pilot of old submarine-hunting Swordfish I had never had occasion to fly really high before. I went up, up, up alone into the deepening blue, until the Spitfire seemed to hang upon her propeller in a remote vast emptiness, and suddenly an awful fear of the loneliness seized me, and with it a painful longing for the earth and homely things. I thought I should go mad if I stayed up there any longer; I eased the stick forward a shade and then Pan took charge altogether. I pressed it hard till the aeroplane plunged like a bronco, the engine revved and roared, the wings began to scream, and the blessed, blessed earth rushed up at me brown and green and dirty-looking but oh! so beautiful in contrast with that cold blue uninhabited sky.

[4] A word I find sinister in a different fashion is the naturalists' term for a caterpillar: "larva," which comes from Latin, in which language it has an uncomfortable, spine-chilling, prickling-at-the-back-of-the-neck connotation. It means the walking spirit of a dead person, but carries the implication that the unresting dead one is in pursuit of the living. Because such a spirit is faceless, the word in Latin acquired the additional meaning of "a mask."

By a most daring fancy, our old naturalists adopted it as the scientific name for a caterpillar; because such a creature wears a disguise, the future insect is not recognisable in the present grub, its form is a "mask" which will one day be cast off. The name dates, of course, from the days before science and the humanities set themselves at odds; a good natural historian was generally a fair classical scholar, and he used the classics to make his communications concerning science more vivid, imaginative, logical and accurate. So science and poetry coexisted,—the use of "larva" for a caterpillar, and of "pupa" for the next metamorphosis, is a truly poetic employment of words. The great naturalist Linnaeus was the first to use "pupa" in this sense, in 1758. It is simply the Latin word for girl-child, hence for a doll; and Linnaeus' adoption of it was a stroke of genius, as you will realise if you look at the underside of a moth's pupa and see the shape of its face, eyes and embryonic wings like little arms sedately crossed in front of its body, all wrapped as if in swaddling-clothes which emphasise its likeness to a doll. Other words from the Latin *pupa* or French *poupée* are puppy (as it were a toy dog, a dog-doll) and pupil, in both senses,—that of the eye is so called because of the tiny image reflected there. From *poupette,* a baby doll, we get puppet and also poppet, the term of endearment.

[5]   Because they are the creatures of our fallible minds, words owe their existence as often to errors, superstitions, confusions and sheer ignorance as they do to our imagination, sharp eyes, keen ears, affections, prejudices, sense of fun, irony or any other of the attributes of this thinking reed, as Pascal described man.

"Hysteria" for example arises out of a medical misconception. Because women were more liable to acute and dramatic emotional disturbances than men, the doctors came to the conclusion that these vapours must be due to the family functioning of some organ which men hadn't got. They decided this could be none other than the uterus; and so "hysteria" gets its name from Greek *hustera,* the womb.

From a medical superstition of the Middle Ages comes the name of a greenish stone which was said to give relief to the pains of colic, especially those which occurred just under the short ribs, or near the groin. For this reason the Spanish doctors called this stone *piedra de ijada,* the stone of the side. Thence by ellipsis and mispronunciation we get our word "jade."

Another superstitious derivation is that of "sinister." The Latin word means "on the left" and the augurs who sought to predict events believed that omens, etc. observed on the left-hand side were unfavourable, wherefore the word gets it uncomfortable meaning.

[6]   Careless pronunciation, the running together of syllables, and our typically English habit of mumbling, combined with ignorance of a word's true meaning and contempt for anything we do not understand, have occasionally enriched the language by accident. "Termagant," for instance, is a corruption of Tervagant or Trivigant, a noisy knockabout character who appeared in the old

morality plays, where he was described as "a Mohammedan deity." A similar corruption gave us "mammet," an image or puppet (now obsolete but familiar in Shakespeare). It derives from the belief that Mahomet was worshipped by his followers. So did we demonstrate our remarkable ignorance concerning the faith which affirms unequivocally: "There is no God but God."

"Ragman rolls" were certain deeds, documents, schedules, catalogues, etc. written upon rolls of parchment, and in particular they were the instruments of homage done by the Spanish nobles to King Edward the First. Slovenly speech turned this into "rigmarole," an excellent word by which we still express our disapproval of legal documents.

Often enough our dislike of foreign pronunciations goes hand in hand with our ignorance; and then perhaps there is born such a word as "nincompoop," possibly from *non compos mentis,* or "dandelion," the happiest of accidents, for whereas *dent-de-lion* described but one not very noticeable characteristic of the plant, its notched leaves, "dandelion" contrives to pack into its nine letters a complete and vivid description of the dandy flower, the show-off, the shaggy-one, golden-maned, bold as a lion and so on.

Another flower-name, "rosemary," provides an even better example of our English way with words. Being partly maritime, the herb was given the Latin name *ros marinus,* "sea-dew." Pleasant enough,—but that *ros* offered a temptation which the English can rarely resist, to make "rose" out of any syllable that sounds remotely like it, while *marinus* naturally suggested "Mary," another name we love. So we dedicated the herb to the Virgin, as it were, and in doing so twisted the Latin out of all semblance of its meaning. Who cares? We made a name for the homely herb that aptly matches it, that has endearing associations, and that is most perfectly suited to our tongue:

> For you there's rosemary and rue; these keep
> Seeming and savour all the winter long.[13]

The learned would perhaps describe the process which gave us "dandelion" as folk-etymology, that is to say "the popular perversion of a form of words in order to render it apparently significant." [14] I am always a bit suspicious about any expression or con-

13. *The Winter's Tale.*
14. *OED.*

cept involving the word "folk," partly because I find it so often associated with the ponderous, patronising and intellectual approach to country people ("folk-speech," "folk-customs," even, ye Gods, "folk-psychology," which, you have probably guessed, is a word invented by the *Herrenvolk* themselves, *völkerpsychologie*) and partly of course because of its nauseous application to fairies: the Little Folk. I have even read a solemn assertion that "foxglove" was originally "folks' glove," fairies' glove, which is precisely the sort of piffle folk-lorists are apt to fall for.

[7]   From time to time in this book we shall have occasion to take note of words which, quite clearly, have been made by poets. The poets may have been individuals, learned or simple but possessed of the seeing eye; or possibly a whole series of imaginations have worked upon a word, polishing it bright as a pebble that has been in the stream for a couple of hundred years. However it happened, nobody can deny the poetry of "dandelion"; nor of "comet," which perhaps occurs to me because it too possesses a flaming mane! *Komē* is Greek for hair; *aster komētes* was a long-haired star; hence via Latin, Old French *comète* for the heavenly body with its hair streaming in the firmament which appears on the Bayeux tapestry. Here is a good example of the pleasure you can get from this hobby of investigating words. "Comet" becomes a word of great splendour when you know its derivation; and whenever you meet with it, especially in poetry, it will "mean more" to you because the image which it calls up in your mind will be more vivid and complete,—

> Incens'd with indignation Satan stood
> Unterrifi'd, and like a comet burn'd
> That fires the length of Ophiucus huge
> In th' arctic sky, and from his horrid hair
> Shakes pestilence and war.[15]

Milton's superb Satan is awesome and terrible and possessed of majesty, because the poet knows that if you allow yourself to think of God's adversary otherwise, you detract from the glory of God. Notice "incens'd," meaning "set on fire" in the literal sense; not just annoyed! And notice "horrid," bearing its older meaning of rough, bristling, shaggy. In fact, Satan's mane of fire streamed out behind him like that of Halley's Comet in 1066!

15. Milton: *Paradise Lost.*

SUMMARY

[1]   Words taken from other languages usually change meanings, and sometimes very dramatically.

[2]   Some of the words we have taken from Greek illustrate this well.

[3]   Words from Greek and Roman mythology are enlivened if one remembers mythological stories.

[4]   Scientific words taken from Latin often show poetic imagination.

[5]   Words from Latin and Greek often reflect old superstitions.

[6]   Others take strange turns because of mispronunciation or misunderstanding.

[7]   Poets often expect us to know something of a word's history.

NOTES

You already know, no doubt, that a very sizable portion of the modern English vocabulary was borrowed from Latin and that many specialized and scientific words are borrowed from Greek. For a generous treatment of these "loan words" you might study such a history of our language as Albert C. Baugh's *History of the English Language,* 2nd ed. (New York: Appleton-Century-Crofts, 1957).

This chapter, by a British journalist and author, is limited to a discussion of only a few of the thousands of words we have borrowed from Greek and Latin, and Mr. Moore is especially concerned with words whose meanings have changed in odd ways or have strange interests for us. The burden of the chapter is, of course, that etymology—the study of the history of a word and its meanings—is a fascinating study. A great dictionary such as the *New English Dictionary* (also called the *Oxford English Dictionary,* since it was published by the Oxford University Press, and known among scholars and librarians as the *NED* or *OED*) is a vast compilation of the histories of the words in our vocabulary.

For that matter, even a small collegiate dictionary is richer in information about words than you may suspect. A useful first step in dictionary study is the careful reading of the front matter (the pages in a dictionary which precede the word list) of a modern collegiate dictionary.

Various Sources

OTTO JESPERSEN

Jens Otto Harry Jespersen, known affectionately among students of the English language as "the great Dane," was professor of English language and literature at the University of Copenhagen for fifty years until his death in 1943. This and the following selection, taken from his Growth and Structure of the English Language *(1905), suggest something of the wide range of sources from which the huge English vocabulary has been derived.*

[1]   Although English has borrowed a great many words from other languages than those mentioned in the preceding chapters, these borrowings need not occupy us long here. For only Scandinavian, French and Latin have left a mark on English deep enough to modify its character and to change its structure, and the language would remain the same in every essential respect even were all the other loan-words to disappear to-morrow.

There is, of course, nothing peculiarly English in the adoption of words denoting animals, plants, products, or institutions originally peculiar to one part of the world, but later known in many countries, such as *gondola, maccaroni* and *lava* from Italian, *matador, siesta* and *sherry* from Spanish, *steppe* and *verst* from Russian, *caravan* and *dervish* from Persian, *hussar* and *shako* from Hungarian, *bey* and *caftan* from Turkish, *harem* and *mufti* from Arabic, *bamboo* and *orangoutang* from Malay, *taboo* from Polynesian, *boomerang* and *wombat* from Australian, *chocolate* and *tomato* from Mexican, *moccasin, tomahawk* and *totem* from other American languages. As a matter of fact, all these words now belong to the whole of the civilized world: like such classical or pseudo-classical words as *nationality, telegram* and *civilization,* they bear

---

Reprinted with permission of The Macmillan Company from *The Growth and Structure of the English Language,* 9th ed. (sections 151–163) by Otto Jespersen. Published in Canada by George Allen & Unwin Ltd.

witness to the sameness of modern culture everywhere: the same products and to a great extent the same ideas are now known all over the globe and many of them have in many languages identical names.

With regard to these as well as to other loan-words it should always be remembered that the ultimate origin of a word is not always the source whence it has penetrated into English. Many exotic words have come to England through Spanish or Portuguese. *Paradise,* originally a Persian word, has come through French; so have *shallop, chaloupe,* originally Dutch *sloep,* in English spelt *sloop,* and *fuchsia,* as shown by the pronunciation: it is derived from the name of a German botanist Fuchs.

[2]   It will be worth our while to consider the loans from a few languages, as they have great cultural importance. First the Dutch.[1] It is significant that this word in English means not German (deutsch), but the inhabitants and the language of the Netherlands, with which the English came into more intimate relations than with the Germans themselves. The Dutch have always been a seafaring nation; hence it is no wonder that many nautical words have come from that source: *yacht, yawl, schooner, bowline, deck, cruise, iceberg; euphroe,* a learned spelling of Du. *juffrouw* "a crowfoot dead-eye," must have been taken over by word of mouth. There are also some military words: *furlough, tattoo, onslaught.* But the most interesting group of Dutch words relates to the fine arts, which flourished in the Low Countries in the 16th and 17th centuries and exercised a strong influence on English artists. Hence such words as *easel, etch, sketch, maulstick, landscape* (whence such English new-formed words as *seascape, cloudscape,* and finally the isolated *scape*). On South African words see [10].

[3]   This leads us naturally to the other great influence on the artistic vocabulary, namely Italian.[2] Attention has already been called to the great number of musical terms derived from Italian.

---

1. See J. F. Bense, *The Anglo-Dutch Relations* ('s-Gravenhage, 1924); Bense, *A Dictionary of the Dutch Element in the English Vocabulary* (The Hague, 1926–1935; a standard work); E. C. Llewellyn, *The Influence of Low Dutch on the English Vocabulary* (Oxford, 1936; based chiefly on Bense); G. N. Clark, *The Dutch Influence on the English Vocabulary* (S. P. E., 44, Oxford, 1935).

2. See Mario Praz, *The Italian Element in English* (Essays and Studies, XV, 20 ff.).

A great many terms of architecture and of the fine arts in general derive from Italy: *balcony, colonnade, cornice, corridor, grotto, loggia, mezzanine, niche, parapet, pilaster, profile;* further *fresco, miniature; improvisatore, dilettante, opera, sonnet.* From related cultural domains we may mention *casino, carnival, milliner* (orig. modistes from Milan). Commercial relations have given us such words as *traffic, risk, magazine, bank* and what belongs to that: *bankrupt* (Latinized from *bancarotta*), *agio, Lombard.* Among military terms may be mentioned *alarm, colonel* (the pronunciation goes back to the form *coronel*), *arsenal, pistol.*

[4]   From Spanish we may mention the military words *armada, escapade* and *embargo,* further designations for persons like *don* (note the curious use in English universities) and *hidalgo; padre* obtained a certain vogue during the first world war. In the world of games we have *quadrille, spade* and other terms for cards. Commerce brought *anchovy, cargo, cordovan* and *lime* (the fruit). In recent times the Californian *cafeteria* has proved exceedingly productive in linguistic offspring: *drugteria, sodateria, fruiteria, shaveteria, shoeteria,* and other more or less ridiculous American words.

[5]   Among Arabic words in English [3]—some of them easily recognizable through the definite article *al*—we must specially mention those relating to mathematics, astronomy, and science in general: *algebra, cipher, zero, nadir, zenith, alchemy, alcohol, alkali, bismuth, elixir, natron.* Some English scientific terms are Arabic in meaning, but not in form, thus the mathematical *sine* from Latin *sinus* "fold," translating Arabic *jaib;* x as a sign for an unknown quantity "was no doubt used first in Spain because it is the letter corresponding etymologically in Spanish to Arabic *shîn,* used in this sense as an abbreviation of the word *shai* thing." Other Arabic words are *alcove, sofa, sash, caraway, sherbet.*

[6]   The British Empire has caused contact with a great many peoples and in consequence loans from many languages. From India we have, among other words, *sahib, begum, maharajah, pundit, baboo* (the curious language spoken by some Hindus is often called Baboo English), *thug; durbar, Swaraj; cot, bungalow, pucka, coolie, pariah, chit, Choki,* originally meaning customs-house, is used for "prison" (folk-etymological connexion with E.

3. Walt Taylor, *Arabic Words in English* (S. P. E., 38, Oxford, 1933).

choke?). For articles of apparel we have *topi, pyjamas* and *bandana*. *Loot* is an interesting parallel to *plunder* [7]. The notorious *dumdum* bullets are named from a place Dum Dum, near Calcutta. Some originally Indian words have come to English through Persian: *divan, khaki, zenana, purdah*. From African languages we have, e.g., *impi* "regiment," *indaba* "conference." From Chinese *kowtow*. But some of these words can hardly be said to belong to ordinary English.

[7]   There are surprisingly few German loan-words in English,[4] and very little can be inferred from them with regard to cultural relations, apart, perhaps, from some philosophical terms the meaning of which was stamped by Kant and his English followers. *Plunder* is due to the English soldiers in the thirty years' war, and *swindler* is said to have been introduced by German Jews about 1726. Some mining terms, such as *feldspar, gneiss* and *quartz*, come from Germany. There are some translation-loans, e.g. *home-sickness* and *one-sided*, also the place-name the *Black Forest*, but otherwise the tendency is to swallow German words raw, even where a translation would have been easy: the *Siebengebirge* and the *Riesengebirge* are much more commonly used than the *Seven Mountains* and the *Giant Mountains*. Thus we have *kindergarten* unchanged, while for the same institution Danish has the literal translation *börnehave* and Norwegian *barnehave*. Similarly English has *rinderpest, landsturm, zollverein, weltpolitik, weltanschauung* and *hinterland*—which may even be used as in "a residential hinterland" (of a town, Kaye-Smith, *Tamarisk Town*, 105), and "a vast hinterland of thoughts and feelings" (Wells, *Marriage*, 2, 121). Here we have come upon something which seems to be characteristic of the English in their relation to foreign words.

[8]   An interesting contrast may be seen between the linguistic behaviour of the Dutch and the English in South Africa. The former, finding there a great many natural objects which were new to them, designated them either by means of existing Dutch words whose meanings were, accordingly, more or less modified, or else by coining new words, generally compounds. Thus *sloot* "ditch" was applied to the peculiar dry rivers of that country, *veld* "field" to the open pasturages, and *kopje* "a little head or cup" to the hills,

4. See Charles T. Carr, *The German Influence on the English Vocabulary* (S. P. E., 42, Oxford, 1934).

etc.; different kinds of animals were called *roodebok* "red-buck," *steenbok* "stonebuck," *springbok* "hopbuck," *springhaas* "hophare," *hartebeest* "hartbeast"; a certain bird was called *slangvreter* "serpent-eater," a certain large shrub *spekboom* "bacon-tree," etc. The English, on the other hand, instead of imitating this principle, have simply taken over all these names into their own language, where they now figure [5] together with some other South African Dutch words, among which may be mentioned *trek* and *spoor* in the special significations of "colonial migration" and "track of wild animal," while the Dutch words are much less specialized (*trekken* "to draw, pull, travel, move"; *spoor* "trace, track, trail"). These examples of borrowings might easily be multiplied from other domains, and we may say of the English what Moth says of Holofernes and Sir Nathaniel that "they have been at a great feast of languages, and stolen the scraps" (*Love's Labours Lost*, V, 1, 39). It will therefore be natural to inquire into the cause of this linguistic omnivorousness.

[9]   It would, of course, be irrational to ascribe the phenomenon to a greater natural gift for learning languages, for in the first place, the English are not usually credited with such a gift, and secondly the best linguists are generally inclined to keep their own language pure rather than adulterate it with scraps of other languages. Consequently, we should be nearer the truth if we were to give as a reason the linguistic incapacity of the average Englishman. As a traveller and a colonizer, however, he is thrown into contact with people of a great many different nations and thus cannot help seeing numerous things and institutions unknown in England. R. L. Stevenson says somewhere about the typical John Bull, that "his is a domineering nature, steady in fight, imperious to command, but neither curious nor quick about the life of others." [6] And perhaps the loan-words we are considering testify to nothing but the most superficial curiosity about the life of other nations and would not have been adopted if John Bull had really in his heart cared any more than this for the foreigners he meets. He is content to pick up a few scattered fragments of their speech —just enough to impart a certain local colouring to his narratives and political discussions, but he goes no further.

---

5. *Roodebok* often spelt in accordance with the actual Dutch pronunciation *rooibok, rooyebok*. *Sloot* often appears in the un-Dutch spelling *sluit*.
6. *Memories and Portraits*, p. 3.

[10] The tendency to adopt words from other languages is due, then, probably to a variety of causes. Foremost among these I think it is right to place the linguistic laziness mentioned in [9] and fostered especially by the preference for words from the classical languages. That the borrowing is not occasioned by an inherent deficiency in the *language* itself is shown by the ease with which new terms actually *are* framed whenever the need of them is really felt, especially by uneducated people who are not tempted to go outside their own language to express their thoughts. Interesting examples of this natural inventiveness may be found in Mr. Edward E. Morris's *Austral English, A dictionary of Australasian words, phrases and usages.* As Mr. Morris says in his preface, "Those who, speaking the tongue of Shakespeare, of Milton, and of Dr. Johnson, came to various parts of Australasia, found a Flora and a Fauna waiting to be named in English. New birds, beasts and fishes, new trees, bushes and flowers, had to receive names for general use. It is probably not too much to say that there never was an instance in history when so many new names were needed, and that there never will be such an occasion again, for never did settlers come, nor can they ever again come, upon Flora and Fauna so completely different from anything seen by them before." The gaps were filled partly by adopting words from the aboriginal languages, e.g. *kangaroo, wombat,* partly by applying English words to objects bearing a real or fancied resemblance to the objects denoted by them in England, e.g. *magpie, oak, beech,* but partly also by new English formations. Accordingly, in turning over the leaves of Mr. Morris's dictionary we come across numerous names of birds like *friar-bird, frogsmouth, honey-eater, ground-lark, forty-spot,*[7] of fishes like *long-fin, trumpeter,* of plants like *sugar-grass, hedge-laurel, ironheart, thousand-jacket.* Most of these show that "the settler must have had an imagination. Whip-bird, or Coach-whip, from the sound of the note, Lyre-bird from the appearance of the outspread tail, are admirable names." (Morris, l. c.). It certainly seems a pity that

7. One story of a curious change of meaning must be recounted in Mr. Morris's words: "The settler heard a bird laugh in what he thought an extremely ridiculous manner, its opening notes suggesting a donkey's bray—he called it the 'laughing jackass.' His descendants have dropped the adjective, and it has come to pass that the word 'jackass' denotes to an Australian something quite different from its meaning to other speakers of our English tongue."

book-learned people when wanting to enrich their mother tongue have not, as a rule, drawn from the same source or shown the same talent for picturesque and "telling" designations.

[11]   Many of our times' new inventions and other innovations have enriched the language.[8] Cinematograph is generally shortened into *cinema,* even *cine,* but people often speak of the *movies.* We have the curious differentiation of *radium* and *radio:* the latter has given a new sense to the old *broadcast* (B.B.C. = British Broadcasting Corporation). For *automobile* the simple word *car* is generally said, or else *motor-car.* We have *aeroplane,* for which some people prefer the form *airplane;* it is also shortened into *plane,* and we have the new *aquaplane* and *seaplane;* further, *airship, aircraft, airman,* etc., also *aerodrome; taxi* is used for crawling along the ground before or after alighting in a plane. Some of the new words introduced with these inventions have taken some time, before their spoken forms in English were quite fixed: *chauffeur* from [ʃouˈfɚ] has now usually become [ˈʃoufə]; *hangar* and *garage* were at first spoken with long [a·] in the last syllable, but now they are generally Anglicized [hæŋgə], [hæŋə], [gæridʒ]. The learned *television* has brought about the verb *televise,* and *televisor* for the apparatus. Let me finally mention *tango* and *jazz.*

[12]   A great many words are nowadays coined by tradespeople to designate new articles of merchandise. Very little regard is generally paid to correctness of formation, the only essential being a name that is good for advertising purposes. Sometimes a mere arbitrary collection of sounds or letters is chosen, as in the case of *kodak,* and sometimes the inventor contents himself with some vague resemblance to some other word, which may assist the buyer to remember the name. A few examples may be given: *bovril* (Latin *bos* + vril, an electrical fluid mentioned in an old novel by Lytton), *vapo-cresolene* (cresolene vaporized), *harlene* (hair), *wincarnis* (a tonic, wine, Latin caro?), *rinso* (for cleaning, rinse), *redux* (reducing herbal tea), *yeast-vite* (tonic), *ceilingite* (whitewash), *elasto* . . . Sometimes these trade names are merely ordinary words disguised by fancy spellings, e.g. *Phiteesi* boots,

8. Recent linguistic innovations are dealt with in H. Spies, *Kultur und Sprache im neun England* (Leipzig, 1925); R. Hittmair, *Wortbildende Kräfte im heutigen Englisch* (Leipzig, 1937); W. E. Collinson, *Contemporary English* (Leipzig, 1927).

Stickphast, Uneeda cigar (= you need a cigar) in England,
Uneeda biscuit in America. Many such names are very short-lived,
but some are there to stay and may even pass into common use
outside the sphere for which they were originally invented. This
is the case with *kodak.*[9]

[13] The Great War (1914–1918) left its mark on language as
on everything.[10] It introduced a certain number of foreign words,
e.g. *camouflage* (in English also as a verb = Fr. *camoufler*), in the
navy called *dazzle-painting;* from German we had *U-boat* = sub-
marine, and the stupid *strafe* (from "Gott strafe England") at the
time often pronounced [streif]; the curious *blighty* is from Hindu
bilayati "foreign," used by soldiers on foreign service for "home,
i.e. England." Old words were provided with new meanings: *ace*
like Fr. *as* came to mean an airman who had brought down a certain number of foreign men; *bus* = aeroplane, further *gas* (be
gassed) and *tank; go West* was used as a euphemism for "die, be
lost." The war even produced a new numeral: *umpteen,* used to
disguise the number of a brigade, later in the sense of a considerable number. The tendency to shorten words is seen in *conchy* =
conscientious objector, *zepp* = Zeppelin, etc. But most of the war
words belong to slang and as such fall outside the scope of this
work.

9. Additional examples in Louise Pound, *Word-Coinage and Modern
Trade Names* (Dialect Notes, LV, 1913), and H. L. Mencken, *The American
Language,* 4th ed., 171 ff.
10. See besides the works by Spies, Hittmair and Collinson mentioned
above, A. Smith, *New Words Self-Defined* (New York, 1920).

NOTES

The general ideas of this essay, as the one preceding, are easy
enough; your study should be concentrated upon learning as many of
the details as you can. It would be wise to learn a good sample of borrowings from each of the sources discussed.
If Jespersen's transcription of words in [11] doesn't make sense to
you, refer to the charts of phonetic alphabets on pages 95–96. Only
one further thing might be added: Jespersen marks a stressed syllable
with an apostrophe-like symbol (') at the *beginning* of the syllable.

Native Resources

OTTO JESPERSEN

*Though a large portion of English words have come from bor-
rowings from other languages, English had considerable native
resources, too, as Professor Jespersen's following chapter makes
clear.*

[1]   However important foreign loan-words are, the chief enrichment of the language is due to those regular processes which are
so familiar that any new word formed by means of them seems
at once an old acquaintance. The whole history of English word-
formation may be summed up as follows—that some formative
elements have been gradually discarded, especially those that presented some difficulty of application, while others have been
continually gaining ground, because they have admitted of being
added to all or nearly all words without occasioning any change
in the kernel of the word. Among the former I shall mention *-en*
to denote female beings (cf. German *-in*). In Old English this
had already become very impracticable because sound changes
had occurred which obscured the connexion between related
words. Corresponding to the masculine *þegn* "retainer," *þeow*
"slave," *wealh* "foreigner," *scealc* "servant," *fox,* we find the feminine *þignen, þiewen, wielen, scielcen, fyxen.* It seems clear that
new generations would find difficulties in forming new feminines
on such indistinct analogies, so we cannot wonder that the ending
ceased to be productive and that the French ending *-ess,* which
presented no difficulties, came to be used extensively. Of the
words in *-en* mentioned, *fyxen* is the only one surviving, and its
connexion with *fox* is now loosened, both through the form *vixen*
(with its *v* from Southern dialects) and through the meaning,
which is now most often "a quarrelsome woman."

Reprinted with permission of The Macmillan Company from Sections 164–
187 of *The Growth and Structure of the English Language,* 9th ed., by Otto
Jespersen. Published in Canada by George Allen & Unwin Ltd.

46

[2] A much more brilliant destiny was reserved for the Old English ending -isc. At first it was added only to nouns indicating nations, whose vowel it changed by mutation; thus *Englisc*, now *English*, from *Angle*, etc. In some adjectives, however, no mutation was possible, e.g. *Irish*, and by analogy the vowel of the primitive word was soon introduced into some of the adjectives, e.g. *Scottish* (earlier *Scyttisc*), *Danish* (earlier *Denisc*). The ending was extended first to words whose meaning was cognate to these national names, *heathenish*, OE. *folcisc* or *þeodisc* "national" (from *folc* or *þeod* "people"); then gradually came *childish*, *churlish*, etc. Each century added new extensions; *foolish* and *feverish*, for instance, date from the 14th, and *boyish* and *girlish* from the 16th century, until now -*ish* can be added to nearly any noun and adjective (swinish, bookish, greenish, biggish, etc.).

[3] We shall see in a later section that the ending -*ing* has still more noticeably broken the bounds of its originally narrow sphere of application. Another case in point is the verbal suffix -*en*. It is now possible to form a verb from any adjective fulfiling certain phonetic conditions by adding -*en* (harden, weaken, sweeten, sharpen, lessen). But this suffix was not used very much before 1500, indeed most of the verbs formed in -*en* belong to the last three centuries. Another extensively used ending is -*er*. Old English had various methods of forming substantives to denote agents; from the verb *huntan* "hunt" it had the noun *hunta* "hunter"; from *beodan* "announce," *boda* "messenger, herald"; from *wealdan* "rule," *weada;* from *beran* "bear," *bora;* from *sceþþan* "injure," *sceaþa;* from *weorcan* "work," *wyrhta* "wright" (in *wheelwright*, etc.), though some of these were used in compounds only; some nouns were formed in -*end: rædend* "ruler," *scieppend* "creator," and others in -*ere: blawere* "one who blows," *blotere* "sacrificer," etc. But it seems as if there were many verbs from which it was impossible to form any agent-noun at all, and the reader will have noticed that even the formation in *a* presented some difficulties, as the vowel was modified according to complicated rules. When the want of new substantives was felt, it was, therefore, more and more the ending -*ere* that was resorted to. But the curious thing is that the function of this ending was at first to make nouns, not from verbs, but from other nouns, thus OE. *bocere* "scribe" from *boc* "book" (already Gothic *bokareis*), compare modern *hatter, tinner, Londoner, New Englander, first-*

nighter. As, however, such a word as fisher, OE. *fiscere,* which is derived from the noun a *fish,* OE. *fisc,* might just as well be analysed as derived from the corresponding verb to *fish,* OE. *fiscian,* it became usual to form new agent-denoting nouns in *-er* from verbs, and in some cases these supplanted older formations (OE. *hunta,* now *hunter*). Now we do not hesitate to make new words in *-er* from any verb, e.g., a *snorer,* a *sitter,* odd *comers* and *goers,* a total *abstainer,* etc. Combinations with an adverb (a *diner-out,* a *looker-on*) go back to Chaucer ("A somnour is a renner up and down With mandements for fornicacioun," D 1284), but do not seem to be very frequent before the Elizabethan period. Note also the extensive use of the suffix to denote instruments and things, as in *slipper, rubber, typewriter, sleeper* (American = sleeping car). A variant of *-er* is *-eer,* which is liable, but only after *t,* to impart a disparaging meaning: this starts perhaps from *garreteer* and *pamphleteer,* hence the contemptuous *sonneteer, profiteer,* famous or infamous during the war, and *patrioteering* (my *Language,* p. 388, not in *NED*). Another variant of *-er* is *-ster,*[1] which is often wrongly supposed to be a specially feminine suffix, though from the earliest times it has been used of men as well as of women, from the old *demestre,* now *deemster* or *dempster* "a judge," and family names like *Baxter, Webster,* down to the more modern *punster, gangster, fibster, youngster,* etc. A *spinster* originally meant one who spins, but is now restricted to unmarried (old) maids. Special feminines are formed in *-stress: seamstress* (*sempstress*), *songstress.*

[4]   Other much-used suffixes for substantives are: *-ness* (goodness, truthfulness), *-dom* (Christendom, boredom, "Swelldom," Thackeray), *-ship* (ownership, companionship, horsemanship), for adjectives: *-ly* (lordly, cowardly), *-y* (fiery, churchy, creepy), *-less* (powerless, dauntless), *-ful* (powerful, fanciful), and *-ed* (blue-eyed, good-natured, renowned, conceited, talented; broad-breasted; level-browed, like the horizon "—thighed and shouldered like the billows—footed like their stealing foam," Ruskin). Prefixes of wide application are *mis-, un-, be-,* and others. By means of these formatives the English vocabulary has been and is being constantly enriched with thousands and thousands of useful new words.

---

1. Jespersen, *Linguistica* (Copenhagen, 1933), p. 420 ff.

[5]   There is one manner of forming verbs from nouns and vice versa which is specifically English and which is of the greatest value on account of the ease with which it is managed, namely that of making them exactly like one another. In Old English there were a certain number of verbs and nouns of the same "root," but distinguished by the endings. Thus "I love" through the three persons singular ran *lufie, lufast, lufaþ,* plural *lufiaþ;* the infinitive was *lufian,* the subjunctive *lufie,* pl. *lufien,* and the imperative was *lufa,* pl. *lufiaþ.* The substantive "love" on the other hand was *lufu,* in the other cases *lufe,* plural *lufa* or *lufe, lufum, lufena* or *lufa.* Similarly "to sleep" was *slæpan,* pres. *slæpe, slæpest, slæp(e)þ, slæpaþ,* subjunctive *slæpe, slæpen,* imperative *slæp, slæpaþ,* while the substantive had the forms *slæp, slæpe* and *slæpes* in the singular and *slæpas, slæpum, slæpa* in the plural. If we were to give the corresponding forms used in the subsequent centuries, we should witness a gradual simplification which had as a further consequence the mutual approximation of the verbal and nominal forms. The *-m* is changed into *-n,* all the vowels of the weak syllables are levelled to one uniform *e,* the plural forms of the verbs in *-þ* give way to forms in *-n,* and all the final *n*'s eventually disappear, while in the nouns *s* is gradually extended so that it becomes the only genitive and almost the only plural ending. The second person singular of the verbs retains its distinctive *-st,* but towards the end of the Middle English period *thou* already begins to be less used, and the polite *ye, you,* which becomes more and more universal, claims no distinctive ending in the verb. In the fifteenth century, the *e* of the endings, which had hitherto been pronounced, ceased to be sounded, and somewhat later *s* became the ordinary ending of the third person singular instead of *th.* These changes brought about the modern scheme:

noun: *love loves—sleep sleeps*
verb: *love loves—sleep sleeps*

where we have perfect formal identity of the two parts of speech, only with the curious cross-relation between them that *s* is the ending of the plural in the nouns and of the singular (third person) in the verbs—an accident which might almost be taken as a device for getting an *s* into most sentences in the present tense (the lover love*s*; the lover*s* love) and for showing by the place of the *s* which of the two numbers is intended.

[6]   As a great many native nouns and verbs had thus come to be identical in form (e.g. *blossom, care, deal, drink, ebb, end, fathom, fight, fish, fire*), and as the same thing happened with numerous originally French words (e.g. *accord,* OFr. acord and acorder, *account, arm, blame, cause, change, charge, charm, claim, combat, comfort, copy, cost, couch*), it was quite natural that the speech-instinct should take it as a matter of course that whenever the need of a verb arose, it might be formed without any derivative ending from the corresponding substantive.[2] Among the innumerable nouns from which verbs have been formed in this manner, we may mention a few: *ape, awe, cook, husband, silence, time, worship.* Nearly every word for the different parts of the body has given rise to a homonym verb, though true it is that some of them are rarely used: *eye, nose* ("you shall nose him as you go up the staires," *Hamlet*), *lip* (= kiss, Shakespeare), *beard, tongue, brain* ("such stuffe as madmen tongue and braine not," Shakespeare, *Cymbeline*), *jaw* (= scold, etc.), *ear* (rare = give ear to), *chin* (American = to chatter), *arm* (= put one's arm round), *shoulder* (arms), *elbow* (one's way through the crowd), *hand, fist* ("fisting each other's throat," Shakespeare), *finger, thumb, breast* (= oppose), *body* (forth), *skin, stomach, limb* ("they limb themselves," Milton), *knee* (= kneel, Shakespeare), *foot.* It would be possible in a similar way to go through a great many other categories of words; everywhere we should see the same facility of forming new verbs from substantives.

[7]   The process is also very often resorted to for "noncewords" in speaking and in writing. Thus, a common form of retort is exemplified by the following quotations: "Trinkets! a bauble

2. It is often said, even by some of the most famous recent writers, that modern English has given up the sharp division into different parts of speech which was characteristic of the earlier stages of our family of speech. This is entirely wrong: even if the same form *love* or *sleep* may be said to belong to more than one word-class, this is true of the isolated form only: in each separate case in which the word is used in actual speech it belongs definitely to one class and to no other. The form *round* is a substantive in "a round of the ladder," "he took his daily round," an adjective in "a round table," a verb in "he failed to round the lamp-post," an adverb in "come round to-morrow," and a preposition in "he walked round the house." Many people will say that in the sentence "we tead at the vicarage" we have a case of a substantive used as a verb. The truth is that we have a real verb, just as real as *dine* or *eat,* though derived from the substantive *tea,* and derived without any distinctive ending in the infinitive. Cf. *Philosophy of Grammar,* pp. 52 and 61 f.

for Lydia! . . . So this was the history of his trinkets! I'll *bauble*
him!" (Sheridan, *Rivals*, V, 2). "I was explaining the Golden Bull
to his Royal Highness." "I'll *Golden Bull* you, you rascal!" roared
the Majesty of Prussia (Macaulay, *Biographical Essay*). "Such a
savage as that, as has just come home from South Africa. Diamonds indeed! I'd *diamond* him" (Trollope, *Old Man's Love*)—
and in a somewhat different manner: "My gracious Uncle.—Tut,
tut, Grace me no Grace, nor Uncle me no Uncle" (Shakespeare,
Richard II, cf. also *Romeo and Juliet*, III, 5, 143). "I heartily wish
I could, but—" "Nay, but me no buts—I have set my heart upon
it" (Scott, *Antiquary*, ch. XI). "Advance and take thy prize, The
diamond; but he answered, Diamond me No diamonds! For God's
love, a little air! Prize me no prizes, for my prize is death" (Tennyson, *Lancelot and Elaine*).

[8]   A still more characteristic peculiarity of the English language is the corresponding freedom with which a form which was
originally a verb is used unchanged as a substantive. This was
not possible till the disappearance of the final -*e* which was found
in most verbal forms, and accordingly we see an ever increasing
number of these formations from about 1500. I shall give some
examples in chronological order, adding the date of the earliest
quotation for the noun in the *NED: glance* 1503, *bend* 1529, *cut*
1530, *fetch* 1530, *hearsay* 1532, *blemish* 1535, *gaze* 1542, *reach*
1542, *drain* 1552, *gather* 1555, *burn* 1563, *lend* 1575, *dislike* 1577,
frown 1581, *dissent* 1585, *fawn* (a servile cringe) 1590, *dismay*
1590, *embrace* 1592, *hatch* 1597, *dip* 1599, *dress* (personal attire)
1606, *flutter* 1641, *divide* 1642, *build* 1667 (before the 19th century
apparently used by Pepys only), *harass* 1667, *haul* 1670, *dive* 1700,
go 1727 (many of the most frequent applications date from the
19th century), *hobble* 1727, *lean* (the act or condition of leaning)
1776, *bid* 1788, *hang* 1797, *dig* 1819, *find* 1825 (in the sense of that
which is found, 1847), *crave* 1830, *kill* (the act of killing) 1825, (a
killed animal) 1878. It will be seen that the 16th century is very
fertile in these nouns, which is only a natural consequence of the
phonological reason given above. As, however, some of the verb-
nouns found in Elizabethan authors have in modern times disappeared or become rare, some grammarians have inferred that we
have here a phenomenon peculiar to that period and due to the
general exuberance of the Renaissance which made people more
free with their language than they have since been. A glance

at our list will show that this is a wrong view; indeed, we use a great many formations of this kind which were unknown to Shakespeare; he had only the substantive *a visitation*, where we say *a visit*, nor did he know our *worries*, our *kicks*, and *moves*, etc., etc.

[9]   In some cases a substantive is formed in this manner in spite of there being already another noun derived from the same verb; thus *a move* has nearly the same meaning as *removal, movement* or *motion* (from which latter a new verb *to motion* is formed); *a resolve* and *resolution,* a *laugh* and *laughter* are nearly the same thing (though an *exhibit* is only one of the things found at an *exhibition*). Hence we get a lively competition started between these substantives and forms in -*ing: meet* (especially in the sporting world) and *meeting, shoot* and *shooting, read* (in the afternoon I like a rest and a read) and *reading*,[3] *row* (let us go out for a row) and *rowing* (he goes in for rowing), *smoke* and *smoking, mend* and *mending, feel* (there was a soft feel of autumn in the air) and *feeling*. The *build* of a house and the *make* of a machine are different from the *building* of the house and the *making* of the machine. The *sit* of a coat may sometimes be spoilt at one *sitting,* and we speak of *dressing,* not of *dress,* in connexion with a salad, etc. The enormous development of these convenient differentiations belongs to the most recent period of the language. Compared with the sets of synonyms mentioned above (§ 133: one of the words borrowed from Latin, etc.) this class of synonyms shows a decided superiority, because here small differences in sense are expressed by small differences in sound, and because all these words are formed in the most regular and easy manner; consequently there is the least possible strain put on the memory.

[10]   In early English a noun and the verb corresponding to it were often similar, although not exactly alike, some historical reason causing a difference in either the vowel or the final consonant or both. In such pairs of words as the following the old relation is kept unchanged: a *life,* to *live;* a *calf,* to *calve;* a *grief,* to *grieve;* a *cloth,* to *clothe;* a *house,* to *house;* a *use,* to *use*—in all these the noun has the voiceless and the verb the voiced consonant. The same alternation has been imitated in a few words

---

3. Darwin says in one of his letters: "I have just finished, after several reads, your paper"; this implies that he did not read it from beginning to end at one sitting; if he had written "after several readings" he would have implied that he had read it through several times.

which had originally the same consonant in the noun as in the verb; thus *belief, proof,* and *excuse* (with voiceless *s*) have supplanted the older substantives in *-ve* and voiced *-se* and inversely the verb *grease* has now often voiced *s* [z] alternating with a voiceless *s*. But in a far greater number of words the tendency to have nouns and verbs of exactly the same sound has prevailed, so that we have to *knife,* to *scarf* (Shakespeare), to *elf* (id.), to *roof,* and with voiceless *s,* to *loose,* to *race,* to *ice,* to *promise,* while the nouns *repose, cruise* (at sea), to *reprieve,* owe their voiced consonants to the corresponding verbs. In this way we get some interesting doublets. Besides the old noun *bath* and verb *bathe* we have the recent verb to *bath* (will you bath baby to-day?) and the substantive *bathe* ("I walked into the sea by myself and had a very decent bathe," Tennyson). Besides *glass* (noun) and *glaze* (verb) we have now also *glass* as a verb and *glaze* as a noun; so also in the case of *grass* and *graze, price* and *prize* (where *praise* verb and noun should be mentioned as etymologically the same word).

[11]   The same forces are at work in the smaller class of words in which the distinction between the noun and the verb is made by the alternation of *ch* and *k,* as in *speech–speak.* Side by side with the old *batch* we have a new noun, a *bake,* besides the noun *stitch* and the verb *stick* we have now also a verb to *stitch* (a book, etc.) and the rare noun a *stick* (the act of sticking); besides the old noun *stench* we have a new one from the verb *stink.* The modern word *ache* (in toothache, etc.) is a curious cross of the old noun, whose spelling has been kept, and the old verb, whose pronunciation (with *k*) has prevailed. Baret (1573) says expressly, "*Ake* is the verb of this substantive *ache, ch* being turned into *k.*" In the Shakespeare folio of 1623 the noun is always spelt with *ch* and the verb with *k;* the verb rimes with *brake* and *sake.* The noun was thus sounded like the name of the letter *h;* and Hart (*An Orthographie,* 1569, p. 35) says expressly, "We abuse the name of h, calling it ache, which sounde serveth very well to expresse a headache, or some bone ache." Indeed, the identity in sound of the noun and the name of the letter gave rise to one of the stock puns of the time: see for instance Shakespeare (*Much Ado about Nothing,* III, 4, 56); "by my troth I am exceeding ill, hey ho.— For a hauke, a horse, or a husband?—For the letter that begins them all, H," and a poem by Heywood: "It is worst among letters in the crosse row, For if thou find him other [= either] in thine

elbow, In thine arme, or leg . . . Where ever you find ache, thou
shalt not like him."

[12]   Numerous substantives and verbs have the same consonants, but a difference in the vowels, due either to gradation
(ablaut) or to mutation (umlaut). But here, too, the creative powers
of language may be observed. Where in old times there was only
a noun *bit* and a verb to *bite*, we have now in addition not only a
verb to *bit* (a horse, to put the bit into its mouth) as in Carlyle's
"the accursed hag 'dyspepsia' had got me bitted and bridled" and
in Coleridge's witty remark (quoted in the *NED*): "It is not women
and Frenchmen only that would rather have their tongues bitten
than bitted"—but also a noun *bite* in various meanings, e.g. in
"his bite is as dangerous as the cobra's" (Kipling) and "she took
a bite out of the apple" (Anthony Hope). From the noun *seat* we
have the new verb to *seat* (to place on a seat), while the verb to
sit has given birth to the noun *sit* (cf. [9]). No longer content with
the old *sale* as the substantive corresponding to *sell*, in slang we
have the new noun *a* (fearful) *sell* (an imposition); cf. also the
American substantive *tell* (according to their tell, see Farmer and
Henley). As *knot* (n.) was to *knit* (v.), so was *coss* to *kiss*, but while
of the former pair both forms have survived and have given rise
to a new verb to *knot* and a new noun, a *knit* (he has a permanent
knit of the brow, *NED*), from the latter the *o*-form has disappeared, the noun being now formed from the verb: a *kiss*. We
have the old *brood* (n.) and *breed* (v.) and the new *brood* (v.) and
breed (n.); a new verb to *blood* exists by the side of the old to
bleed, and a new noun *feed* by the side of the old *food*. It is obvious that the language has been enriched by acquiring all these
newly formed words; but it should also be admitted that there has
been a positive gain in ease and simplicity in all those cases where
there was no occasion for turning the existing phonetic difference
to account by creating new verbs or nouns in new significations,
and where, accordingly, one of the phonetic forms has simply disappeared, as when the old verbs *sniwan, scrydan, swierman* have
given way to the new *snows, shroud, swarm*, which are like the
nouns, or when the noun *swat, swot* (he swette blodes swot,
Ancrene Riwle) has been discarded in favour of *sweat*, which has
the same vowel as the verb.

[13]   In some cases the place of the stress serves to distinguish
substantives from verbs, the former having initial and the latter

final stress. Thus some native words with prefixes: 'forecast (sb.), fore'cast (v.), similarly overthrow, underline. In the same way a great many Romanic words are differentiated, the substantives (adjectives) having fore-stress, the corresponding verbs end-stress: e.g. absent, accent, conduct, frequent, object, present, rebel, record, subject, interdict. Words like compliment, experiment have an obscure vowel [ə] in the substantive, but a full vowel [e] in the verb, even if the final syllable has not full stress.

[14] Among the other points of interest presented by the formations occupying us here I may mention the curious oscillation found in some instances between noun and verb. Smoke is first a noun (the smoke from the chimney), then a verb (the chimney smokes, he smokes a pipe); then a new noun is formed from the verb in the last sense (let us have a smoke). Similarly gossip (a) noun: godfather, intimate friend, idle talker, (b) verb: to talk idly, (c) new noun: idle talk; dart (a) a weapon, (b) to throw (a dart), to move rapidly (like a dart), (c) a sudden motion; brush (a) an instrument, (b) to use that instrument, (c) the action of using it (your hat wants a brush); sail (a) a piece of canvas, (b) to sail, (c) a sailing excursion; wire (a) a metallic thread, (b) to telegraph, (c) a telegram; so also cable; in vulgar language a verb is formed to jaw and from that a second noun a jaw ("what speech do you mean?" "Why that grand jaw that you sputtered forth just now about reputation," F. C. Philips). Sometimes the starting point is a verb, e.g., frame (a) to form, (b) noun: a fabric, a border for a picture, etc., (c) verb: to set in a frame; and sometimes an adjective, e.g., faint (a) weak, (b) to become weak, (c) a fainting fit.

[15] To those who might see in the obliteration of the old distinctive marks of the different parts of speech a danger of ambiguity, I would answer that this danger is more imaginary than real. I open at random a modern novel and count on one page 34 nouns which can be used as infinitives without any change, and 38 verbs the forms of which can be used as nouns,[4] while only 22 nouns and 9 verbs cannot be thus used. As some of the ambiguous

4. Answer, brother, reply, father, room, key, haste, gate, time, head, pavement, man, waste, truth, thunder, clap, storey, bed, book, night, face, point, shame, while, eye, top, hook, finger, bell, land, lamp, tapen, shelf, church,— whisper, wait, return, go, keep, call, look, leave, reproach, do, pass, come, cry, open, sing, fall, hurry, reach, snatch, lie, regard, creep, lend, say, try, steal, hold, swell, wonder, interest, see, choke, shake, place, escape, ring, take, light. (I have not counted auxiliary verbs.)

nouns and verbs occur more than once, and as the same page contains adverbs, prepositions, and conjunctions [5] which are identical with nouns (adjectives) or verbs, or both, the theoretical possibilities of mistakes arising from confusion of parts of speech would seem to be very numerous. And yet no one reading that page would feel the slightest hesitation about understanding every word correctly, as either the ending or the context shows at once whether a verb is meant or not. Even such an extreme case as this line, which is actually found in a modern song, "Her eyes like angels watch them still," is not obscure, although *her* might be both accusative and possessive, *eyes* both noun and verb, *like* adjective, conjunction, and verb, *watch* noun and verb, and *still* adjective, verb and adverb. A modern Englishman, realizing the great advantage his language possesses in its power of making words serve in new functions, might make Shakespeare's lines his own in a different sense:

> So all my best is dressing old words new,
> spending againe what is already spent.[6]

[16]   Word-composition plays a very important part in English. Compounds are either fixed or free, i.e. such that when the need arises any speaker can form new compounds after the pattern of already existing combinations. The former tend to be felt as independent units, isolated from the component parts in sound and (or) in meaning. *Daisy* was originally *dayes eye*, but no one nowadays connects the word with either *day* or *eye*. *Woman* was originally *wif* + *man;* a reminder of the [i]-sound is kept in the plural *women; nostril,* OE. *nosuþyrel* (the latter part means "hole"), *fifteen, Monday, Christmas* show shortening of the first element as compared with *nose, five, moon, Christ.* Compare the treatment of the second element in the numerous place-names in *-ton,* from *town,* and in *-mouth,* pronounced [-meþ]. *Cupboard* is pronounced [kʌbəd]. Sometimes there is recomposition as a reaction against isolation: OE. *hūs* + *wif* in course of time lost *w,* both vowels were shortened, *s* was sounded [z], and *f* became *v* or was even lost; in the derived meanings "needle-case" and "jade" we find the forms *huzzif, huzzive* and *huzzy.* But in the original sense the word was constantly revived: *housewife.* With free com-

---

5. Back, down, still, out, home, except, like, while, straight.
6. Sonnet 76.

pounds we may have even long strings, like *railway refreshment room, New Year Eve fancy dress ball,* his *twopence a week pocket-money,* etc.

[17] With regard to the logical relation of the parts of a compound very few are of the same type as *tiptoe* = tip of the toe. In the majority the first part determines the second: a *garden flower* is a kind of flower, but a *flower garden* a kind of garden. The relation of the two parts may be very different, and is left to be inferred from the meaning of each. Compare for instance *lifeboat* on the one hand with *life-insurance, life member, lifetime, life class* (class of painters drawing from life) and on the other hand *steamboat, pilot boat, iron boat,* etc. *Home letters* (from h.), *home voyage* (to), *home life* (at). Sometimes a compound means "at the same time A and B": *servantman* = *man servant, queen-dowager, deaf-mute* = deaf and dumb.

[18] A special type of compounds is exemplified in *pick-pocket* = "one who picks pockets." This type (verb + object) seems to have originated in Romanic languages, but has in modern times proved very fertile in English: *cut-purse, know-nothing, sawbones, breakwater, stopgap, scare-crow,* etc. Such compounds are very often used as first parts of new compounds, in which case they may be considered adjectives: *breakneck* pace, a very *telltale* face, a *lack-lustre* eye, a *make-shift* dinner.[7]

[19] While in the old type of fixed compounds the first part had strong and the second weak stress, the stress tends in free compounds, such as *gold coin, coat tail, lead pencil, headmaster,* to be more level, so that it often varies rhythmically according to the context. Each part of the compound is felt as independent of and of equal weight with the other. As an adjective before a substantive is now just as uninflected as a substantive forming the first part of a compound, the two combinations are also made syntactically equal. They are co-ordinated in "her Christian and *family* name," "all national, *State, county,* and municipal offices," "a *Boston* young lady." The prop-word *one* may be used as in "two *gold* watches and a *silver* one," "give me a paper, one of the *Sunday* ones." The likeness with adjectives is made even more obvious when an adverb is used as in "from a too exclusively *London* standpoint," "in purely *Government* work," "in the most *matter-of-*

7. *MEG,* II, 8, 6 and 14, 7.

fact way." From being often used as first parts of compounds some substantives have really become regular adjectives and are recognized as such by everybody: *chief, choice, commonplace;* they may even form adverbs: *choicely,* and substantives like *commonplaceness. Dainty,* originally a substantive meaning a delicacy (Old French *daintie* from L. *dignitatem*), and *bridal* (originally *brydealu* "bride-ale") are now practically nothing but adjectives: note in both their seemingly adjectival endings.[8]

[20]   Having thus considered the modes of forming new words by adding something to existing words, by adding to them nothing at all, and by composition, we shall end this chapter by some remarks on the formation of new words by subtracting something from old ones.[9] Such "back-formations," as they are very conveniently termed by Dr. Murray,* owe their origin to one part of a word being mistaken for some derivative suffix (or, more rarely, prefix). The adverbs *sideling, groveling* and *darkling* were originally formed by means of the adverbial ending *-ling,* but in such phrases as *he walks sideling, he lies groveling,* etc., they looked exactly like participles in *-ing,* and the consequence was that the new verbs to *sidle,* to *grovel,* and to *darkle* were derived from them by the subtraction of *-ing.* The *Banting* cure was named after one Mr. Banting; the occasional verb to *bant* is, accordingly, a back-formation. The ending *-y* is often subtracted; from *greedy* is thus formed the noun *greed* (about 1600), from *lazy* and *cosy* the two verbs *laze* and *cose* (Kingsley), and from *jeopardy* (French *jeu parti*) the verb *jeopard.* The old adjective corresponding to *difficulty* was *difficile* as in French, but about 1600 the adjective *difficult* = the noun minus *y*) makes its appearance. *Puppy* from French *poupée* was thought to be formed by means of the petting suffix *y,* and thus *pup* was created; similarly I think that *cad* is from *caddy, caddie* = Fr. *cadet* (a youngster) and *pet* from *petty* = Fr. *petit,* the transition in meaning from "little" to "favourite" being easily accounted for. Several verbs originate from nouns in *-er* (*-ar, -or*), which were not originally "agent nouns"; *butcher* is the French *boucher,* derived from *bouc*

8. See *MEG,* II, ch. XI.

9. Otto Jespersen, "Om subtraktionsdannelser, særligt på dansk og engelsk," in *Festskrift til Vilh Thomsen* (Copenhagen, 1894). I have treated a few classes of back-formations in *Engl. Studien* 70, pp. 117 ff.

[* Sir James A. Murray, editor of the *Oxford English Dictionary* from 1879 to 1915.—Editor's note.]

"a buck, goat" with no corresponding verb, but in English it has given rise to the rare verb to *butch* and to the noun a *butch-knife*. Similarly *harbinger, rover, pedlar, burglar, hawker*, and probably *beggar*, call into existence the verbs to *harbinge* (Whitman), *rove, peddle, burgle, hawk*, and *beg*; and the Latin words *editor, donator, vivisector*, produce the un-Latin verbs to *edit, donate* (American), *vivisect* (Meredith), etc., which look as if they came from Latin participles. Some of these back-formations have been more successful than others in being generally recognized in Standard English.

[21] It is not usual in Germanic languages to form compounds with a verb as the second, and an object or a predicative as the first, part. Hence, when we find such verbs as to *housekeep* (Kipling, Merriman), the explanation must be that *-er* has been subtracted from the perfectly legitimate noun a *housekeeper* (or *-ing* from *housekeeping*). The oldest examples I know of this formation are to *backbite* (1300), to *partake* (*parttake*, 16th century) and to *soothsay* and *conycatch* (Shakespeare); others are to *hutkeep*, common in Australia, *book-keep* (Shaw), to *dressmake*, to *matchmake* ("women will match-make, you know," A. Hope), to *thoughtread* ("Why don't they thoughtread each other?" H. G. Wells), to *typewrite* ("I could typewrite if I had a machine," id., also in B. Shaw's *Candida*), to *merrymake* ("you merrymake together," Du Maurier). It will be seen that most of these are nonce-words. The verbs to *henpeck* and to *sunburn* are back-formations from the participles *henpecked* and *sunburnt*; and Browning even says "*moonstrike* him!" (*Pippa Passes*) for "let him be moonstruck."

[22] We have seen that monosyllabism is one of the most characteristic features of modern English, and this chapter has shown us some of the morphological processes by which the original stock of monosyllables has been in course of time considerably increased. It may not, therefore, be out of place here briefly to give an account of some of the other modes by which such short words have been developed. Some are simply longer words which have been shortened by regular phonetic development (cf. *love*, [5], p. 49); e.g. *eight* OE. *eahta, dear* OE. *deore, fowl* OE. *fugol, hawk* OE. *hafoc, lord* OE. *hlaford, not* and *nought* OE. *nawiht, pence* OE. *penigas, ant* OE. *æmette*, etc. *Miss* before the names of unmarried ladies is a somewhat irregular shortening of "missis" (mistress); though found here and there in the seventeenth century,

Miss was not yet recognized in the middle of the eighteenth century (cf. Fielding's Mrs. Bridgit, Mrs. Honour, etc.).

[23]   This leads us to the numerous popular clippings of long foreign words, of which rarely the middle (as in *Tench* "the House of *Detention*" and *teck* "detective") or the end (as in *bus* "omnibus," *baccer, baccy* "tobacco," *phone,* "telephone"), but more often the beginning only subsists. Some of these stump-words have never passed beyond slang, such as *sov* "sovereign," *pub* "public-house," *confab* "confabulation," *pop* "popular concert," *vet* "veterinary surgeon," *Jap* "Japanese," *guv* "Governor," *Mods* "Moderations," an Oxford examination, *matric* "matriculation," *prep* "preparation," and *impot* or *impo* "imposition" in schoolboys' slang, *sup* "supernumerary," *props* "properties" in theatrical slang, *perks* "perquisites," *comp* "compositor," *caps* "capital letters," etc., etc. Some are perhaps now in a fair way to become recognized in ordinary speech, such as *exam* "examination," and *bike* "bicycle"; and some words have become so firmly established as to make the full words pass completely into oblivion, e.g. *cab* (cabriolet), *fad* (fadaise), *navvy* (navigator in the sense of canal-digger and later railway labourer) and and *mob* (mobile vulgus).

[24]   A last group of English monosyllables comprises a certain number of words the etymology of which has hitherto baffled all the endeavours of philologists. At a certain moment such a word suddenly comes into the language, nobody knowing from where, so that we must feel really inclined to think of a creation *ex nihilo.* I am not particularly thinking of words denoting sounds or movements in a more or less onomatopoetic way, for their origin is psychologically easy to account for, but of such words as the following, some of which belong now to the most indispensable speech material: *bad,*[10] *big,*[11] *lad* and *lass,* all appearing towards the end of the thirteenth century; *fit* adjective and *fit* substantive, probably two mutually independent words, the adjective dating from 1440, the substantive in the now current sense from 1547; *dad* "father," *jump, crease* "fold, wrinkle," *gloat,* and *bet* from the sixteenth century; *job, fun* (and *pun*), *blight, chum* and *hump* from the seventeenth century; *fuss, jam* verb and substantive, and *hoax*

10. See Zupita's attempt at an explanation in the *NED,* which does not account for the origin of *bæddel.*
11. The best explanation is Björkman's, see *Scand. Loan Words,* pp. 157 and 259; but even he does not claim to have solved the mystery completely.

from the eighteenth, and *slum, stunt* and *blurb* from the nineteenth and twentieth centuries. Anyone who has watched small children carefully must have noticed that they sometimes create some such words without any apparent reason; sometimes they stick to it only for a day or two as the name of some plaything, etc., and then forget it; but sometimes a funny sound takes lastingly their fancy and may even be adopted by their playmates or parents as a real word.[12] Without pretending that such is the origin of all the words just mentioned I yet venture to throw out the suggestion that some of them may be due to children's playful inventiveness—while others may have sprung from the corresponding linguistic playfulness of grown-up people which forms the fundamental essence of the phenomenon called *slang.*

12. Cf. my book *Language,* pp. 151 ff. On the general theory of slang see ib., pp. 298 ff., and *Mankind, Nation and Individual,* pp. 149 ff.

SUMMARY

As great as our borrowings from foreign languages have been, the chief source of enrichment of the English vocabulary has been the regular processes of the native tongue, which fall into four categories:
1. Adding to words [1–4], such as suffixes like *-en, -ish, -er (-eer, -ster)* and others.
2. Interchanging of word functions without any addition at all [5–15], from nouns to verbs or verbs to nouns especially but not exclusively; sometimes these changes are accompanied by change of stress [13].
3. Compounding words [16–19], especially two nouns [16–17], but also verb-noun combinations [18].
4. Subtracting from words [20–24], especially such subtractings as are known as back-formations [20–22] and as clippings [23–24].

NOTES

This is the first selection in the text which is very demanding. Jespersen presents a wealth of materials; but more importantly, he assumes that his reader has a certain amount of knowledge.

First, one must know some dates and be able to associate some names with them. Since this essay deals with periods of the English language, the following chart may prove helpful (*c.* stands for Latin *circa* and means "around, about"):

Old English (O.E.): English up to *c.* A.D. 1150.

Middle English: English from *c.* 1150 to *c.* 1500.

Modern English: English from *c.* 1500 to the present. Sometimes subdivided as Early Modern English, *c.* 1500 to *c.* 1700, and Modern English, *c.* 1700 to the present.

62   OTTO JESPERSEN

Next, a rough dating of authors and works cited may help:
13th century: *Ancren Riwle*
14th century: Chaucer
16th century: Baret, Hart, Heywood
(Shakespeare, 1564–1616; Elizabeth I reigned 1558–1603)
17th century: Milton, Pepys
18th century: Sheridan, Fielding
19th century: Scott, Coleridge, Carlyle, Macauley, Thackeray, Darwin, Ruskin, Browning, Tennyson, Trollope
20th century: Kipling, Murray, Wells, Merriman, du Maurier, Hope, Phillips

In connection with dates and history, Jespersen assumes that one is aware that in 1066 the Norman French king William conquered England, that in the next two centuries French was the official language of the country, and that a great number of French words were, as a result, added to the English vocabulary—most of them, but not all by any means, words of business, administration, law, and the king's court. Notice that cuts of meat are still named with French words (beef, veal, pork, mutton) while the animals keep English names (cow or steer, calf, pig, sheep).

Second, Jespersen expects one to know the traditional parts of speech: nouns and pronouns (together called substantives), verbs, adjectives, adverbs, prepositions, and conjunctions. Professor Myers's essay beginning on page 135 and the notes following it will supply the information.

Third, he expects one to know a few things about Old English: that *sc* was pronounced as we pronounce *sh* today, that the "thorn" (þ) was pronounced as we pronounce the *th* in *thin,* and that an OE *f* was pronounced as we pronounce *v* when it fell between two vowels (hence *lufie* was pronounced "loo-vee-ay"). He also expects one to know something about verb conjugations and noun declensions in Old English. An example of each follows:

VERB CONJUGATION

Present Tense

ic lufie	(I love)	we lufiaþ	(we love)
þu lufast	(thou lovest)	ge lufiaþ	(ye love)
he lufaþ	(he loveth)	hie lufiaþ	(they love)

NOUN DECLENSION

Singular Number

Nominative case (subject)	lufe	(love)	slæp	(sleep)
Genitive case (possessive)	lufu	(love)	slæpes	(sleep's)
Dative case (indirect object)	lufe	(love's)	slæpe	(to, for sleep)
Accusative case (direct object)	lufe	(to, for love)	slæp	(sleep)

Plural Number

Nominative case	lufa, lufe	(loves)	slæpas	(sleeps)
Genitive case	lufa, lufena	(loves')	slæpa	(sleeps')
Dative case	lufum	(to, for loves)	slæpum	(to, for sleeps)
Accusative case	lufa, lufe	(loves)	slæpas	(sleeps)

Fourth, Jespersen assumes that we know that *NED* means the *New (Oxford) English Dictionary*. He also refers to his own *Modern English Grammar (MEG)*, by all odds the largest grammar of modern English (6 volumes as published in Heidelberg; 7 volumes as published in Copenhagen). He assumes that we know such abbreviations as *cf.* (compare), *e.g.* (for example), *f.* (and following page), *ff.* (and following pages), *id.* (the same; from the same source), OE (Old English), L. (Latin), Fr. (French), and OFr. (Old French).

Finally, the reference in [9] (to Sect. 133) to sets of synonyms in our language, one of which is native, the other Latin, may be illustrated by the following pairs:

youthful – juvenile knowledge – science
weighty – ponderous wretched – miserable

American Slang

H. L. MENCKEN

Henry Louis Mencken (1880–1956) was an almost incredibly productive commentator on the American scene for the first half of the twentieth century—newspaperman, editor, author, and scholar. His American Language *(first edition 1918), from which this selection is taken, is one of the most delicious books on language ever written, combining long and careful research with brilliant style and sparkling wit.*

[1] Slang is defined by the Oxford Dictionary as "language of a highly colloquial type, considered as below the level of standard educated speech, and consisting either of new words or of current words employed in some special sense." The origin of the word is unknown. Ernest Weekley, in his "Etymological Dictionary of Modern English," 1921, suggests that it may have some relation to the verb *to sling,* and cites two Norwegian dialect words, based upon the cognate verb *slenge* or *slengje,* that appear to be its brothers: *slengjeord,* a neologism, and *slengjenamn,* a nickname. But he is not sure, so he adds the note that "some regard it as an argotic perversion of the French *langue,* language." A German philologian, O. Ritter, believes that it may be derived, not from *langue,* but from *language* itself, most probably by a combination of blending and shortening, as in *thieve(s' lang)uage, beggar(s' lang)uage,* and so on.[1] "Webster's New International," 1934, follows somewhat haltingly after Weekley. The Oxford Dictionary, 1919, evades the question by dismissing *slang* as "a word of cant

---

1. *Archiv für das Studium der neueren Sprachen,* Vol. CXVI, 1906. I am indebted for the reference to Concerning the Etymology of Slang, by Fr. Klaeber, *American Speech,* April, 1926. The process is not unfamiliar in English: *tawdry,* from *Saint Audrey,* offers an example.

Reprinted from H. L. Mencken's *The American Language* (pp. 555–575), 4th ed., by permission of Alfred A. Knopf, Inc. Copyright 1919, 1936, by Alfred A. Knopf, Inc. Renewed, 1947, by H. L. Mencken.

origin, the ultimate source of which is not apparent." When it first appeared in English, about the middle of the Eighteenth Century,[2] it was employed as a synonym of *cant,* and so designated "the special vocabulary used by any set of persons of a low or disreputable character"; and half a century later it began to be used interchangeably with *argot,* which means the vocabulary special to any group, trade or profession. But during the past fifty years the three terms have tended to be more or less clearly distinguished. The jargon of criminals is both a kind of slang and a kind of argot, but it is best described as *cant,* a word derived from the Latin *cantus,* and going back, in its present sense, to c. 1540. One of the principal aims of cant is to make what is said unintelligible to persons outside the group, a purpose that is absent from most forms of argot and slang. Argot often includes slang, as when a circus man calls his patrons *suckers* and speaks of refunding money to one full of complaints as *squaring the beef,* but when he calls the circus grounds the *lot* and the manager's quarters the *white wagon,* he is simply using the special language of his trade, and it is quite as respectable as the argot of lawyers or diplomats. The essence of slang is that it is of general dispersion, but still stands outside the accepted canon of the language. It is, says George H. McKnight,[3] "a form of colloquial speech created in a spirit of defiance and aiming at freshness and novelty. . . . Its figures are consciously farfetched and are intentionally drawn from the most ignoble of sources. Closely akin to profanity in its spirit, its aim is to shock." Among the impulses leading to its invention, adds Henry Bradley,[4] "the two more important seem to be the desire to secure increased vivacity and the desire to secure increased sense of intimacy in the use of language." "It seldom attempts," says the London *Times,* "to supply deficiencies in conventional language; its object is nearly always to provide a new and different way of saying what can be perfectly well said without it." [5] What chiefly lies behind it is simply a kind of linguistic

2. It has since appeared in German, French and Swedish, as is shown by the titles of Deutsches Slang, by Arnold Genthe; Strassburg, 1892; Le Slang, by J. Manchon; Paris, 1923; and Stockholmska Slang, by W. P. Uhrström; Stockholm, 1911.
3. English Words and Their Background; New York, 1923, p. 43.
4. *Art.* Slang, Encyclopaedia Britannica, 14 ed.; New York, 1929.
5. American Slang (leading article), May 11, 1931. Many other definitions of *slang* are quoted in What is Slang? by H. F. Reves, *American Speech,*

exuberance, an excess of word-making energy. It relates itself to the standard language a great deal as dancing relates itself to music. But there is also something else. The best slang is not only ingenious and amusing; it also embodies a kind of social criticism. It not only provides new names for a series of everyday concepts, some new and some old; it also says something about them. "Words which produce the slang effect," observes Frank K. Sechrist,[6] "arouse associations which are incongruous or incompatible with those of customary thinking."

[2]   Everyone, including even the metaphysician in his study and the eremite in his cell, has a large vocabulary of slang, but the vocabulary of the vulgar is likely to be larger than that of the cultured, and it is harder worked. Its content may be divided into two categories: (a) old words, whether used singly or in combination, that have been put to new uses, usually metaphorical, and (b) new words that have not yet been admitted to the standard vocabulary. Examples of the first type are *rubberneck*, for a gaping and prying person, and *iceberg*, for a cold woman; examples of the second are *hoosegow*, *flimflam*, *blurb*, *bazoo* and *blah*. There is a constant movement of slang terms into accepted usage.

Jan., 1926. A few by literati may be added. "Slang," said Carl Sandburg, "is language that takes off its coat, spits on its hands, and gets to work." "Slang," said Victor Hugo, "is a dressing-room in which language, having an evil deed to prepare, puts on a disguise." "Slang," said Ambrose Bierce, "is the speech of him who robs the literary garbage-carts on their way to the dumps." Emerson and Whitman were its partisans. "What can describe the folly and emptiness of scolding," asked the former (Journals, 1840), "like the word *jawing?*" "Slang," said Whitman, "is the wholesome fermentation or eructation of those processes eternally active in language, by which the froth and specks are thrown up, mostly to pass away, though occasionally to settle and permanently crystalize." (Slang in America, 1885.) And again: "These words ought to be collected—the bad words as well as the good. Many of these bad words are fine." (An American Primer, c. 1856.)

6. The Psychology of Unconventional Language, *Pedagogical Seminary*, Dec., 1913, p. 443. "Our feeling and reactions to slang words," continues Sechrist, "may be due to the word as such, to the use it is put to, to the individual using it, to the group using it, to the thing tabooed to which it applies, or to the context in which it is found. . . . Unconventional language keeps close to the objective world of things. It keeps oriented to the sense of touch, contact, pressure, preferring a language material which is ultimately verifiable by the most realistic sense." This last, I fear, is somewhat dubious. See also An Investigation of the Function and Use of Slang, by A. H. Melville, *Pedagogical Seminary*, March, 1912; and La Psychologie de l'argot, by Raoul de La Grasserie, *Revue Philosophique* (Paris), Vol. LX, 1905.

Nice, as an adjective of all work, signifying anything satisfactory, was once in slang use only, and the purists denounced it,[7] but today no one would question "a *nice* day," "a *nice* time," or "a *nice* hotel." The French word *tête* has been a sound name for the human head for many centuries, but its origin was in *testa,* meaning a pot, a favorite slang word of the soldiers of the decaying Roman Empire, exactly analogous to our *block, nut* and *bean.* The verb-phrase *to hold up* is now perfectly good American, but so recently as 1901 the late Brander Matthews was sneering at it as slang. In the same way many other verb-phrases, *e.g., to cave in, to fill the bill* and *to fly off the handle,* once viewed askance, have gradually worked their way to a relatively high level of the standard speech. On some indeterminate tomorrow *to stick up* and *to take for a ride* may follow them. "Even the greatest purist," says Robert Lynd, "does not object today to the inclusion of the word *bogus* in a literary English vocabulary, though a hundred years ago *bogus* was an American slang word meaning an apparatus for coining false money. *Carpetbagger* and *bunkum* are other American slang words that have naturalized themselves in English speech, and *mob* is an example of English slang that was once as vulgar as *incog* or *photo.*" [8] Sometimes a word comes in below the salt, gradually wins respectability, and then drops to the level of slang, and is worked to death. An example is offered by *strenuous.* It was first used by John Marston, the dramatist, in 1599, and apparently he invented it, as he invented *puffy, chilblained, spurious* and *clumsy.* As strange as it may seem to us today, all these words were frowned on by the purists of the time as uncouth and vulgar, and Ben Jonson attacked them with violence in his "Poetaster," written in 1601. In particular, Ben was upset by *strenuous.* But it made its way despite him, and during the next three centuries it was used by a multitude of impeccable authors, including Milton, Swift, Burke, Hazlitt, and Macaulay. And then Theodore Roosevelt invented and announced the Strenuous Life, the adjective struck the American fancy and passed into slang, and in a little while it was so horribly threadbare that all persons of careful

7. It came in about 1765. During the early Eighteenth Century *elegant* was commonly used, and in Shakespeare's day the favorite was *fine. Nice* has had many rival, *e.g., ripping* and *topping* in England, and *grand* and *swell* in America, but it hangs on.

8. The King's English and the Prince's American, *Living Age,* March 15, 1928.

speech sickened of it, and to this day it bears the ridiculous connotation that hangs about most slang, and is seldom used seriously.

All neologisms, of course, are not slang. At about the time the
word *hoosegow,* derived from the Spanish, came into American
slang use, the word *rodeo,* also Spanish, came into the standard
vocabulary. The distinction between the two is not hard to make
out. *Hoosegow* was really not needed. We had plenty of words to
designate a jail, and they were old and good words. *Hoosegow*
came in simply because there was something arresting and out-
landish about it—and the users of slang have a great liking for
pungent novelties. *Rodeo,* on the other hand, designated something for which there was no other word in American—something,
indeed, of which the generality of Americans had just become
aware—and so it was accepted at once. Many neologisms have
been the deliberate inventions of quite serious men, *e.g., gas,
kodak, vaseline. Scientist* was concocted in 1840 by William
Whewell, professor of moral theology and casuistical divinity at
Cambridge. *Ampere* was proposed solemnly by the Electric Con-
gress which met in Paris in 1881, and was taken into all civilized
languages instantly. *Radio* was suggested for wireless telegrams
by an international convention held in Berlin in 1906, and was
extended to wireless broadcasts in the United States about 1920,
though the English prefer *wireless* in the latter sense. But such
words as these were never slang; they came into general and respectable use at once, along with *argon, x-ray, carburetor, strato-
sphere, bacillus,* and many another of the sort. These words were
all sorely needed; it was impossible to convey the ideas behind
them without them, save by clumsy circumlocutions. It is one of
the functions of slang, also, to serve a short cut, but it is seldom
if ever really necessary. Instead, as W. D. Whitney once said, it
is only a wanton product of "the exuberance of mental activity,
and the natural delight of language-making." [9] This mental activity, of course, is the function of a relatively small class. "The unconscious genius of the people," said Paul Shorey, "no more invents slang than it invents epics. It is coined in the sweat of their
brow by smart writers who, as they would say, are *out for the
coin.*" [10] Or, if not out for the coin, then at least out for notice,

9. The Life and Growth of Language; New York, 1897, p. 113.
10. The American Language, in Academy Papers; New York, 1925, p. 149.
Henry Bradley says (*Art.* Slang, Encyclopaedia Britannica, 14th ed.; 1929)

kudos, admiration, or maybe simply for satisfaction of the "natural delight of language-making." Some of the best slang emerges from the argot of college students, but everyone who has observed the process of its gestation knows that the general run of students have nothing to do with the matter, save maybe to provide an eager welcome for the novelties set before them. College slang is actually made by the campus wits, just as general slang is made by the wits of the newspapers and theaters. The idea of calling an engagement-ring a *handcuff* did not occur to the young gentlemen of Harvard by mass inspiration; it occurred to a certain definite one of them, probably after long and deliberate cogitation, and he gave it to the rest and to his country.

[3]   Toward the end of 1933 W. J. Funk of the Funk and Wagnalls Company, publishers of the Standard Dictionary and the *Literary Digest,* undertook to supply the newspapers with the names of the ten most fecund makers of the American slang then current. He nominated T. A. (Tad) Dorgan, the cartoonist; Sime Silverman, editor of the theatrical weekly, *Variety;* Gene Buck, the song writer; Damon Runyon, the sports writer; Walter Winchell and Arthur (Bugs) Baer, newspaper columnists; George Ade, Ring Lardner and Gelett Burgess.[11] He should have added Jack Conway and Johnny O'Connor of the staff of *Variety;* James Gleason, author of "Is Zat So?"; Rube Goldberg, the cartoonist; Johnny Stanley and Johnny Lyman, Broadway figures; Wilson Mizner and Milt Gross. Conway, who died in 1928, is credited with the invention of *palooka* (a third-rater), *belly-laugh, Arab* (for Jew), *S.A.*

---

that "slang develops most freely in groups with a strong realization of group activity and interest, and groups without this interest, *e.g.,* farmers, rarely invent slang terms." The real reason why farmers seldom invent them, of course, is that farmers, as a class, are extremely stupid. They never invent anything else.

11. Mr. Funk added my own name to the list, but this, apparently, was only a fraternal courtesy, for I have never devised anything properly describable as slang, save maybe *booboisie.* This was a deliberate invention. One evening in February, 1922, Ernest Boyd and I were the guests of Harry C. Black at his home in Baltimore. We fell to talking of the paucity of words to describe the victims of the Depression then current, and decided to remedy it. So we put together a list of about fifty terms, and on Feb. 15 I published it in the Baltimore *Evening Sun.* It included *boobariat, booberati, boobarian, boobomaniac, boobuli,* and *booboisie.* Only booboisie, which happened to be one of my contributions, caught on. A bit lated I added *Homo boobus,* and Boyd, who is learned in the tongues, corrected it to *Homo boobiens.* This also had its day, but its use was confined to the *intelligentsia,* and it was hardly slang. Even *booboisie* lies rather outside the bounds.

(sex appeal), *high-hat, pushover, boloney* (for buncombe, later adopted by Alfred E. Smith), *headache* (wife), and the verbs *to scram, to click* (meaning to succeed), and *to laugh that off.*[12] Winchell, if he did not actually invent *whoopee,* at least gave it the popularity it enjoyed, *c.* 1930.[13] He is also the father of *Chicagorilla, Joosh* (for Jewish), *pash* (for passion) and *shafts* (for legs), and he has devised a great many nonce words and phrases, some of them euphemistic and others far from it, *e.g.,* for married: *welded, sealed, lohengrined, merged* and *middle-aisled;* for divorced: *Reno-vated;* for contemplating divorce: *telling it to a judge, soured, curdled, in husband trouble, this-and-that-way,* and *on the verge;* for in love: *on the merge, on fire, uh-huh, that way, cupiding, Adam-and-Eveing,* and *man-and-womaning it;* for expecting young: *infanticipating, baby-bound* and *storked.* I add a few other characteristic specimens of his art: *go-ghetto, debutramp, phffft, foofff* (a pest), *Wildeman* (a homosexual), *heheheh* (a mocking laugh), *Hard-Times Square* (Times Square), *blessed-event* (the birth of young), *the Hardened Artery* (Broadway), *radiodor* (a radio announcer), *moom-pitcher* (moving picture), *girl-mad, Park Rowgue* (a newspaper reporter) and *intelligentlemen.* Most of these, of course, had only their brief days, but a few promise to survive. Dorgan, who died in 1929, was the begetter of *applesauce, twenty-three, skiddoo,*[14] *ball-and-chain* (for wife),

12. Conway's coinages are listed by Walter Winchell in Your Broadway and Mine, New York *Graphic,* Oct. 4, 1928, and in A Primer of Broadway Slang, *Vanity Fair,* Nov., 1927. On December 29, 1926, under the title of Why I Write Slang, Conway contributed a very shrewd article to *Variety.* In it he differentiated clearly between the cant of criminals, which is unintelligible to the general, and what he called Broadway slang. The latter differs from the former, he said, "as much as Bostonese from hog Latin."

13. Lexicographical explorers have found *whoopee* in a cowboy song published by John A. Lomax in 1910, in Kipling's Loot (Barrack-Room Ballads), 1892, and in Mark Twain's A Tramp Abroad, 1880. *Whoope* was common in the English literature of the Fifteenth, Sixteenth and Seventeenth Centuries, but it was probably only our *whoop* with a silent final *e.* Said Winchell in the New York *Mirror,* Jan. 17, 1935: "They contend *whoopee* is older than Shakespeare. Well, all right. I never claimed it, anyhow. But let 'em take *makin' whoopee* from me and look out!"

14. Dorgan's claims to both *twenty-three* and its brother *skiddoo* have been disputed. An editorial in the Louisville *Times,* May 9, 1929, credits Frank Parker Stockbridge with the theory that *twenty-three* was launched by The Only Way, a dramatization of Dickens's Tale of Two Cities, presented by Henry Miller in New York in 1899. In the last act an old woman counted the victims of the guillotine, and Sydney Carton was the twenty-third. According to Stockbridge, her solemn "Twenty-three!" was borrowed by Broad-

cake-eater, dumb Dora, dumbell (for stupid person), *nobody home,* and *you said it.* He also gave the world "Yes, we have no bananas," though he did not write the song, and he seems to have originated *the cat's pajamas,* which was followed by a long series of similar superlatives.[15] The sports writers, of course, are all assiduous makers of slang, and many of their inventions are taken into the general vocabulary. Thus, those who specialize in boxing have contributed, in recent years, *kayo, cauliflower-ear, prelim, shadow-boxing, slug-fest, title-holder, punch drunk,*[16] *brother-act, punk, to side-step* and *to go the limit;* [17] those who cover baseball have made many additions to the list of baseball terms given in Chapter V; [18] and those who follow the golf tournaments have

---

way, and quickly became popular. He says that *skiddoo,* derived from *skedaddle,* was "added for the enlightenment of any who hadn't seen the play."

15. See Tad Dorgan is Dead, by W. L. Werner, *American Speech,* Aug., 1929. *The flea's eyebrows, the bee's knees, the snake's hips* and *the canary's tusks* will be recalled. A writer in *Liberty,* quoted in *American Speech,* Feb., 1927, p. 258, says that Dorgan also helped to popularize *hard-boiled,* the invention of Jack Doyle, keeper of a billiard academy in New York.

16. For a learned discourse on the pathological meaning of this term see *Punch Drunk,* by Harrison S. Martland, *Journal of the American Medical Association,* Oct. 13, 1928. In severe cases "there may develop a peculiar tilting of the head, a marked dragging of one or both legs, a staggering, propulsive gait with facial characteristics of the parkinsonian syndrome, or a backward swaying of the body, tremors, vertigo and deafness." Some of the synonyms are *cuckoo, goofy, cutting paper-dolls* and *slug-nutty.*

17. See Jargon of Fistiana, by Robert E. Creighton, *American Speech,* Oct., 1933, and Color Stuff, by Harold E. Rockwell, the same, Oct., 1927. William Henry Nugent, in The Sports Section, *American Mercury,* March, 1929, says that the father of them all was Pierce Egan, who established *Pierce Egan's Life in London and Sporting Guide* in 1824. A year earlier Egan printed a revised edition of Francis Grose's Classical Dictionary of the Vulgar Tongues, 1785. In it appeared *to stall off, cheese it, to trim* (in the sense of to swindle), *to pony up, squealer, sucker, yellow-belly,* and many other locutions still in use.

18. See Baseball Slang, by V. Samuels, *American Speech,* Feb., 1927, p. 255. Hugh Fullerton, one of the rev. elders of the fraternity, says that the first baseball reports to be adorned with neologisms, *e.g., south-paw, initial-sack, grass-cutter, shut-out* and *circus-play,* were written by Charlie Seymour of the Chicago *Inter-Ocean* and Lennie Washburn of the Chicago *Herald* during the 80's. Some years ago the Chicago *Record-Herald,* apparently alarmed by the extravagant fancy of its baseball reporters, asked its readers if they would prefer a return to plain English. Such of them as were literate enough to send in their votes were almost unanimously against a change. As one of them said, "One is nearer the park when Schulte *slams the pill* than when he merely *hits the ball.*" For the argot of baseball players, as opposed to the slang of sports writers, see Baseball Terminology, by Henry J. Heck, *American Speech,* April, 1930.

given currency to *birdie, fore, par, bunker, divot, fairway, to tee off, stance,* and *onesome, twosome, threesome* and so on—some of them received into the standard speech but the majority lingering in the twilight of slang.[19]

[4]   George Philip Krapp attempts to distinguish between slang and sound idiom by setting up the doctrine that the former is "more expressive than the situation demands." "It is," he says, "a kind of hyperesthesia in the use of language. *To laugh in your sleeve* is idiom because it arises out of a natural situation; it is a metaphor derived from the picture of one raising his sleeve to his face to hide a smile, a metaphor which arose naturally enough in early periods when sleeves were long and flowing; but *to talk through your hat* is slang, not only because it is new, but also because it is a grotesque exaggeration of the truth." [20] The theory, unluckily, is combated by many plain facts. *To hand it to him, to get away with it* and even *to hand him a lemon* are certainly not metaphors that transcend the practicable and probable, and yet all are undoubtedly slang. On the other hand, there is palpable exaggeration in such phrases as "he is not worth the powder it would take to kill him," in such adjectives as *breakbone* (fever), and in such compounds as *fire-eater,* and yet it would be absurd to dismiss them as slang. Between *blockhead* and *bonehead* there is little to choose, but the former is sound English, whereas the latter is American slang. So with many familiar similes, *e.g., like greased lightning, as scarce as hen's teeth:* they are grotesque hyperboles, but hardly slang.

The true distinction, in so far as any distinction exists at all, is that indicated by Whitney, Bradley, Sechrist and McKnight. Slang originates in the effort of ingenious individuals to make the language more pungent and picturesque—to increase the store of terse and striking words, to widen the boundaries of metaphor, and to provide a vocabulary for new shades of difference in meaning. As Dr. Otto Jespersen has pointed out,[21] this is also the aim of

19. See Golf Gab, by Anne Angel, *American Speech,* Sept., 1926. In 1934 Willis Stork, a student of Dr. Louise Pound at the University of Nebraska, prepared a paper on The Jargon of the Sports Writers, mainly confined to an examination of the sports pages of two Lincoln, Neb., papers, the *State Journal* and the *Star* from July 1, 1933 to July 15, 1934. So far it has not been published. See also Our Golf Lingo Peeves the British, *Literary Digest,* April 11, 1931.

20. Modern English; New York, 1910, p. 211.

21. Language: Its Nature, Development and Origin; London, 1922, p. 300.

poets (as, indeed, it is of prose writers), but they are restrained by consideration of taste and decorum, and also, not infrequently, by historical or logical considerations. The maker of slang is under no such limitations: he is free to confect his neologism by any process that can be grasped by his customers, and out of any materials available, whether native or foreign. He may adopt any of the traditional devices of metaphor. Making an attribute do duty for the whole gives him *stiff* for corpse, *flat-foot* for policeman, *smoke-eater* for fireman, *skirt* for woman, *lunger* for consumptive, and *yes-man* for sycophant. Hidden resemblances give him *morgue* for a newspaper's file of clippings, *bean* for head, and *sinker* for a doughnut. The substitution of far-fetched figures for literal description gives him *glad-rags* for fine clothing, *bonehead* for ignoramus, *booze-foundry* for saloon, and *cart-wheel* for dollar, and the contrary resort to a brutal literalness gives him *kill-joy, low-life* and *hand-out*. He makes abbreviations with a free hand—*beaut* for beauty, *gas* for gasoline, and so on. He makes bold avail of composition, as in *attaboy* and *whatdyecallem*, and of onomatopoeia, as in *biff, zowie, honky-tonk* and *wow*. He enriches the ancient counters of speech with picturesque synonyms, as in *guy, gink, duck, bird* and *bozo* for fellow. He transfers proper names to common usage, as in *ostermoor* for mattress, and then sometimes gives them remote figurative significances, as in *ostermoors* for whiskers. Above all, he enriches the vocabulary of action with many new verbs and verb-phrases, *e.g., to burp, to neck, to gang, to frame up, to hit the pipe, to give him the works*, and so on. If, by the fortunes that condition language-making, his neologism acquires a special and limited meaning, not served by any existing locution, it enters into sound idiom and is presently wholly legitimatized; if, on the contrary, it is adopted by the populace as a counter-word and employed with such banal imitativeness that it soon loses any definite significance whatever, then it remains slang and is avoided by the finical. An example of the former process is afforded by *tommy-rot*. It first appeared as English school-boy slang, but its obvious utility soon brought it into good usage. In one of Jerome K. Jerome's books, "Paul Kelver," there is the following dialogue:

> "The wonderful songs that nobody ever sings, the wonderful pictures that nobody ever paints, and all the rest of it. It's *tommy-rot!*"
> "I wish you wouldn't use slang."

"Well, you know what I mean. What is the proper word? Give it to me."

"I suppose you mean *cant*."

"No, I don't. *Cant* is something that you don't believe in yourself.[22] It's *tommy-rot;* there isn't any other word."

Nor were there any other words for *hubbub, fireworks, foppish, fretful, sportive, dog-weary, to bump* and *to dwindle* in Shakespeare's time; he adopted and dignified them because they met genuine needs.[23] Nor was there any other satisfactory word for *graft* when it came in, nor for *rowdy,* nor for *boom,* nor for *joyride,* nor for *slacker,* nor for *trust-buster.* Such words often retain a humorous quality; they are used satirically and hence appear but seldom in wholly serious discourse. But they have standing in the language nevertheless, and only a prig would hesitate to use them as George Saintsbury used *the best of the bunch* and *jokesmith.* So recently as 1929 the Encyclopaedia Britannica listed *bootlegger, speakeasy, dry, wet, crook, fake, fizzle, hike, hobo, poppycock, racketeer* and *O.K.* as American slang terms but today most of them are in perfectly good usage. What would one call a racketeer if *racketeer* were actually forbidden? It would take a phrase of four or five words at least, and they would certainly not express the idea clearly.[24]

On the other hand, many an apt and ingenious neologism, by falling too quickly into the gaping maw of the proletariat, is spoiled forthwith and forever. Once it becomes, in Oliver Wendell Holmes's phrase, "a cheap generic term, a substitute for differentiated specific expressions," it quickly acquires such flatness that the fastidious flee it as a plague. The case of *strenuous* I have al-

---

22. This sense of the word, of course, is to be differentiated sharply from the philological sense of a more or less secret jargon.

23. A long list of his contributions to the vocabulary, including a number borrowed from the slang of his time, is to be found in Modern English in the Making, by George H. McKnight; New York, 1928, p. 188 *ff.*

24. In 1932–33 Dr. Walter Barnes of the New York University set four of his associates to canvassing 100 college, high school and elementary teachers on the subject of slang. They were asked to scrutinize a list of 432 slang terms, and to estimate them as acceptable, trite and forceless, doubtful, or offensive. Those chosen as most acceptable were *pep, fake, stiff upper lip, double-cross* and *booster.* All these, in ordinary discourse, are nearly if not quite irreplaceable. Others high on the list were *speakeasy, bone-dry, broke, fan, go-getter, snappy, to make the grade, pull* (in the sense of influence), *come-back, frame-up, racket, give-away, cinch* and *to turn down.* The results of the inquiry were issued in mimeograph as Studies in Current Colloquial Usage; New York, 1933.

ready mentioned. One recalls, too, many capital verb-phrases, thus ruined by unintelligent appreciation, e.g., *to freeze on to, to have the goods, to cut no ice, to fall for,* and *to get by;* and some excellent substantives, *e.g., dope* and *dub,* and compounds, *e.g., come-on* and *easy-mark,* and simple verbs, *e.g., to neck* and *to vamp.* These are all quite as sound in structure as the great majority of our most familiar words and phrases—*to cut no ice,* for example, is certainly as good as *to butter no parsnips*—, but their adoption by the ignorant and their endless use and misuse in all sorts of situations have left them tattered and obnoxious, and soon or late they will probably go the way, as Brander Matthews once said, of all the other "temporary phrases which spring up, one scarcely knows how, and flourish unaccountably for a few months, and then disappear forever, leaving no sign." Matthews was wrong in two particulars here. They do not arrive by any mysterious parthenogenesis, but come from sources which, in many cases, may be determined. And they last, alas, a good deal more than a month. *Shoo-fly* afflicted the American people for four or five years, and "I *don't* think," *aber nit, over the left, good night* and *oh yeah* were scarcely less long-lived.[25] There are, indeed, slang terms that have survived for centuries, never dropping quite out of use and yet never attaining to good usage. Among verbs, *to do* for to cheat has been traced to 1789, *to frisk* for to search to 1781, *to grease* for to bribe to 1557, and *to blow* for to boast to c. 1400.[26] Among nouns, *gas* for empty talk has been traced to 1847, *jug* for prison to 1834, *lip* for insolence to 1821, *sap* for fool to 1815, *murphy* for potato to 1811, *racket* to 1785, *bread-basket*

25. The life of such a word or phrase seems to depend, at least to some extent, upon its logical content. When it is sheer silliness the populace quickly tires of it. Thus "Ah there, my size, I'll steal you," "Where did you get that hat?", "How'd you like to be the ice-man?", "Would you for fifty cents?", "Let her go, Gallegher," "So's your old man" and their congeners were all short-lived. Many such vacuities have a faintly obscene significance. It is their function to conceal the speaker's lack of a logical retort by raising a snicker. Those of rather more sense and appositeness, *e.g.,* "Tell your troubles to a policeman," "How do you get that way?", "Where do you get that stuff?", "I'll say so" and "You said a mouthful," seem to last longer. In 1932 a Bridgeport, Conn., high-school teacher, Miss Julia Farnam, told the Bridgeport *Post* on returning from a visit to England that she had met there "the daughter of an earl" who thought "You said a mouthful" "the cleverest expression she ever heard." (*Post,* Oct. 3.)

26. These and the following examples are taken from The Age of Slang, by J. Louis Kuethe, Baltimore *Evening Sun,* July 3, 1934.

for stomach to 1753, *hush-money* to 1709, *hick* to 1690, *gold-mine* for profitable venture to 1664, *grub* for food to 1659, *rot-gut* to 1597 and *bones* for dice to *c.* 1386. Among the adjectives, *lousy* in the sense of inferior goes back to 1690; when it burst into American slang in 1910 or thereabout it was already more than two centuries old. *Booze* has never got into Standard English, but it was known to slang in the first years of the Fourteenth Century. When *nuts* in the sense revealed by "Chicago was *nuts* for the Giants" came into popularity in the United States *c.* 1920, it was treated by most of the newspaper commentators on current slang as a neologism, but in truth it had been used in precisely the same sense by R. H. Dana, Jr., in "Two Years Before the Mast," 1840, and by Mark Twain in "Following the Equator," 1897.[27] Sometimes an old slang word suddenly acquires a new meaning. An example is offered by *to chisel.* In the sense of to cheat, as in "He *chiseled* me out of $3," it goes back to the first years of the Nineteenth Century, but with the advent of the N.R.A., in the late Summer of 1933, it took on the new meaning of to evade compliance with the law by concealment or stealth. It has been credited to Franklin D. Roosevelt, but I believe that its true father was General Hugh S. Johnson, J.D.

[5]   With the possible exception of the French, the Americans now produce more slang than any other people, and put it to heavier use in their daily affairs. But they entered upon its concoction relatively late, and down to the second decade of the Nineteenth Century they were content to take their supply from England. American slang, says George Philip Krapp, "is the child of the new nationalism, the new spirit of joyous adventure that entered American life after the close of the War of 1812."[28] There was, during the colonial and early republican periods, a great production of neologisms, as we have seen in Chapter III, but very little of it was properly describable as slang. I find *to boost,* defined as to raise us, to lift up, to exalt, in the glossary appended to David Humphreys's "The Yankey in England," 1815,[29] but all the other slang terms listed, *e.g., duds* for clothes, *spunk* for courage, and *uppish,* are in Francis Grose's "Classical Dictionary of the

27. For this I am indebted to Mr. James D. Hart of Cambridge, Mass.
28. Is American English Archaic?, *Southwest Review,* Summer, 1927, p. 302.
29. The first example in the Supplement to the Oxford Dictionary is from John Neal's Brother Jonathan, 1825.

Vulgar Tongue," published in London thirty years before. The Rev. John Witherspoon's denunciation of slang in "The Druid," 1781, is a denunciation of English slang, though he is discussing the speech habits of Americans. But with the great movement into the West, following the War of 1812, the American vulgate came into its own, and soon the men of the ever-receding frontier were pouring out a copious stream of neologisms, many of them showing the audacious fancy of true slang. When these novelties penetrated to the East they produced a sort of linguistic shock, and the finicky were as much upset by the "tall talk" in which they were embodied as English pedants are today by the slang of Hollywood.[30] That some of them were extremely extravagant is a fact: I need point only to *blustiferous, clam-jamphrie, conbobberation, helliferocious, mollagausauger, peedoodles, ripsniptiously, slang-whanger, sockdolager, to exflunctify, to flummuck, to giraffe, to hornswoggle, to obflisticate* and *to puckerstopple*.[31] Most of these, of course, had their brief days and then disappeared, but there were others that got into the common vocabulary and still survive, e.g., *blizzard, to hornswoggle, sockdolager* and *rambunctious,* the last-named the final step in a process which began with *robustious* and ran through *rumbustious* and *rambustious* in England before Americans took a hand in it. With them came many verb-phrases, e.g., *to pick a crow with, to cut one's eye-teeth, to go the whole hog.* This "tall talk," despite the horror of the delicate, was a great success in the East, and its salient practitioners—for example, David Crockett—were popular heroes. Its example encouraged the production of like neologisms everywhere, and by 1840 the use of slang was very widespread. It is to those days before the Civil War that we owe many of the colorful American terms for strong drink, still current, e.g., *panther-sweat, nose-paint, red-eye, corn-juice, forty-rod, mountain-dew, coffin-varnish, bust-head, stagger-soup, tonsil-paint, squirrel-whiskey* and so on, and for drunk, e.g., *boiled, canned, cock-eyed, frazzled, fried, oiled, ossified, pifflicated, pie-eyed, plastered, snozzled, stewed, stuccoed, tanked, woozy.*[32] "Perhaps the most striking difference between British and Ameri-

30. Specimens of this tall talk are given in Chapter IV, Section 1.
31. For these examples I am indebted to M. M. Mathews, who prints a longer list in The Beginnings of American English; Chicago, 1931, pp. 114–15.
32. For a much longer list see Slang Synonyms for *Drunk,* by Manuel Prenner, *American Speech,* Dec., 1928.

can slang," says Krapp,[33] "is that the former is more largely merely a matter of the use of queer-sounding words, like *bally* and *swank*, whereas American slang suggests vivid images and pictures." This was hardly true in the heyday of "tall talk," but that it is true now is revealed by a comparison of current English and American college slang. The vocabulary of Oxford and Cambridge seems inordinately obvious and banal to an American undergraduate. At Oxford it is made up in large part of a series of childish perversions of common and proper nouns, effected by adding *-er* or inserting *gg*. Thus, breakfast becomes *brekker*, collection becomes *collecker*, the Queen Street Cinema becomes the *Queener*, St. John's becomes *Jaggers* and the Prince of Wales becomes the *Pragger-Wagger*. The rest of the vocabulary is equally feeble. To match the magnificent American *lounge-lizard* the best the Oxonians can achieve is *a bit of a lad*, and in place of the multitudinous American synonyms for *girl* [34] there are only *bint* (Arabic for *woman*) and a few other such flabby terms.[35] All college slang, of course, borrows heavily from the general slang vocabulary. For example, *chicken*, which designated a young girl on most Ameri-

---

33. The English Language in America; New York, 1925, Vol. I, p. 114.

34. There is a list of them in English Words and Their Background, by George H. McKnight; New York, 1923, p. 61.

35. I am indebted here to Mr. Hiram D. Blauvelt. The literature dealing with American college slang begins with A Collection of College Words and Customs, by B. H. Hall; Cambridge, Mass., 1851. Its contents are summarized in College Slang of a Century Ago, by Joseph C. Smith, *Delta Kappa Epsilon Quarterly*, May, 1933. For the slang in vogue at the beginning of the present century see College Words and Phrases, by Eugene H. Babbitt, *Dialect Notes*, Vol. II, Pt. I, 1900, a very valuable compilation. For later periods see College Slang, by M. C. McPhee, *American Speech*, Dec., 1927, and College Abbreviations, by W. E. Schultz, the same, Feb., 1930. There are many monographs on the slang of definite colleges, for example: College Slang Words and Phrases from Bryn Mawr College, by Howard J. Savage, *Dialect Notes*, Vol. V, Pt. V, 1922; Colgate University Slang, by J. A. Russell, *American Speech*, Feb., 1930; A Babylonish Cruise [Girard College], by Carroll H. Frey, *Steel and Garnet*, Dec., 1922; Johns Hopkins Jargon, by J. Louis Kuethe, *American Speech*, June, 1932; Kansas University Slang, by Carl Pingry and Vance Randolph, the same, Feb., 1928; Midshipman Jargon, by Mary B. Peterson, the same, Aug., 1928; Negro Slang in Lincoln University, by Hugh Sebastian, the same, Dec., 1934; University of Missouri Slang, by Virginia Carter, the same, Feb., 1931; Slang at Smith, by M. L. Farrand, *Delineator*, Oct., 1920; Stanford Expressions, by W. R. Morse, *American Speech*, March, 1927; Stanfordiana, by John A. Shidler and R. M. Clarke, Jr., the same, Feb., 1932; More Stanford Expressions, by John A. Shidler, the same, Aug., 1932; and College Slang Words and Phrases from Western Reserve University, *Dialect Notes*, Vol. IV, Pt. III, 1915.

can campuses until 1921 or thereabout,[36] was used by Steele in 1711, and, in the form of *no chicken*, by Swift in 1720. It had acquired a disparaging significance in the United States by 1788, as the following lines show:

> From visiting bagnios, those seats of despair,
> Where *chickens* will call you *my duck* and *my dear*
> In hopes that your purse may fall to their share,
> Deliver me! [37]

[6] Like the vulgar language in general, popular American slang has got very little sober study from the professional philologians. The only existing glossary of it by a native scholar—"A Dictionary of American Slang," by Maurice H. Weseen, associate professor of English at the University of Nebraska—is an extremely slipshod and even ridiculous work.[38] There are several collections by laymen, but most of them are still worse.[39] The best, and by far, is "Slang Today and Yesterday," by Eric Partridge,[40] which deals principally with English slang, but also has a valuable section on American slang. All the dictionaries of Americanisms, of course, include words reasonably describable as slang,

36. I take the date from Slang Today and Yesterday, by Eric Partridge; 2nd ed.; London, 1935, p. 429. Partridge says that it was displaced, at least for a time, by the English *flapper*.

37. The Married Man's Litany, *New Hampshire Spy*, June 10. I am indebted for the quotation to Dr. James Truslow Adams.

38. New York, 1934. Dr. Weseen seems to be uncertain about the meaning of the word *slang*. He extends it to embrace trade and class argots, the technical vocabularies of various arts and mysteries, common mispronunciations, and the general body of nonce-words. On what theory does he hold that *A No. 1*, *boss*, and *close call* are slang? Or *chaw*, *snoot* and *coupla*? Or *cold snap*, *eternal triangle* and *dead as a doornail*? Or *moron*, *journalese* and *Hoosier*? Or such painful artificialities as *Emersonthusiast*, *mound mainstay* ("the chief pitcher for a baseball team"), and *powerphobe* ("a person who fears the political power of public companies"). Some of his definitions are howlers, as, for example, "an uncouth person" for *leatherneck* (Tell it to the Marines!), and "the home of a newly married couple"—just that, and nothing more—for *love-nest*.

39. For example, A Thesaurus of Slang, by Howard N. Rose; New York, 1934. Rose's aim is the lowly one of aiding writers of pulp fiction. The ordinary English words are listed alphabetically, and the equivalents in slang or argot follow them. Thus the fictioneer who yearns to give verisimilitude to his otherwise bald and unconvincing narrative may learn readily what college students call a library or a lavatory, and how hoboes distinguish between the professional levels of their trade.

40. 2nd ed.; London, 1935. It contains a long and interesting history of modern slang, and separate chapters on various varieties of cant and argot.

but they appear only incidentally, and not in large numbers. Thornton, for example, bars out a great deal of interesting and amusing material by confining his researches to written records. In England the literature of the subject is far more extensive. It began in the Sixteenth Century with the publication of several vocabularies of thieves' argot, and has been enriched in recent years by a number of valuable works, notably the Partridge volume just cited, "Slang, Phrase and Idiom in Colloquial English and Their Use," by Thomas R. G. Lyell,[41] and the monumental "Slang and Its Analogues," by John S. Farmer and W. E. Henley.[42] Before the completion of the last-named, the chief authorities on English slang were "A Dictionary of Slang, Jargon and Cant," by Albert Barrère and Charles G. Leland,[43] and "A Dictionary of Modern Cant, Slang and Vulgar Words," by J. C. Hotten.[44] Relatively little attention is paid to slang in the philological journals, but it is frequently discussed in the magazines of general circulation and in the newspapers.[45] When the English papers denounce Americanisms, which is very often, it is commonly slang that arouses their most violent dudgeon. This dudgeon, of course, is grounded upon its very success: the American movies and talkies have implanted American slang in England even more copiously than they have implanted more decorous American

41. Tokyo, 1931.

42. In seven volumes; London, 1890–1904. This huge work is mainly devoted to cant, but it also contains a great deal of English and American slang. About 15,000 terms are listed. In many cases there are dated quotations, but the dates are not always accurate. In his preface Farmer promised to include a bibliography, a vocabulary of foreign slang, and a study of comparative slang, but this intention seems to have been abandoned. An abridgment in one volume by the same authors appeared in London in 1905. Farmer alone printed a Dictionary of Americanisms in London in 1889. It included relatively little slang.

43. In two volumes; London, 1889–90. It listed about 4800 terms, and like Slang and Its Analogues was privately printed. There was a second edition in 1897.

44. Usually called simply the Slang Dictionary. The first edition appeared in London in 1859. There were later editions in 1860, 1864, and 1874, and many reprints.

45. The more respectable literature, running down to 1922, is listed in A Bibliography of Writings on the English Language, by Arthur G. Kennedy; Cambridge and New Haven, 1927, p. 419 ff. There is a briefer bibliography in the third edition of the present work; New York, 1928, p. 463 ff. For the period since 1922, the bibliographies printed in each issue of *American Speech* and annually in the *Publications of the Modern Language Association* are useful, though they are far from complete.

neologisms. As the *Spectator* was saying lately, its influence "on the British Empire continues, ever more rapidly, to increase—a portent frequently mentioned and almost as frequently deplored." [46] Sometimes it is belabored as intolerably vulgar, indecent and against God, as when the *Christian World* [47] blamed it for the prevalence of "dishonest and debased thought" and ascribed its use to "a sneaking fear and dislike of calling beautiful things by their beautiful names and of calling ugly things by their ugly names"; sometimes it is sneered at as empty and puerile, signifying nothing, as when Allan Monkhouse [48] demanded piously "What is the good of all this?" and answered "Such words are the ghosts of old facetiousness, and the world would be better without them"; and sometimes efforts are made to dispose of it by proving that it is all stolen from England, as when Dr. C. T. Onions, one of the editors of the Oxford Dictionary, offered to show a London reporter that the dictionary listed any American slang term he could name.[49] Alas, for Dr. Onions, after making good with *to grill, fresh, to figure* (in the sense of to conclude), *bunkum* (he apparently forgot its clearly American origin) and *rake-off* (he had to fall back upon an American example), he came to grief with *boloney* and *nerts*. One of the favorite forms of this latter enterprise is a letter to the editor announcing the discovery that this or that locution, lately come into popularity by way of the talkies, is to be found in Shakespeare,[50] or the Authorized Version of the Bible, or maybe even in Piers Plowman. There are also the specialists who devote themselves to demonstrating that American slang is simply a series of borrowings from the Continental languages, particularly French—for example, that *and how* is a translation of *et comment*, that *you're telling me* is from *à qui le dites-vous*, and that *to get one's goat* is from *prendre sa chèvre*.[51] But not all Englishmen, of course, oppose and deride

46. In a review of the Weseen Dictionary of American Slang, March 15, 1935.
47. May 14, 1931.
48. American Slang, Manchester *Guardian Weekly*, March 8, 1935.
49. London *Evening News*, April 30, 1934.
50. The same quest is sometimes pursued by Americans. See, for example, Shakespeare and American Slang, by Frederic S. Marquardt, *American Speech*, Dec., 1928, and Slang from Shakespeare, by Anderson M. Baten; Hammond, Ind., 1931.
51. *Prendre sa chèvre* has been traced to Henri Estienne's Satires, *c.* 1585. It is to be found also in Montaigne and Molière, and was included in the

the American invasion, whether of slang or of novelties on high levels. Not a few agree with Horace Annesley Vachell that "American slanguage is not a tyranny, but a beneficent autocracy. . . . *Lounge-lizard*, for example, is excellent. . . . It is humiliating to reflect that English slang at its best has to curtsey to American slang." To which "Jackdaw" adds in *John O'London's Weekly:* [52] "We do but pick up the crumbs that fall from Jonathan's table."

[7] During the [First] World War there was some compensatory borrowing of English army slang and argot by the American troops, but it did not go very far. Indeed, the list of loan-words that came into anything approaching general use in the A.E.F. was about limited to *ace, blimp, cootie, Frog, Jack Johnson, Jerry, blotto, over the top* and *whizz-bang,* Some of the favorites of the British soldiers, *e.g., fag, blighty, cheerio, to strafe, funk-hole* and *righto,* were seldom if ever used by the Americans. The greater part of the American vocabulary came from the Regular Army, and some of it was of very respectable antiquity, *e.g., hand-shaker, Holy Joe* (for chaplain), *slum* (stew), *corned willie* (corned beef hash), *outfit, belly-robber, dog-robber* (an officer's servant or orderly),[53] *doughboy, jawbone* (meaning credit, or anything spurious or dubious), *mud-splasher* (artilleryman), *buck-private, top-kick, gold-fish* (canned salmon), *gob, leatherneck,*

1776 edition of the Dictionnaire de l'Académie. Mr. Rowland M. Myers, to whom I am indebted here, suggests that Estienne may have picked it up in the course of his Greek studies. I have been told that the locution originated, in America, in the fact that the old-time horse-trainers, having a nervous horse to handle, put a goat in its stall to give it company. When the goat was taken away the horse yielded to the heebie-jeebies, and so was easily beaten on the track. A variant etymology was printed in the London *Morning Post,* Jan. 31, 1935. It was so precious that it deserves to be embalmed: "Among the Negroes in Harlem it is the custom for each household to keep a goat to act as general scavenger. Occasionally one man will steal another's goat, and the household debris then accumulates, to the general annoyance." The phrase "Let George do it," once so popular in the United States, is said by some to have been only a translation of "Laissez faire à Georges," which originated in France during the Fifteenth Century, and at the start had satirical reference to the multiform activities of Cardinal Georges d'Amboise, Prime Minister to Louis XII.

52. The Way They Talk Over There, Dec. 10, 1927.

53. I am informed by Staff Sergeant J. R. Ulmer, U. S. A., that *dog-robber* is an enlisted man's term; the officers commonly use *striker.* In the same way, the enlisted men speak of *civvies* and the officers of *cits* (civilian clothes). Sergeant Ulmer says that the Regular Army makes little use of a number of terms that are commonly believed to be in its vocabulary, *e.g., rookie:* it prefers *John* or *dumb John.*

padre, chow, outfit and *punk* (bread). A few novelties came in, *e.g., tin-hat* and *a.w.o.l.*, and there was some fashioning of counterwords and phrases from French materials, *e.g., boocoo* or *boocoup* (beaucoup), *toot sweet* (tout de suite) and *trez beans* (très bien), but neither class was numerous. Naturally enough, a large part of the daily conversation of the troops was obscene, or, at all events, excessively vulgar. Their common name for cavalryman, for example, could hardly be printed here. The English called the military police *red-caps*, but the American name was *M.P.'s*. The British used *O.C.* for Officer Commanding; the Americans used *C.O.* for Commanding Officer. The British were fond of a number of Americanisms, *e.g., cold-feet, kibosh, nix, pal* and *to chew the rag*, but whether they were borrowed from the A.E.F. or acquired by some less direct route I do not know.[54] About *gob, leatherneck* and *doughboy* there have been bitter etymological wrangles. *Gob* has been traced variously to a Chinese word (*gobshite*), of unknown meaning and probably mythical; to *gobble*, an allusion to the somewhat earnest methods of feeding prevailing among sailors; and to *gob*, an archaic English dialect word signifying expectoration. The English coast-guardsmen, who are said to be free spitters, are often called *gobbies*. In May, 1928, Admiral H. A. Wiley, then commander-in-chief of the United

---

54. I am indebted here to Dr. H. K. Croessman and to Mr. Elrick B. Davis. See A. E. F. English, by Mary Paxton Keeley, *American Speech*, 1930, and Soldier Slang by Capt. Elbridge Colby, U. S. A., eight articles, *Our Army*, Oct. 1929–June 1930. An anonymous article in the *Stars and Stripes*, the newspaper of the A.E.F., for April 12, 1918, is also worth consulting. For British War slang see Songs and Slang of the British Soldier, 1914–18, by John Brophy and Eric Partridge; London, 1930; Soldier and Sailor Words and Phrases, by Edward Fraser and John Gibbons; and War Words, in Contemporary English, by W. E. Collinson; Leipzig, 1927, p. 91 *ff*. The book by Brophy and Partridge also includes American terms, but there are many omissions, and a few gross errors. Its vocabulary is amplified in Additions to a Volume on the Slang and the Idioms of the World War, by Eugene S. McCartney, Papers of the *Michigan Academy of Science, Arts and Letters*, Vol. X, 1928. See also Linguistic Processes as Illustrated by War Slang, by the same, the same, Vol. III, 1923. (For the last two I am indebted to Dr. W. W. Bishop, librarian of the University of Michigan.) For French war slang see The Slang of the Poilu, by Eric Partridge, *Quarterly Review*, April, 1932; L'Argot de la guerre, by Albert Dauzet; Paris, 1918; L'Argot des poilus, by François Dechelette; Paris, 1918; Le Langage des poilus, by Claude Lambert; Bordeaux, 1915; L'Argot des tranchées, by Lazar Saineau; Paris, 1915; and Le Poilu tel qu'il se parle, by Gaston Esnault; Paris, 1919. For German, see Wie der Feldgraue spricht, by Karl Bergmann; Giessen, 1916, and Deutsche Soldatensprache, by O. Mausser; Strasburg, 1917.

States Fleet, forbade the use of *gob* in ship's newspapers, calling is "undignified and unworthy." But the gobs continue to cherish it. *Leatherneck,* I have been told, originated in the fact that the collar of the Marines used to be lined with leather. But the Navy prefers to believe that it has something to do with the fact that a sailor, when he washes, strips to the waist and renovates his whole upper works, whereas a Marine simply rolls up his sleeves and washes in the scantier manner of a civilian. It is the theory of all gobs that all Marines are dirty fellows. But the step from unwashed necks to leather seems to me to be somewhat long and perilous. The term *devil-dogs,* often applied to the Marines during the World War, was supposed to be a translation of the German *teufelhunde.* During the fighting around Chateau Thierry, in June and July, 1918, the Marines were heavily engaged, and the story went at the time that the Germans, finding them very formidable, called them *teufelhunde.* But I have been told by German officers who were in that fighting that no such word was known in the German army. *Doughboy* is an old English navy term for dumpling. It was formerly applied to the infantry only, and its use is said to have originated in the fact that the infantrymen once pipe-clayed parts of their uniforms, with the result that they became covered with a doughy mass when it rained.[55]

55. There have been several studies of the use of slang by the authors of fiction, British and American, but rather curiously all of them are by foreigners, *e.g.,* Slang bei Sinclair Lewis, Hanes-Werner Wasmuth; Hamburg, 1935; Slang and Cant in Jerome K. Jerome's Works, by Olaf E. Bosson; Cambridge (England), 1911; Das Prinzip der Verwendung des Slang bei Dickens, by Karl Westendorff; Greifswald, 1923. Dickens himself printed an article on slang in *Household Words,* Sept. 24, 1853.

SUMMARY

[1]   Slang, like cant and argot, is substantially colloquial language (that is, spoken, not written) below the level of standard educated speech, but unlike cant it is not meant to be unintelligible, and unlike argot it is not restricted to a trade or profession.

[2]   Slang is made by giving old words new meanings or by coining new words. But not all new meanings nor all new words are slang.

[3]   Slang is the invention of individuals—chiefly, in America, of writers and journalists, especially columnists and sports writers.

[4]   Slang differs from standard idiom in its freedom from restrictions; it employs the devices of metaphor, abbreviation, and composition.

[5]   American slang, largely borrowed from British until after the War of 1812, got its real start in the tall talk of the frontier; it is now marked by vivid and striking images.

[6]   Slang has not been studied very thoroughly but it has been widely deprecated in the public press.

[7]   During World War I both the American and the British produced a great deal of slang, but there was very little interchange of the slang vocabulary.

PART THREE   Sounds and Symbols

The Vowels of American English

HENRY LEE SMITH, JR.

Henry Lee Smith, Jr., is professor of linguistics at the University of Buffalo. Long interested in the application of the science of linguistics to the teaching of English and other languages, Professor Smith is now working on the application of linguistics to the teaching of reading in elementary schools. This selection is from a series of lectures given at the Harvard Graduate School of Education.

In order to see how unaware we traditionally educated people really are of the structure of our language and how much we are confused between the system that is *language* and the derived system that is *writing* we can use no better illustration than the English vowels. Ask any linguistically naïve but literate speaker of English, "How many vowels are there in English?" and you will get the reply, "Five, *a, e, i, o,* and *u,* and sometimes *y* and *w.*" But only a moment's reflection will make us realize that if we mean by "vowels" vowel sounds rather than vowel letters, there are obviously many more. But how many more? Any speaker can quickly arrive at six contrasts of *short* or *simple* vowels, as for example in the words *pit, pet, pat, put, putt,* and *pot.* Immediately the inconsistency of our writing system is revealed when we notice that *put* and *putt*—words with contrasting vowel sounds —are spelled with the same vowel letter. True, we do add an extra *t* in the word having to do with golf, and this might be a very useful convention in signaling that the vowel letter preceding stands for a different vowel sound, were we always to follow the practice. But we don't, as for example in *but* which rhymes with *putt* but isn't spelled with the extra *t*. It is not hard to see what the foreigner means when he says, "English isn't such a hard language as far as the grammar goes, it's just such a hard language to pronounce." Here he, also being confused between language and writing, is telling us of our inconsistent and incomplete spelling system.

So we obviously have at least six short or simple contrasting vowel sounds in the over-all pattern of English. But how many more are there? There is not space here to go into detail concerning the rigorous process of analysis that linguists go through in arriving at their statements in answer to that question, but we can at least try to show the kind of arrangement that linguists use in seeing the relationships between the structure points of the vocalic part of the sound-systems of languages. Speaking in very simple terms, linguists classify the vowels of languages according to the use made of the tongue and lips in relation to the mouth cavity. Thus a vowel pronounced with the front part of the tongue raised high and almost touching the ridge behind the upper teeth or the upper teeth themselves, is called a "high front vowel." If the lips are spread the vowel is designated "unrounded"; if the lips are pursed, the vowel is classified as "rounded." Likewise a vowel sound uttered with the *back* of the tongue raised and under muscular tension is called a "back vowel"; and, depending again upon how the lips are used, "rounded" or "unrounded." For example, the vowel sound in French *titre* or *machine* is a high, front, unrounded vowel; the vowel sound in French *rue* or *tu* is a high, front, rounded vowel. And again the vowel in French *tout* or *boue* is a high, back, rounded vowel. A vowel as in English *but* or *putt* is designated as "mid, central, unrounded," and the vowels in English *put* and *pat* are designated respectively as "high, back, rounded" (though the rounding is slight) and "low, front, unrounded." A chart of the English short, or simple, vowels we have already mentioned will be helpful.

We notice that in our chart there are three blank boxes with no exemplifying words. A little more digging and we find that speakers of English from various dialect regions furnish us examples of vowels in these areas. For instance, the adverb *just* as in "Just as I came in" or "Just as he got there" is pronounced by most speakers from all dialect regions with a high, central, vowel.

	Front	Central	Back
High	p*i*t		p*u*t
Mid	p*e*t	p*u*tt b*u*t	
Low	p*a*t	p*o*t	

Fig. 1

The word used here does not rhyme with *gist* or with *jest* or with *just* (as said in the phrase "the *just* man"). We have no symbol for this vowel in our writing system, so I will use an *i* with a little bar through it to represent it, ɨ. This vowel occurs very frequently in all varieties of English in stressed as well as unstressed positions and you will frequently hear it, for example, in the words *children, this,* and *which.* It is the vowel heard in the substandard form for the pronoun *you,* often misspelled "youse," but frequently occurring in the gossip columns spelled "yiz" or "yez," as in "I thought I told yiz to come." On the other hand, it is heard in the speech of Eastern Seaboard dowagers in such a sentence as, "We're having my s*i*ster for d*i*nner," where again the vowels are not the same as heard in *pit* or *bit,* but pronounced with the tongue's highest position nearer the center of the mouth rather than nearer the front.

For those of us who distinguish the weak or unstressed form of the pronouns *him* and *them* or who distinguish the possessive of *Rosa* from the plural of *rose,* it is this high, central vowel we employ. For example, "I told'im to come" is contrasted with "I told'em to come" in many dialects by the use of the high, front, vowel as in *bit* or *pit* for the first pronoun and the high, central vowel for the second. And in "Rosa's roses," many speakers will use the mid, central vowel in the possessive of the girl's name and the high, central vowel in the plural ending.

One of the important things to remember in speaking about vowels in English is that not all speakers of the standard language are going to use the same vowels in the same words. It is this different selection, which can be correlated with geographical regions and with position in the social "scale," that helps us to "locate" people by their speech. Carrying this idea further, we can readily see an excellent example of regional difference in the pronunciation of words like *pot, lot, not,* etc. Most persons from the area of coastal New England will pronounce these words not with a low, central vowel but a low, back vowel, slightly rounded. This vowel, but pronounced with more tenseness of the aural musculature, is also the vowel used by most British speakers in these words. It is also very frequently heard in the speech of Americans from the central and western parts of the country in such words as *sorry, orange,* and *forest.* In my own dialect this vowel is relatively rare; I find it in *one* of my pronunciations of words like "alcohol" and "Nujol." The symbol I will use for this vowel is ɔ, a *c* turned backwards and frequently referred to as "open *o.*"

We have now identified eight vowels in the over-all pattern, and because of the few vowel letters we have to represent them, and in order to be consistent, I am going to suggest the following symbolization: *i* as in *pit, e* as in *pet,* æ as in *pat,* ɨ as in "jist," ə as in *putt* and *but, a* as in *pot* (outside of New England), *u* as in *put* and *look,* and ɔ as in *pot,* and *lot* in New England and Great Britain. But we still have one box on our chart with no examples to illustrate it. This is the box we would read "mid, back vowel." It so happens that this vowel is also extremely common in New England. It has in fact frequently been referred to as the New England "short *o.*" It is the vowel we hear in the typical "Down Easter's" pronunciation in "I'm gonna be home the whole day," or "I'll put on my coat and go down the road." Here *whole* and *home, coat* and *road* do not rhyme with *hull* and *hum* and *cut* and *rud,* though to non-New England speakers this is often the impression. In my own speech, I have this vowel regularly only in "gonna," which is a very frequently occurring pronunciation of this "contraction." Many speakers, however, use ə, the vowel in *but* or *cut,* in the form spelled "gonna," and many others use the high, central vowel, ɨ.

We have now filled out our chart and placed our symbols where they belong. But we all know this is not the whole story of the vowel sounds in the over-all pattern of English. What about the so-called long vowels and diphthongs? Further rigorous analysis of the speech of persons all over the English-speaking world leads

	Front	Central	Back
High	*i* pit	*ɨ* "jɨst"	*u* put
Mid	*e* pet	*ə* putt	*o* "gonna" home (N. E.)
Low	*æ* pat	*a* pot	*ɔ* pot (N. E.) sorry (C. and W. U. S.)

FIG. 2

us to the conclusion that English—like the other Germanic languages—has a vowel system that can be described as consisting of simple or short vowels and what are called "complex nuclei." Complex nuclei are of three types. First are those composed of any one of the simple vowels followed by a *glide* to a *higher* and *fronter* tongue position. Second, we have the simple vowel followed by a *glide* to a *higher* and *backer* tongue position, and, third, we have any one of the simple vowels followed by a *glide* to a more *central* tongue position. These glides are termed "semivowels," because they pattern like consonants, on the one hand, but fill out the vowel nuclei on the other. They are the sounds we familiarly represent with the letters *y*, *w*, and *h* as heard in such words as *ye*, *woo*, and *hah*.

In *ye* and *woo* and *hah* we have excellent examples of our semivowels *y*, *w*, and *h* used in both initial and final positions, that is, both preceding and following a simple vowel. For if we both listen to and feel what goes on inside our mouths when we say, for example, *ye*, we will notice that we start in a very high, front position and drop to a slightly higher occurrence of the vowel in *pit* and then return by gliding to a higher and fronter position. *Ye*, then, is composed of three segments, *y*, *i*, *y*. Similarly *yay* is composed of semivowel *y* followed by the vowel in *pet*, followed by a return to a higher and fronter position—*y, e, y*. By the same analysis, *woo* is heard to be composed of a very high, back, fully rounded sound followed by a slightly higher variety of the simple vowel in *put*, followed by a return, through gliding, back to the very high, very rounded sound. Again we have three segments—*w, u, w*. Similarly, *woe* would be *w, o, w*, and *wow*, *w, a, w*, or *w, æ, w*.

This analysis of simple vowels plus the semivowels *y* and *w* allows us to handle twenty-seven vocalic syllable nuclei in English—the nine simple vowels already taken up, and each of these followed by *y* and *w*. Examples of all occurrences of complex nuclei with *y* and *w* follow, first with *y*:

iy as in *be, me, see, keep, eat*.

ey as in *day, bay, pay, gate*.

æy as in certain Southern pronunciations of *I, July, half*.

iy as in Philadelphia and other central dialects for *me, see, be*.

əy as in *first* and *bird* as heard quite typically in certain New York City and Southern coastal dialects (quite often spelled "foist," "boid," in dialect stories and comic strips).

ay as in *I, my, sigh, might*, in Northern and Western speech.

uy as in *push* in certain Southern and Western dialects.

oy as in *joy, boy, Hoyt*.

ɔy as in *time, life*, in northern Eastern Seaboard dialects and in Ireland.

With *w*:

iw as in *new, few, too, food*, in certain speakers in the northern Middle West (instead of the usual *uw*).

ew as in the extreme Southern coastal (Tidewater Virginia) pronunciation of *house, out, about* (often erroneously rendered as "hoose" and "oot" in dialect stories). This is also heard in the extreme form of the "British accent" in such words as *oh, no*, and *go*.

æw as in *how, now, cow, out, around* in most standard speakers, though variations too tense and too nasalized are frowned on by elocution and speech teachers in favor of a nucleus consisting of *aw*.

iw as in *food, moon, spoon* in most central dialects, in contrast to the Northern and Western structuring with *uw*.

əw as in *go, no, so, note,* particularly in Eastern Central dialects (Philadelphia) and as in many British dialects, in contrast with a structuring of *ow.*

aw as in *house, out, about, around, cow, now,* in Northern and
Western speech (see æw above).

uw as in *food, moon, spoon,* in Northern and Western speech
(see *iw, ɨw* above).

ow as in *go, so, no, boat,* in most of the United States (see *ew*
and *əw* above).

ɔw as in the pronunciation of "you all" as a one-syllable utterance in many Southern dialects.

Now for a quick rundown on the complex nuclei with *h.* The
h, we remember, represents a glide to the center from one of our
simple vowel positions. In *hah,* we note that the initial sound has
some friction noise along with it, and it starts off without the
vocal cords vibrating (or, to use the technical term, "voiceless").
The sound represented by the final *h,* however, is accompanied
by no friction voice and is "voiced" all the way through. We have
all learned to associate the friction noise, which characterizes
initial h's in English, with the letter symbol *h,* and so it comes as
a slight shock to see the symbol used to represent the semivowel
glide to the center after a simple vowel. In other words, *hah, ah,
pa,* and *ma* all rhyme; all end in *h* though the final *h* is seldom
represented in our writing system. It takes only a little careful
listening, however, to realize that the initial *h's* in *he* and in *hot,*
though noticeably different in tongue position, are actually starting *nearer the center* of the mouth than the simple vowels that
follow them. Even more easily can we notice the gliding to the
center from the simple vowel position when *h* follows, as in *idea,
poor* and *law.* Examples of the nine simple vowels followed by
h are:

ih as in *idea, peer, fear* (in New England where "final *r* is not
pronounced" the composition of the nuclei with *h* are particularly easy to hear).

eh as in *yeah, Mary, bath, past, grass, hand,* though many
coastal New Englanders use *ey* in *Mary* and *æh,* or *ah* in
bath, grass, etc.

æh as in *past, grass, bath,* in coastal New England and certain
British dialects. Also heard in cultured speech all along the

Atlantic Seaboard.

ih as in *first, girl, murder* in less privileged speakers of the coastal New England area, where cultured speakers will use *əh.*

əh as in *first, girl, murder, fur.* This pronunciation without a noticeable retraction of the tongue (represented by *r*) is the usual one along the North Atlantic Coast and in cultured British speech. It is also heard in Southern coastal dialects, though it there frequently alternates with *əy.*

ah as in *calm, balm, ah'd, ma, pa, ah.* Also heard in *past, last, grass,* by those speakers both in Britain and America who are said to use "the broad *a.*"

uh as in *poor, sure, cure.* Again in those dialect areas where "*r* is not pronounced" as in coastal New England, the structure of these nuclei is very easy to hear.

oh as in *law, off, often, saw,* in most of the Central Atlantic Seaboard dialects and in many coastal New England dialects. In Western speech, these words quite frequently are pronounced with *ɔh,* or even *ah* (see below).

ɔh as in *law, often, collar, caller,* in many Northern and Western dialects (see *oh* above).

This very brief set of examples at least begins to give us some idea of the complexity of the structuring of English vowel nuclei. Thirty-six possible "vowels" in the over-all pattern is quite a long way from "five vowels—*a, e, i, o, u,* and sometimes *y* and *w.*" The advantage of the teacher's knowing something about the structuring of the vowel system in the teaching of reading is immediately apparent. In the first place, the preparation of materials which will introduce the child to the printed page through the regularities between the language and its spelling is obvious and has already been mentioned. In the second place, lots of needless confusion and frustration can be avoided if the teacher can be made to understand that *standard* pronunciation varies geographically and that just because Johnny pronounces *bad* as *behd* when the teacher pronounces it *bæhd* doesn't make Johnny "wrong" and the teacher "right." And again, for example, in many standard Southern pronunciations no distinction is made between *e* and *i* before a nasal consonant, so *pen* and *pin* are pronounced to rhyme. To tell standard speakers that this is wrong "because the two words are spelled with two different letters" is as misleading and erroneous as to say that by far the larger majority of educated speakers in the country are "wrong" because they pronounce *merry, marry* and *Mary* so that all three words rhyme.

SUMMARY

Speakers of American English distinguish nine basic vowels and, with glides to three "semivowels," twenty-seven "long" vowels or vowel nuclei. No one speaker uses all of these vowel sounds, but American speakers from various parts of the country, taken together, do.

NOTES

Professor Smith's essay needs no explanation. But before you proceed to the next essays, a word should be said about two things: (1) other ways of indicating spoken vowel sounds and (2) ways of indicating "consonant" sounds of modern English. What we are explaining in all this is a "phonetic"—or, more properly, a "phonemic"—alphabet: a system of symbols to represent the sounds of a language. Strictly speaking, a "phonetic" alphabet will provide a means of distinguishing all the different sounds made in a language, whether the differences are significant or not.

An example may show what is meant. If you listen as you say such words as *pop, babe, dad,* and *tot,* you will hear that you say the first consonant in each word differently from the way you say the last one; that is, the first *p* in *pop* is comparatively exploded, the second one much less so—one, the linguist says, is aspirated and the other unaspirated. An alphabet which is intended to distinguish all the sounds in a language would have to provide means of distinguishing these two *p*'s; and the "phonetic" alphabet does so, by writing the first *p* with a superscript *h* (p^h) and the second *p* with a little equal sign ($p^=$). But these two *p*'s are not significantly different in modern English; we do not use the two to distinguish different words. In fact, we never say either one or the other at the same place, but faithfully pop *p*'s at beginnings of words and faithfully don't pop them at ends of words. They are, the linguist says, in "complementary distribution": where p^h appears, $p^=$ does not, and vice versa. Therefore, if we are interested in in a "phonemic" alphabet (one in which only significant sound differences are represented), one symbol will suffice for both these *p*'s. The alphabets discussed below, though variously called "phonetic" and "phonemic" are really "phonemic" in character. (Linguists use the tags *-etic* and *-emic* consistently to distinguish "the possible group" from "that part of the possible group which has meaning in a given language.")

(1) The vowel system here explained is known widely as the

Trager-Smith system (after Professors Smith and George L. Trager). Another commonly used system of transcribing the vowels is called the IPA (International Phonetic Alphabet) system. It utilizes the following characters for the various sounds indicated:

IPA VOWELS

i for the sound of *ee* in *beet*
ɪ for the sound of *i* in *sit*
e for the sound of *a* in *chaotic*
ei for the sound of *a* in *cave*
ε for the sound of *e* in *set*
æ for the sound of *a* in *sat*
ɑ for the sound of *a* in *father*
a for the sound of *a* in *ask,* as often pronounced in American (between æ and ɑ)
ɔ for the sound of *a* in *all* or *o* in *horse*
ɒ for the sound of *o* in *sorry* as pronounced in England and often in America (between ɑ and ɔ)
o for the sound of *o* in *notation*
ou for the sound of *o* in *go*
ʊ for the sound of *u* in *pull*
u for the sound of *oo* in *pool*
ʌ for the sound of *u* in *sun* (stressed)
ə for the sound of *a* in *sofa* (unstressed)
з for the sound of *ir* in *bird* as pronounced in Southern England, Eastern and Southern U. S.

If we chart this vowel system as Professor Smith charts his basic vowels, we get this sort of chart:

i (b*ee*t)			u (p*oo*l)	
ɪ (s*i*t)			ʊ (p*u*ll)	
e (ch*a*otic)		ʌ (s*u*n)	o (n*o*tation)	
ε (s*e*t)		ə (sof*a*)		
æ (s*a*t)	a (*a*sk)	ɑ (f*a*ther)	ɒ (s*o*rry)	ɔ (*a*ll)

Two glides or nuclei are listed: ei (for the *a* in *cave*) and ou (for the *o* in *go*).

(2) The symbols generally used by linguists for the consonant sounds in English are less controversial. The following chart lists them, with the few variants which do occur:

CONSONANTS

p   as in *pip* (voiceless)
b   as in *bib* (voiced)

t	as in *tat* (voiceless)
d	as in *did* (voiced)
k	as in *kick* (voiceless)
g	as in *gag* (voiced)
f	as in *fife* (voiceless)
v	as in *valve* (voiced)
θ	as in *th*in streng*th* (voiceless)
ð	as in *th*ey ba*th*e (voiced)
š or ʃ	as in *shush* (voiceless)
č or tʃ	as in *ch*ur*ch* (voiced)
ž or ʒ	as in a*z*ure (voiceless)
ǰ or dʒ	as in *ju*d*ge* (voiced)
l	as in *lull* (voiced)
m	as in *mom* (voiced)
n	as in *nun* (voiced)
ŋ	as in si*ng* (voiced)
h	as in *h*at (voiceless)
j	as in *y*ield (voiced)
r	as in *rear* (voiced)
w	as in *w*ield (voiced)
s	as in *sass* (voiceless)
z	as in *z*eroe*s* (voiced)

Now, running one's eye down these charts may be pleasant and easy. But it will not get you really acquainted with phonemic transcription. Unless you practice both the reading and the writing of these symbols, you will never sufficiently master them to make them worthwhile for your study of languages. If your instructor does not pose exercises for you, prepare some for yourself, and ask your instructor to look at them, to make sure you understand.

Writing

LEONARD ROBERT PALMER

Professor of comparative philology at Oxford University, Leonard Robert Palmer has written books on Greek and Latin as well as on the study of language generally. This excerpt from his Introduction to Modern Linguistics *outlines the development of our writing system.*

[1]   Our consideration of language and its problems in the previous chapters has been based upon the fact that languages are systems of significant *sounds*. We must now approach our subject from a new angle. It is a remarkable fact that in a civilized community linguistic behaviour, both active and passive, that is to say linguistic expression and understanding, are carried on without the use of vocal sounds at all. In this book, in which the author is behaving linguistically in order to influence the mind of you, his reader, there is no contact from mouth to ear such as we have assumed in our previous disquisitions. Instead of this the writer has caused marks to be made on paper and the reader sees these marks, and from these visual impressions he interprets the author's meaning. Yet we call this *linguistic* behaviour; and the book or rather its contents constitutes *linguistic* matter, although the tongue (*lingua*) has not been called upon to articulate a single sound.

Our ability to perform such acts of communication and interpretation again rests upon training in early childhood. After the laborious process of learning the auditory symbols that constitute our language, we were next compelled to acquire a new system of symbols. By an intricate pedagogic apparatus of picture-books, letter-boxes, chalks and slates our minds were impressed with the fact that certain intricate shapes refer to particular sounds. In

Pp. 115–125 from L. R. Palmer, *Introduction to Modern Linguistics* (London: Macmillan & Co., 1936). Reprinted by permission of the author.

other words, we were compelled to submit our linguistic knowledge to a process of phonetic analysis, to realize that all our speech
may be reduced to a series of easily distinguishable sounds and
that these sounds may be represented by visual symbols. This system of writing and the different mode of linguistic behaviour
which it makes possible open up a series of new problems. To approach them we must first consider how this remarkable alignment
of writing and sound, of visual and auditory impressions, came
into being. We must trace the history of the alphabet.

[2]   The earliest and most primitive stage of graphic symbolization consists of picture writing. A more or less complicated event
is depicted as a totality without reference to any linguistic analysis or description of that event. The accompanying figure, 1, which

Fig. 1

reproduces part of a famous Egyptian document, will illustrate
what is meant. The flattened oval at the base of the complex represents a land, and this land is further identified by papyrus growing on it—it is the papyrus land, the Nile delta. The head attached
to it represents the inhabitants of that land. The falcon is the
symbol for the king, and the fact that he is leading the head by a
string indicates that he conquered the land and took its inhabitants prisoners. It must be emphasized that in this type of graphic
representation there is little or no connection with the *linguistic*
expression of the idea or event. There is no articulation of the
picture to correspond to the words into which the sentence may

be analysed. Nevertheless the very fact that the event must be symbolized stimulates the mind to analysis. For symbolization implies schematization; that is, the choice of the most significant factors and moments in the event-complex. Such an analysis constitutes the next stage in the development of writing. The picture, instead of being conceived as a totality referring as such to a complex event, now denotes a single idea or object. Figure 2 gives

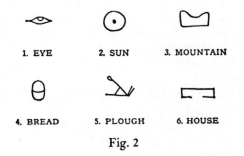

1. EYE   2. SUN   3. MOUNTAIN

4. BREAD   5. PLOUGH   6. HOUSE

Fig. 2

a selection of such *ideographic* hieroglyphs, as they are called. Here again stress must be laid upon the fact that at this stage the graphic symbol refers directly to the idea. It has as yet no connection with the linguistic sound symbol—the word. Writing and speech are, in fact, still two independent systems of symbols that serve to represent ideas. This fact may be schematized in the accompanying figure 3. The most significant step in the history of

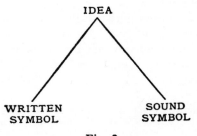

Fig. 3

writing was taken when the third side of the triangle was completed, and the graphic symbol was taken to represent not the idea but the sounds of the corresponding word.[1] Writing is now not an ideographic but a *phonetic* system. Suppose in an ideographic system we have two symbols, one denoting man and denoting age; in the new system these symbols will merely represent the groups of sounds *m a n* and *a g e*, so that by their juxtaposition we could represent the word *manage*. A further advance in technique was made when the pictures were taken to represent not the whole phonetic word, but merely the first syllable of that words. In this way the so-called syllabaries, such as we find in Cyprus and in Japan, most probably evolved. The alphabetic stage was finally reached when the symbol was used to denote the first sound of the word of which it is a sketch. This is known as the acrophonic principle.

[3]   After this preliminary survey we can approach the problem of our own alphabet. The nations of western Europe have derived their systems of writing from the Romans, who in their turn learned it from Greek sources. The Greeks themselves believed that they owed their alphabet to the Phoenicians, a Semitic people who from the cities of Tyre and Sidon engaged in mercantile activities which took them as far as the coasts of our own island. Until recent years, however, no one had been successful in connecting the Semitic scripts (of which Phoenician was one variety) with the Egyptian hieroglyphic system. In 1916, however, Gardiner, a leading English Egyptologist, succeeded in reading certain inscriptions that had been found in the peninsula of Sinai. The script in which these inscriptions are written proved to be the missing link. The symbols resemble the Egyptian hieroglyphs and, like them, may be written horizontally or vertically, and from left to right or from right to left. Figure 4 demonstrates without the need of further comment the fact that the form of the symbols themselves is based on Egyptian models, and that they have a close resemblance to the oldest Semitic scripts. The only difficulty

1. This is a convenient point to refute possible objections to my definition of language. To those scholars who will remark that it makes no allowance for "written language," I would reply that writing in its first stage can only be metaphorically called "language." It is a system of symbols on the same level as the postage stamps and flowers we discussed above. When, however, writing becomes phonetic, i.e. when the third side of the triangle is completed, then these visual symbols have only meaning in so far as they refer to the sound symbols and so fall within our definition.

EGYPTIAN	SINAI SCRIPT	SEMITIC TYPES		EARLY GREEK	GR. NAME	SEM. NAME	MEANING OF SEM. NAME
			MOABITE STONE		ἄλφα	'ALF	OX
				△	δέλτα	DELT	DOOR
					Κάππα	KAF	BENT HAND
					μῦ	MEM	WATER
					ρῶ	ROSH	HEAD

FIG. 4

is that they have a different phonetic value. A dazzling light was thrown on this problem when it was realized that the *names* of the Semitic symbols designate the *objects* which the Sinai symbols depict. That is to say, the Sinai symbols refer to the *Semitic names* of the objects which the Egyptian hieroglyphs represented. This can only mean that a Semitic-speaking people adopted the Egyptian script, but made it refer to the corresponding words of their own language. By the acrophonic principle the symbols were made to represent the first sounds of these Semitic words and so the alphabet was evolved. The accompanying table (Fig. 4) illustrates the whole history of our letters A, D, K, M, R, down to the earliest Greek types.

In the alphabet we seem to have reached a solution of the problem of written representation of speech that is at once simple and adequate. This is made clear if we compare an alphabetic system with the syllabaries which were their immediate predecessors in the line of evolution. If a language has five vowel sounds, then it must have a separate symbol to render the combination of each consonant with each vowel. Thus there must be a separate symbol for the sound combinations *pa, pe, pi, po, pu;* so that a language with 16 consonants would require a syllabary with 80 signs to represent all combinations with its 5 vowels. The alphabetic system, on the other hand, with its one-sound-one-symbol principle, finds 16 + 5 symbols adequate to perform the same task. With this invention perfection seems to have been reached. Yet in England the indignant foreigner and the harassed schoolboy may with justice ask why this conformity of writing with pronunciation no longer exists, and why the golden age was allowed to pass. Here we hit upon the essential difference between speech and writing. The development of the written language is governed by very different conditions from that of spoken language. The act of writing and the different mnemonic conditions of the visual and the auditory symbol give the written language a greater stability and a more rigid conservatism. The spoken language, on the other hand, by that process called linguistic drift, alters by imperceptible changes. If writing remains unchanged, in the course of time a complete rupture will be made between the written and spoken forms of a language. This has actually happened in modern Greece, where the traveller finds the debased Attic of the newspapers of little use in conversation with the natives. But English is in similar case. Why do we write *gh* in *light, right, sight?* The answer is that our modern English spelling represents the pronunciation of the fifteenth century, and at that time *gh* was meant to render a palatal fricative which is still pronounced in Lowland Scotch and may still be heard in the corresponding German word *Licht.* Our spelling has remained practically unaltered since that date, while pronunciation has undergone such profound changes that the link between speech and writing has almost been severed. Irish is in an even worse plight. Where *saoghal* = sil, *oidhche* = i, we may indeed say that one writes Oxford and pronounces Cambridge. The difficulties of such spellings are so great for certain types of people that there has been at regular intervals a great clamour for spelling reform. But there are several considerations which should deter from precipitate action. A problem of a similar kind exists in China, where the authorities have often been urged to abandon their own cumbersome method of writing and to adopt the western European alphabetic script. The reflections of an eminent Sinologist on this question are relevant to our own problem. I paraphrase and supplement them in the following paragraph.[2]

In China, as in early Egypt, the script was nothing more than a system of stylized and simplified pictures. That is to say, the visual symbols referred directly to the idea and not to the idea *via* the spoken word. This means that the written language is inde-

2. B. Karlgren, *Sound and Symbol in Chinese.* Oxford, 1923.

pendent of the changes and modifications of speech. It means that the literature of 4000 years is at once opened to the student who learns the 4000-odd visual symbols which we are told is sufficient for everyday use. He is not burdened with the task of learning Middle Chinese and Old Chinese. No dialect complications arise such as trouble the student of classical Greek, who, to appreciate Homer, Sappho, Herodotus and Demosthenes, must learn as many varieties of speech. Moreover, though the different parts of China have spoken dialects that are mutually unintelligible, an edict written in the ancient characters is immediately comprehensible to the literate in every province. Yet we are told that if a Cantonese were to read it aloud, the sounds would convey absolutely nothing to a speaker of the Pekinese dialect. Thus the Chinese script is the sole instrument of universal communication in China, and as such it is the backbone of Chinese culture. If they were to yield to the importunities of Western states and introduced an alphabetic script, the schoolboy (and the European) would be saved at most a year or two of study. But for this slight gain the Chinese would lose the heritage of a literature that has endured and grown for 4000 years. Moreover, a phonetic document written in the Pekin dialect would be unintelligible elsewhere. The unity of China, as of all administrative areas, depends entirely on the existence of a common means of communication. This work has hitherto been performed through the medium of the universally intelligible script. If this is abandoned, where is the *koine* that would take its place? Karlgren has well said: "If China does not abandon its peculiar script in favour of our alphabetic writing, this is not due to any stupid or obdurate conservatism . . . the day the Chinese discard it they will surrender the very foundation of their culture."

The same warning holds good for our problem. The student of language is aware that in the first place any reformed system of spelling would be out of date in fifty years. Secondly, in what orthography are we to print the masterpieces of English literature? To ascribe modern pronunciation to Shakespeare would be a falsification. Yet if we preserved the old spelling for such works and applied the modern orthography only to modern texts, teaching it in the primary schools, then English literature would become a closed book to all who had not the time and patience to learn the old orthography. To those who have learned to read *lite* the old *light* will be as foreign as the German *Licht*. The traditional orthography, like Chinese script, is a unifying bond which holds together the whole of English literature since the fifteenth century. Any adequate attempt at modernization will lock the doors of English literature to all except the erudite.

SUMMARY

[1]   Learning to read a language forces us to analyze the sounds of the language and their relationship to written shapes. To approach these relationships sensibly we must trace the history of the alphabet.

[2]   Writing began with picture-writing, which pictured an event without reference to any spoken language. The second step was the development of ideographic hieroglyphs, which used certain limited symbols to represent limited ideas, but still without reference to the spoken language. The third step was the association of an ideograph with the sounds of the word associated with the event. In this way "syllabaries" (making connections between signs and spoken syllables) were probably developed. When the symbol became associated with only the first sound of the syllable (the so-called "acrophonic principle"), the alphabet came into being.

[3]   Our own alphabet came to us through the Romans, Greeks, and presumably the Phoenicians. The connection between Semitic scripts and Egyptian hieroglyphs was discovered by Gardiner in 1916. Semitic-speaking people had adopted the Egyptian ideographs but associated them with spoken sounds, and indeed the first sounds in words, thus creating a much more efficient system than that of the "syllabary." A written language gives great stability to a language's writing, but spoken language tends to change—hence the problem of a spelling "reform" for English today. The Chinese, who have stuck to a written language of ideographs (isolated from spoken dialects), find that their written language is their only means of communication; we find ours our only means of preserving our literary heritage.

NOTES

Perhaps a word should be said about two items in this essay, the "syllabary" and the "acrophonic principle." A syllabary develops when symbols are created to represent the various syllables of a language. Thus, in English we have nine basic vowels. If our writing had not developed past the syllabary stage, we would have a separate symbol for each of these sound combinations, made with the basic vowels and the consonant *b*:

/bi/	/bɨ/	/bu/
/be/	/bə/	/bo/
/bæ/	/ba/	/bɔ/

—to say nothing of yet other "long-vowel" combinations and to say nothing of the 23 consonants besides *b*! The 24 consonants and 9 basic vowels in English would require a syllabary of at least 216 characters. If the "long vowels" were counted, we should need a syllabary of 864 symbols!

The so-called "acrophonic (first-sound) principle" was an amazing discovery. It consisted of associating a symbol not with the whole syllable but with only the first sound of the syllable—as, for example, the symbol for /ba/ with only the /b/ sound and the symbol for the syllable /em/ with only the /e/ sound. This discovery allowed the reduction of the written symbols to the basic sounds in a language. In terms of our imagined English syllabary of from 216 to 864 symbols, the acrophonic principle would allow us to reduce to the 36-character alphabet which our present language should have to be written phonemically. The fact that we try to get by with only 26 letters means that our spelling is necessarily unphonetic to some extent.

English as a Phonetic Language

Since 1946, Ralph M. Williams has taught at Trinity College, where he is now professor of English. His Phonetic Spelling for College Students, *from which this selection is taken, applies modern linguistic knowledg to the problems of English spelling.*

[1]   One of the commonest excuses offered for the prevalence of bad spelling today is the idea that English is not a phonetic language. That is perhaps putting the cart before the horse. English *is* a phonetic language; every language which uses an alphabet or other set of phonetic symbols is phonetic. But the history of the English language has been one of continual change, and as these changes often affect you as a speller of modern English, we propose to give you a very brief history of the language, emphasizing and illustrating most fully those changes which concern you most.

❖   ❖   ❖

[2]   The history of English as a distinct Teutonic language may be said to begin about 449 A.D., the traditional date for the arrival of the first contingent of Angles, Saxons, and Jutes in what is now known as England (Angle-land). England, or Britain as it had been known, was previously inhabited by people speaking different languages of the Celtic branch of the Indo-European family. For roughly four hundred years many of these people had been under the rule of the Romans, and had been protected and civilized by them. But when, about 410 A.D., the Romans withdrew their last forces, the untrained native population (although of Celtic stock for the most part, they thought of themselves as Romans, of course) was left at the mercy of the related but wilder

Pp. 130–137 from *Phonetic Spelling for College Students* by Ralph M. Williams. © 1960 by Oxford University Press, Inc. Reprinted by permission.

and more uncivilized tribes who had never been subjugated by the Romans and who had been harassing the Britons with raids for some time. According to legend, the former Roman subjects sought aid from the Angles, Saxons, and Jutes, and those who came to help stayed to conquer. In any event, it took the newcomers little more than a century to drive the Celts back up into Scotland, where 150,000 people still speak Gaelic, west into the mountains of Wales, where a Celtic language spoken by over two million people still flourishes, southwest into Cornwall, where a Celtic language survived until the eighteenth century, and across the Channel into Brittany, the northwestern corner of France, where many people still speak a Celtic tongue, Breton.

Although the earliest written records of Anglo-Saxon or Old English preserved date from about the seventh century, from them it is abundantly clear that these immigrants from the North Sea coastal areas of what are now Germany and Denmark brought with them a language highly inflected in comparison with modern English, and very limited in vocabulary. The noun, for example, was declined for four cases in both singular and plural. There were two main declensions of nouns, each subdivided into several classes. Gender was grammatical, not natural as it is today. Every adjective had to agree with the noun it modified in number, case, and gender. It could do this in two ways; after a definite article or a demonstrative pronoun it took what is known as a *weak* form, and when it stood alone it was declined in the *strong* form. For example, "these young boys" would be translated *þas geongan cnapan,* but "young boys" would be *geonge cnapan.* Other examples could be given from the verbs, adverbs, and pronouns to show how much more complicated the system of inflection was in the Old English period, but this will perhaps suffice to suggest to you that one reason why we have trouble at times with inflectional endings is that we have grown so accustomed to doing without them except in a few places, that we tend to forget even the few that are left.

When the Anglo-Saxons came to their new home, they probably brought with them their old runic alphabet, but by the time our records begin it had been largely replaced by the Latin one. Only five runic letters remained: eth (ð) and thorn (þ), for the voiced and voiceless sounds of *th* (though even when the preserved written records begin the two phonograms seem to be used interchangeably); wen (ƿ) for /w/; the digraph which we use in our phonetic alphabet for the simple or short *a*, /æ/, represented the same sound in Old English; and finally *g* was represented in at least some of its uses by ʒ. Our table of consonants shows that, as today, there were 24 consonant sounds. Although we use the same phonetic symbols, these were not necessarily always exactly the same as the corresponding ones today, having been made a little bit farther forward in the mouth in some cases, or a little bit farther back in others. One sound, /ž/ had not yet been introduced, and another, the voiced counterpart of /h/, which we represent by /x/, has disappeared in modern English. This last sound, pronounced like the final consonant in the Scots *loch*, was usually written *h*, as in *þurh* (modern *through*).

These 24 consonant sounds had to be represented by 17 letters, so that from the very beginning English has not had enough single symbols to go around and has had to use digraphs or make letters represent more than one sound. As today, *c*, *g*, and *s* were the ones which did the most double duty. The letter *c* represented /k/ most commonly, as in *cēne* (*bold*); it also represented /č/ as in *cirice* (*church*). This latter use was primarily before the front vowels /i/ and /e/. The letter also served as part of various digraphs: in *cg* to represent /j/ as in *brycg* (*bridge*), and in *sc* to represent /š/, as in *scip* (*ship*). The letter *g* or its runic counterpart, ʒ, represented three sounds by itself: its modern sound /g/, as in *glæd* (*glad*); /y/ as in *geard* (*yard*); and rarely /j/ as in *sengan* (*singe*). The voiceless spirants /f/, /θ/, and /s/ became voiced when standing between vowels or between *r* or *l* and a vowel, as in *drifan* (*drive*) and *freosan* (*freeze*), but with no change in spelling; hence /v/ and /z/ were represented by *f* and *s* respectively, and þ became the commoner representative of the two middle slit spirants. The sound /ŋ/ was represented by *n* and occurred only before /g/ and /k/. The following /g/ was always pronounced in Old English, as it is today in *finger*, but is not in *singer*. The voiceless aspirated stops (/p, t, k/) were often doubled before /r/ and /l/, as in *bitter* (*bitter*), *æppel* (*apple*), *miccle* (*great*), and occasionally their voiced counterparts were too, as in *næddre* (*serpent, adder*), thus creating the third largest group of double letters in English.

The vowels form a very rough approximation of our present system also. The short, or simple vowels were /æ, e, i, ɔ, a, u/ with the other three being dialectal additions or variations. /æ, e, i, a, u/ were represented in Old English by their present phonetic symbols, and /ɔ/ by o. The complex vowels are a bit more complicated. /aH/ was represented by ā (the diacritical mark to indicate

CONSONANT SOUNDS OF EARLY OLD ENGLISH
(with their commonest phonograms in parentheses)

	FRONT	MIDDLE	BACK
STOPS			
Aspirated			
voiced	/b/ (b)	/d/ (d)	/g/ (g, ȝ)
voiceless	/p/ (p)	/t/ (t)	/k/ (c)
Affricated			
voiced		/ǰ/ (cg,g)	
voiceless		/č/ (c)	
SPIRANTS			
Slit			
voiced	/v/ (f)	/ð/ (þ, ð)	/x/ (h)
voiceless	/f/ (f)	/θ/ (þ, ð)	/h/ (h)
Grooved			
voiced		/z/ (s)	
voiceless		/s/ (s)	/š/ (sc)
RESONANTS			
Lateral, voiced		/l/ (l)	
Nasal, voiced	/m/ (m)	/n/ (n)	/ŋ/ (n)
Median, voiced	/w/ (ƿ)	/r/ (r)	/y/ (g)

length was not used in the old manuscripts, of course, but it is customary to indicate length in modern editions of the ancient texts); /ey/ by ē, /iy/ by ī, /ow/ by ō, /uw/ by ū, and /uy/ (not a common nucleus in modern English) by ȳ. In addition to these six long vowels, Old English had three common diphthongs, *ea, eo,* and *ie,* in which the first vowel could be either long or short, thus making really six diphthongs.

[3] The breakdown of the Old English inflectional system began about the tenth century, and is still going on (consider what is happening to the apostrophe in the possessive case). In the first place, there was no great literature in the language, either in quality or in quantity, to be revered and thus serve as a conservative force as it did, for example, in Latin. The arts of reading and writing were not widespread, and there were few schools and few teachers to serve as another conserving force. And finally, in the

eighth century the Anglo-Saxons were themselves subjected to the same kind of treatment they had given to the Celts; they were invaded by the Danes, and after almost a century of fighting had been driven out of most of the northeastern third of England. A long period of warfare of this sort will produce social and political unrest enough to allow a language to develop in an untrammeled and popular way. Another theory is that once they stopped fighting and learned to live peaceably together, the two groups realized that they spoke very similar languages, words often having the same root and differing only in inflectional ending. Thus, the conjecture is, they were led to drop the endings in order to understand one another better. Whatever the reason, the speakers of Old English certainly began to pronounce their inflectional endings less carefully, perhaps giving more accent to the root than before, and even less to the ending, which had always been unaccented.

In addition to beginning the degeneration of inflectional endings, the Old Norse language spoken by the Danish invaders left one or two permanent marks on English spelling. Although the Danes still used a completely runic alphabet, they may well have encouraged the introduction of the letter *k* from the continent at this time. As *sc* customarily represented /š/, Old English had no way of representing the combination /sk/, yet at this time it was borrowing a number of words such as *skin* (from Old Norse *skinn*) which had this combination. And it was about the time of the invasions of the Danes or a little later that the old manuscripts begin to use *k* before *e* and *i*. Although the introduction of *k* may have been designed primarily to alleviate some of the confusion caused by having *c* represent both /k/ and /č/, it did not always succeed, as the modern words *shirt* and *skirt* testify. *Skirt* is derived from the Old Norse word *skyrta*, which meant "shirt"; *shirt* is descended from Old English *scyrte* (pronounced /širte/), meaning "skirt"!

The tendency to drop inflections was furthered by the Norman invasion of 1066, which made the dominant language in England a dialect of French and again allowed English to develop in an uninhibited and popular manner. Various non-linguistic causes helped in the revival of English as the dominant language of England after three hundred years of being the language of serfs. As long as they could go back and forth between Normandy and England easily, the Anglo-Norman aristocracy got along very well without the English language. But early in the thirteenth century

French military successes, and a decree by the French king that no one could hold both an English and a French title and lands, tended to cut them off from France. Then the Plague, respecting no particular language, appeared in the fourteenth century, and made the need for Englishmen in every walk of life acute. Ultimately, by 1400 English was again the language in general use. During the period since 1066, however, the old inflectional system of the Teutonic language had almost completely broken down.

The Old English vocabulary, which had been slender, was enriched by the addition of many new words from French, especially during the fourteenth century, when the social barriers between Norman and English were rapidly breaking down and Englishmen were first able to aspire to high positions. The French spoken by Englishmen was laughed at on the Continent (those of you who have read the Prologue to the *Canterbury Tales* will remember Chaucer's gentle joke about the Prioress, who spoke the French of "Stratford atte Bowe" for the French of Paris was unknown to her [1]); yet enough prestige clung to this language of the upper classes to make the English want to lard their language with French words. The same linguistic phenomenon is observable today, though on a much smaller scale, in our use of *fiancee*, *foyer*, *debutante*, and other words which have a synonym already established the language but lacking in the distinction words are felt to receive from the French.

Perhaps of most interest to modern students of spelling, however, are the new phonograms introduced into the language by the Norman scribes (who were for many years almost the only people in England able to write), struggling to deal with a strange language and strange phonograms. The most important were those replacing the old runic symbols. The digraph æ was replaced by *a*, and the wen (ƿ) by *w*—this last being one of the first changes to occur. /g/ came to be represented by the Roman *g*, and *g*'s /y/ sound ultimately became *y*, although ȝ survived in handwriting down to the end of the period. One phonogram, *th*, replaced both the eth (ð) and the thorn (þ) late in the Middle English Period (1100-1500); earlier *th* was used only in learned words and proper names, and was pronounced /t/ as in *Thomas*,

1. For other contemporary references to the poor quality of French spoken in England, see Albert C. Baugh, *A History of the English Language*, 2nd ed., New York, Appleton-Century-Crofts, 1957, pp. 167–8.

and, as we have noted, þ became the popular symbol for both these runic phonograms. But the introduction of printing into England in the 1470's put an end to the use of these distinctive phonograms, as all the type used in England was for some time made on the continent where these symbols were not used.

Several other phonograms were introduced by Norman scribes as being more familiar than some of the symbols used in the English manuscripts they were copying. For example, in Old English *cg* represented /ǰ/; the Norman scribes introduced the letter *ʒ* to take its place. The old English *cw* in the same fashion became *qu*, /uw/ became *ou* (pronounced much as in modern French, not modern English), and *sc* became *sh*. And through borrowings from French which already had the sounds /v/ or /z/ represented by *v* or *z*, these two new phonograms for the voiced spirants were introduced into English. The phonogram *ph*, which, like *th*, was also used mainly in learned words (primarily Latin borrowings from Greek which had then come down into French) and proper names, was first introduced at this time. /č/, being close to the sound represented by *ch* in French, took over this phonogram. *C*, however took on a new sound, beginning at this time to represent /s/

CONSONANT SOUNDS OF MIDDLE ENGLISH *c*. 1400
(with their commonest phonograms in parentheses)

	FRONT	MIDDLE	BACK
STOPS			
Aspirated			
voiced	/b/ (*b*)	/d/ (*d*)	/g/ (*g*)
voiceless	/p/ (*p*)	/t/ (*t*)	/k/ (*c, k*)
Affricated			
voiced		/ǰ/ (*j, cg*)	
voiceless		/č/ (*ch*)	
SPIRANTS			
Slit			
voiced	/v/ (*f, v*)	/ð/ (þ, *th*)	/x/ (*gh*)
voiceless	/f/ (*f, ph*)	/θ/ (þ, *th*)	/h/ (*h*)
Grooved			
voiced		/z/ (*s, z*)	/ž/ (*z*)
voiceless		/s/ (*s, c*)	/š/ (*sh*)
RESONANTS			
Lateral, voiced		/l/ (*l*)	
Nasal, voiced	/m/ (*m*)	/n/ (*n*)	/ŋ/ (*n*)
Median, voiced	/w/ (*w*)	/r/ (*r*)	/y/ (*y, ʒ*)

in words borrowed from French, as *face*. In other borrowings from French, /ž/ first appeared, as in *azure*. And the voiced back slit spirant /x/ was finally represented by *gh* (Old English *dohtor* became *doghtor*, modern *daughter*).

[4] The re-establishment of English as the dominant language did not mean the end of change, however. The fifteenth century was another period of political and social unrest, marked by the last half of the Hundred Years War, and the long-drawn-out civil strife known as the War of the Roses. During this century what is known as the Great Vowel Shift in English was completed; although parts of it at least may have had their beginnings much earlier, the major portion of the change took place during this century. While all vowel sounds may have been changing somewhat, the most important changes were in the long vowels, as follows:

/aH/ → /ow/	(hām	→ home)
/ow/ → /uw/	(mōd	→ mood)
/uw/ → /aw/	(hūs	→ house)
/ey/ → /iy/	(slēpan → sleep)
/iy/ → /ay/	(hwīt	→ white)

In other words, each vowel moved forward a little in position, and the spelling adapted itself to the new sounds. This left the single letters *a* and *e* not representing long vowels, and the sounds /aH/ and /ey/ vacant. This situation was taken care of by new borrowings, and, more importantly, by other vowel changes in English itself. At this same time, the short vowels except /i/ and /u/ were lengthened before a single consonant followed by a weak or unaccented vowel. In this way, for example, Old English *nama* became *name*, the *a* having the sound of the continental long *e*. Later, in very early modern English, when all the inflectional vowel endings had been leveled to *-e*, the letter was retained even when it was no longer pronounced when it would distinguish between two potential homonymns, at *hate* and *hat*, or *hope* and *hop*, and thus the final silent *e* came to be regarded as a sign of length in the preceding vowel, as it is today.

With the beginning of modern English, grammatical changes ceased to be so great, but sound changes and additions to the vocabulary kept on. It is these two, in fact, that are largely responsible for much of the speller's woe today. As early as the first part of the Modern English Period (i.e. 1500–1600), there was a strong feeling that a standardized spelling would be desirable. Most individuals kept their own spelling fairly consistent, but there was great variation from one person to another in spite of the standardizing influence of a number of spelling reformers and, not least, of the printers. During this century "long" or double consonants were shortened, and came to be pronounced as they are today, like single consonants. But as the double letter showed that the preceding vowel was short, the spelling was retained, and the doubling extended to many letters not previously doubled: *penny, copper, herring,* for example. Unfortunately this doubling was not carried out too consistently, and we have modern *rabbit* and *habit* (which rhyme) coming from Middle English *rabett* and *habit.* As the letters *u* and *v* were used interchangeably, it became customary to keep the silent *e* after *v* even when the vowel was short, to avoid confusion (*lou* or *lov* could otherwise be interpreted as either *love* or *low*).

During the seventeenth century a further weakening of some sounds occurred: /w/ was dropped (in pronunciation) in unaccented syllables, as in *towards,* and became silent before /r/ as in *write;* /t/ preceded by /s/ or /f/ and followed by /l/, /m/, or /n/ became silent, as in *thistle, Christmas, often, chestnut.*

By the eighteenth century, gradual but steady changes in sound and the influence of printers had created an atmosphere receptive to a standardization of spelling. Early in the century Swift proposed an Academy to "fix" the language, i.e. to stabilize it and keep it from changing. The poets Mark Akenside and Thomas Edwards and others proposed spelling reforms. But it took the authority and prestige of Dr. Johnson's famous *Dictionary* (1755) to standardize English spelling for the first time. Except for a few American variations on British usage, proposed by Noah Webster in his spelling books and dictionary, our spelling follows essentially the pattern set up by Dr. Johnson over two hundred years ago.

[5]   But the language has gone on changing in sound and adding new words in these two centuries. Anyone who reads much of the poetry of Alexander Pope (1688–1744) will notice rhymes which were true in his day but are false today (familiar examples are *tea* and *obey,* and *join* and *divine*). And the increase in our scientific learning and our knowledge of the world in general has led to the coining of many new technical terms based mainly on

Latin and Greek roots, and to increased borrowings from many different languages. In these more recent borrowings the tendency has been to preserve the original spelling, thus bringing into English many new and unnecessary phonograms. This has made some knowledge of the etymology of words, and an understanding of the proper way to use a dictionary, essential to a modern speller.

Fortunately the answer to this complexity lies in what too many students try to employ without knowing how—phonetic spelling. The newspapers recently carried an account of a young soldier whose report of an adventure illustrates what untutored phonetic spelling can be like:

> I . . . will on duddy on the 20 Sept 1957 at approx 2255 I was walking post 6 witch is loketed on the south side of the matence hanger at the south end of the parkind airia. I was woking est by the wase of the paved ramp at approx the senter of the parkind airia when a radil snack sounded his worning I druw my weppen and fired.[2]

This passage illustrates a number of things. It shows how badly one can misspell and still be understood. Spelling, as long as it "approxes" the sound, does not have to be "correct" so far as communication is concerned—except that this young soldier was communicating a lot about himself that was not contained in the denotations of his words. It also shows how badly many people associate sound with symbol; we trust you were duly horrified to see *dd* and *ck* following a long vowel. Even worse, however, is the obvious failure to hear or be aware of the sounds one is using. Unless his speech was more slovenly than most, he was not hearing in "matence" all the sounds he was using. And the use of *will* for (presumably) *went* indicates further lack of consciousness of the sounds he is representing.

2. New York *Herald Tribune*, Sept. 6, 1959, Section 1, p. 18.

SUMMARY

[1] English is a phonetic language, but it is not perfectly so and for historical reasons.

[2] English derives from the languages of the Angles, Saxons, and Jutes, who came to England in the fifth century. The highly inflected Germanic tongue they developed was first written with a combination of Latin alphabet and runic characters. In all they had only 17 characters to represent 24 wounds, so the written language was in a sense "unphonetic" from the outset.

[3]   The invading Danes and Normans both hurried the breakdown of the English inflectional system and altered the writing of the English language by introducing new characters to represent some of the sounds of the language.

[4]   The Great Vowel Shift, beginning in the sixteenth century, brought about a major change in the relations between spoken and written English, and efforts toward standardized spelling began, but were neither successful nor uniform. English spelling did not become "fixed" until Johnson's *Dictionary* appeared in 1755.

[5]   Borrowings from foreign languages, because the foreign spellings are retained, have tended to increase the varieties of English spellings of many sounds. "Phonetic" spelling today is dependent upon a considerable knowledge of the language, its history, and its sources.

NOTES

The new terms should not be troublesome. A phonogram is, in common parlance, a "spelling"; literally, it is a "sound-writing."

Perhaps another word or so about the Great Vowel Shift will be helpful. If we remember our vowel chart of "long" vowels, we can chart the shift something like this:

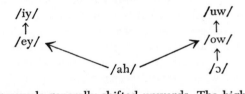

That is, long vowels generally shifted upwards. The high vowels /iy/ and /uw/ diphthonized became /ay/ and /aw/, respectively.

These words from the opening lines of the Prolog to Chaucer's *Canterbury Tales* will illustrate the shifts in pronunciation from Chaucer's day to ours:

	/ah/→/ow/ or /ey/
April	/ahpril/→/eypril/
bathed	/baðəd/→/beyðd/
make	/mahkə/→/meyk/

	/ɔ/→/ow/
open	/ɔpən/→/owpən/
folk	/fɔlk/→/fowk/
holy	/hɔli/→/howli/

	/ey/→/iy/
pierced	/peyrsəd/→/piyrst/
sweet	/sweyt/→/swiyt/
heath	/heyθ/→/hiyθ/
seek	/seyk/→/siyk/

root   /rowt/→/ruwt/   (/ow/→/uw/)

inspired   /inspiyrəd/→/inspayrd/   (/iy/→/ay/)
eye   /iy/→/ay/

showers   /ʃuwrəs/→/ʃawərz/   (/uw/→/aw/ (or /æw/))
flower   /fluwr/→/flawər/
fowl   /fuwl/→/fawl/

How Shall We Spell?

WILLIAM DWIGHT WHITNEY

William Dwight Whitney (1827–1894) edited the greatest Ameri-can dictionary, The Century Dictionary and Cyclopedia (6 vol-umes, 1889–1891), *and hence could bring the weight of very considerable authority to the question of "simplified spelling." You may find his views on American spelling surprising.*

[1] How our English words shall be spelt is a matter concerning which the great mass of those to whom the language is native ap-pear to have pretty fully made up their minds. They intend to tolerate no change in the present orthography. * * * And yet there are, from time to time, voices raised also upon the other side of the question; even efforts seriously made—doubtless with some hope of a successful issue—to bring about that sweeping revolution which we, the English-speakers at large, are determined neither to encourage nor to allow. To mention only one or two of those which have last come under our notice: a company has been formed at Mendota, in Illinois, "with a capital of $35,000," for carrying through the great national reform in spelling, and introducing a new and strictly phonetic alphabet;" * * * and a senator of the United States has moved to devote a part of the superfluous public funds to paying a mixed commission, which shall devise and re-port a plan for a consistent orthography. The subject, then, is still in some degree an open one before the public mind. Or, if we are to regard the influence of these few unquiet spirits as too insignifi-cant to be made much account of, we may at any rate take a satis-faction in reviewing the position we hold against them, and realizing anew its strength and security.

[2] No one, we presume, will be found to question that one very important reason why we cleave to our present modes of

From *Oriental and Linguistic Studies* by William Dwight Whitney (New York: Scribner, Armstrong & Co., 1874).

spelling is the simple fact that they are ours. We have learned them, by dint of diligent study, if not of painful effort; we are used to them; our spoken words in any other garb would look to us strange and quaint, or even ridiculous. To give them up would imply a revolution—such an overthrow of a grand institution, firmly rooted in the usages and predilections of a wide community, as no race or generation has ever yet been willing to permit, save under the pressure of some great and profoundly felt necessity. And we acknowledge no such necessity; far from this, we think we see a variety of reasons why our favorite institution is preferable to any that could be put in its place. Precisely here, however, we ought to feel most distrustful of the ground we stand upon. It is so easy to overvalue, or even wholly to misinterpret, reasons apparently favoring conclusions which we are already determined to reach! Let us, then, enter into a summary examination of the alleged advantages of our present English orthography, for the purpose of determining both what is their actual worth, and how far we rely upon them in our defense of the institution.

[3] First to be noticed among the advantages referred to is the convenient discrimination to the eye of homonyms, or words which are pronounced alike, but have a different origin and meaning. A familiar example is afforded us in the written distinction of *meet, meat,* and *mete;* and another that of *to, too,* and *two;* such triplets, as every one knows, are not very rare in our language, and couples of the same sort are to be counted by scores. Now, we have to observe that any credit which is given to our written language in this particular must be taken away from our spoken language. We gain nothing by writing the uttered syllables *meet* and *too* in a variety of ways, unless, when uttered, they are of ambiguous meaning. If our minds are for even the briefest moment puzzled by such expressions as "he goes *to* Boston," "he goes *two* miles," "he goes *too far,*" not knowing which *too* is meant in either case, then it is worth while to avoid a like difficulty in our reading by spelling the word differently. But who will consent to make so damaging an admission? There is a language in the world, the Chinese, where the words are so few, and their meanings so many, that orthographic differences are brought in as an important aid to comprehension, and the writing follows, upon a grand scale, not the utterance alone, but the signification also. Thus, there are more

than eleven hundred ways of writing the word *ē*, and other words count their representatives by hundreds, by scores, or by tens. A host of devices have to be resorted to there in spoken speech to get rid of ambiguities which are wholly avoided in written. Our English, however, is not afflicted with such poverty of expression as to be brought to this strait. We have also three different *founds*— *found* from *find*, *found* meaning "establish," and *found* meaning "cast, mould"—between which, we venture to say, no soul ever thought of making a confusion, though they are all spelt with the same letters. Is there any one who cannot tell, by the ear or by the eye, when *cleave* means "stick together," and when it means "part asunder"? Who ever finds any more difficulty in separating *bear*, "bruin," from *bear*, "carry," than in separating either of these from *bare*, "naked"? Of how infinitesimal value, then, is the Chinese principle, as introduced into English usage! We may blot out every vestige of it from our vocabulary tomorrow, and it will never be missed; the written language will still continue to be as good as the spoken; and if any one is not content with that, let him migrate and learn another tongue. If the principle is to be kept and made much of, let us agree to give it a more consistent application: let us not spell alike words so different in history and use as the three *founds;* when the same vocable diverges into meanings widely dissimilar, let us vary its spelling a little to match, not writing in the same way "she *became* ill" and "her dress *became* her," nor letting the lawyer and the lover go to *court* in the same orthographic fashion—yet more, when there has been a divergence of pronunciation as well, as when a *minúte* portion of time has become a *mínute*. Let us separate he *rĕad* from he *rēads*, as we have separated he *lĕd* from he *lēads;* above all, let us not confound together in spelling words distinct in every respect—derivation, sense, and utterance—like the verb *lēad* and the metal *lĕad*.

[4]   Consistency, however, of any kind in English spelling we have taught ourselves to regard as of little or no consequence; its value is quite overborne and thrown into the shade for us by that of the "historic" principle. If there is any one thing more than another that makes us content with, even proud of, our orthography, it is the fact that it is "historic." But wherein, again, lies the worth of the historic principle? Why, in its interesting suggestiveness, of course; in its exceeding importance to etymology. Very extreme claims have been made in its behalf in this latter respect

by the enemies of the *Fonetik Nuz* party. Thus, an English Quarterly reviewer, taking Max Müller to task for the few words in favor of the inherent desirableness of a phonetic mode of spelling boldly spoken by him in the last series of his lectures on language, asks "who would have either time or energy enough to master the history of this single language" if we strike out the traces of the origin of its words still preserved in their spelling? and he adds that the introduction of a phonetic system "in the second generation would break the backs of philological students, and in the third render their existence impossible" (the latter catastrophe, as we may remark, being a very natural consequence of the former). And a very recent American writer on the English language echoes these sentiments, maintaining that, "if the form were to follow the sound, there would soon not a single trace be left of the language used by our forefathers;" and that, "if the *Fonetik Nuz* had been started a thousand years ago, it is safe to assert that nobody would have had either the courage or the time to attempt mastering the history of our language." Now, we doubt not that these gentlemen conceived themselves to be making a stout fight in defense of the guild of etymologists, threatened with the cutting off of one of its chief sources of gain, and to be winning a title to its collective and profound gratitude. But save us from such champions! They may be allowed to speak for themselves, since they know best their own infirmity of back and need of braces; the rest of the guild, however, will thank them for nothing. If the English were like the Tibetan, for example, a dialect of unknown history and of exceedingly obscure character and relations, the philologists who first came upon it would naturally be delighted to find its words, like the Tibetan, crowded full of silent consonants and built about mispronounced vowels—all relics, or at least presumed ones, of former modes of utterance. But the two cases are not, in fact, altogether parallel. Of the English we have abundant monuments coming from nearly every century since before the time of Alfred, or say for eleven or twelve hundred years; and the chief fault which we have to find with them as illustrations of the history of the language is that they are so little regardful of the phonetic principle. The confused orthography of the Anglo-Saxon itself is an obstacle in the way of our fully understanding its orthoëpic aspect, and the difficulty grows constantly worse from that time to the present. Painful researches into the history of the changes in English pronunciation are now in progress which would be rendered unnecessary if the written literature of each period had represented in an orderly and consistent manner its own modes of utterance. There is in existence a manuscript poem, the "Ormulum," of the "Semi-Saxon" period of our literature (A.D. 1150–1250), apparently in the author's own hand, no one else having ever thought well enough of it to copy it; and a tedious work it is, indeed; but for us it has a high and peculiar value, just for the reason that its author was a phonetic fanatic, and wrote it out in a consistent mode of spelling of his own devising, one that throws a deal of light upon the condition of the spoken language of his time. While we have the sources of our English fully within our reach in the Anglo-Saxon and Old French literatures, it is the height of unreason to assert that our reading of English etymologies is in any manner dependent upon the current "historic" orthography.

But further, were this dependence as great as is claimed, we are still puzzled to see how it should have any bearing upon the present practical question of a reform in spelling. Should even the Tibetan people desire to carry through such a reform—to write, for example, *dag* instead of *bsgrags*, *mre* instead of *smras*—the philologist would rather admire their good sense than quarrel with its results; having once obtained a record of the old written form, he is indifferent as to whether it be or be not longer kept up in popular usage. Do the writers whom we have quoted above imagine that, the moment we adopt a new mode of spelling, all the literature written in the old is to pass in a twinkling out of existence and out of memory? Certainly there are agencies which might be made use of to avert so bewildering a catastrophe. A Society for the Preservation of English Etymologies might perhaps be organized, which should make a provident selection of old-style dictionaries and grammars, and store them away in a triply fireproof library, for the young philologists of future times to be nursed upon until they could bear stronger food. It might even be found practicable, by ingenious and careful management, to procure the construction of a dictionary of the new-fangled idiom in which the former spelling of every word should be set alongside its modern substitute, in order to render possible the historic comprehension of the latter. Thus, to take an extreme case or two, the new word *sam* (*a* as in *far*), by having the explanation "anciently, *psalm*" added to it, would be sufficiently insured against any such

shocking suppositions on the part of the future student of English
as that it pointed to Samuel instead of David as author of the
sacred lyrics, or that it was a development out of the mystical letters "S. M." placed in the singing-books at the head of so many of
their number; *him* (*hymn*) would be, by like means, saved from
confusion with the personal pronoun—and so on. We do not wish
to show an unbecoming levity or disrespect, but it is very hard to
answer with anything approaching to seriousness such arguments
as those we are combating; "absurd" and "preposterous," and such
impolite epithets, fit them better than any others we can find in
the English vocabulary. They are extreme examples of the fallacies
to which learned men will sometimes resort in support of a favorite
prejudice.

[5]   Many, however, who have too much insight and caution
to put their advocacy of the "historic" or Tibetan principle in
English orthography upon the false ground of its indispensable-
ness to etymologic science, will yet defend it as calculated to lead
on the writer or speaker of our language to inquire into the history
of the words he uses, thus favoring the development of an ety-
mologizing tendency. He who now pronounces *sam* and *him*, they
think, would be liable, if he also wrote those syllables phonetically, to just simply accept them as names of the things they designate, like *pig* and *pen*, without giving a thought to their derivation;
whereas, if he knows that they are and must be spelt *psalm* and
hymn, his natural curiosity to discover the cause of so singular a
phenomenon may plunge him into the Greek language, and make
a philologist of him almost before he suspects what he is about.
There is more show of reason in this argument; but whether more
reason, admits of doubt. The anomalies of our othography, unfortunately, are far from being calculated, in the gross, to guide
the unlearned to etymological research. For one of them which is
of value in the way of incitement and instruction, there are many
which can only confuse and discourage. In the first place, there
are not a few downright blunders among them. Thus, to cite a
familiar instance or two, the *g* of *sovereign* (French *souverain*,
Italian *sovrano*) has no business there, since the word has nothing
whatever to do with *reigning*; *island* (from Anglo-Saxon *ealand* is
spelt with an *s* out of ignorant imitation of *isle* (Latin *insula*), with
which it is wholly unconnected; in like manner, an *l* has stumbled
into *could*, in order to assimilate it in look to its comrades in office,

would and *should; women* is for an original *wif-men,* and its phonetic spelling would be also more truly historical. Again, another part, and not a small one, seem to the ordinary speller the merest confusion (and are often, in fact, nothing better), calculated to lead him to nothing but lamentation over his hard lot, that he is compelled to master them. Take a series of words like *believer, receiver, weaver, fever, reever,* and try how many of the community are even accessible to proof that their orthographic discordances are bottomed on anything tangible. There is in some persons, as we well know, an exquisite etymologic sensibility which can feel and relish a historical reminiscence wholly imperceptible to men of common mould; to which, for instance, the *u* of *honour* is a precious and never-to-be-relinquished token that the word is derived from the Latin *honor* not directly, but through the medium of the French *honneur:* and we look upon it with a kind of wondering awe, as we do upon the superhuman delicacy of organization of the "true princess" in Andersen's story, who felt the pea so painfully through twenty mattresses and twenty eiderdown beds; but it is so far beyond us that we cannot pretend to sympathize with it, or even to covet its possession. If we are to use a suggestive historic orthography, we should like to have our words remodeled a little in its favor: if we must retain and value the *b* of *doubt* (Latin *dubitare*), as sign of its descent, we crave also a *p* in *count* (French *compter,* Latin *computare*), and at least a *b* if not an *r* also, in *priest* (Greek *presbuteros*); we are not content with but one silent letter in *alms,* as relic of the stately Greek word *eleēmosunē;* we contemplate with only partial satisfaction the *l* of *calm* and *walk,* while we miss it in *such* and *which* (derivatives from *so-like* and *who-like*). Why, too, should we limit the suggestiveness of our terms to the latest stages of their history? Now that the modern school of linguistic science, with the aid of the Sanskrit and other distant and barbarous tongues, claims to have penetrated back to the very earliest roots out of which our language has grown, let us take due account of its results, and cunningly convert our English spelling into a complete course of philological training.

We have, however, no intention of taking upon ourselves here the character of reformers or of proposers of reforms; only, when this and the other principle are put forward as valuable, we cannot well help stepping aside a moment to see where we should be led to if, like true men, we attempted to carry out our principles. As regards the historic element in English orthography, we think it evident enough that its worth and interest do not at all lie in its instructing effect upon the general public who use the language, but rather in its tendency to call up pleasing associations in the minds of the learned, of those who are already more or less familiar with the sources from which our words come. It is much more an aristocratic luxury than a popular benefit. To the instrument which is in every one's hands for constant use it adds a new kind of suggestiveness for those who know what it means, and gives them the satisfaction of feeling that, though they may not wield the instrument more successfully than others, there are peculiarities in its structure which they alone appreciate. Such a satisfaction is a selfish one, and improperly and wrongly obtained, if bought by a sacrifice of any measure of convenience or advantage to the great public of speakers and writers.

[6]   What may be the general loss in these respects we will not now stop to inquire. For it is incontrovertibly true that, whether the natural merits of the two principles we have been considering —the Chinese and the Tibetan, the differentiation of homonymous words and the retention in writing of former modes of utterance— be greater or less, they are practically held in the most complete subordination to another, namely a simple conservation of the modes of spelling now current. All that is said in their defense is as much aside from the true point as were the pleas put forth a few years since by the Southern slave-owners respecting the curse of Canaan and the separate origin and inferior endowments of the negro race. Those pleas were urged, no doubt, with a certain kind of sincerity; but we have yet to hear of the ethnologically learned or the devout Southerner who ever set a slave free because the blood of the superior race predominated in him, or because only the sixteenth part of his lineage was to be traced to Ham, while the rest went back to Shem or Japhet, or both. "Possession is nine points of the law" and *partus sequitur ventrem*" were the true proof-texts and scientific principles on which the master's right reposed; and so also "whatever is, is right" constitutes the complete ethical code of him who is defending English spelling. Anything else is mere casuistry, a casting of dust in the eyes of the objector. The paramount consideration, which really decides every case, is that the existing orthography must be perpetuated; if for this and that word any other apparently supporting considerations

of any kind soever can be found, they may be made the most of—
yet without creating a precedent, or establishing a principle which
is to be heeded in any other case, where it would make in favor of
a change. The advocate of "historic" spelling insists as strongly
upon retaining the *l* of *could* as that of *would,* and fights against a
p in *count* not less vehemently than in favor of a *b* in *doubt;* the
difference of *receive* and *believe* is no more sacred in his eyes than
the sameness of *cleave* and *cleave.* Now, we have no quarrel with
any one who plants himself squarely and openly upon the conservative ground, and declares that our English spelling is, with all
its faults and inconsistencies, good enough for its purpose, that
every item of it is consecrated by usage and enshrined in predilections, and therefore must and shall be maintained. What we cannot abide is that he who means this, and this only, should give
himself the airs of one who is defending important principles, and
keeping off from the fabric of English speech rude hands that
would fain mar its beauty and usefulness. Orthographic purism is,
of all kinds of purism, the lowest and the cheapest, as is verbal
criticism of all kinds of criticism, and word-faith of all kinds of
orthodoxy. As Mephistopheles urges upon the Student, when per-
suading him to pin his belief upon the letter,—"*Von einem Wort
lässt sich kein Iota rauben*" ("every iota of the written word may
be fought for")—that, too, even by the tyro who has well conned
his spelling-book, though his knowledge of his native speech end
chiefly there. Many a man who could not put together a single
paragraph of nervous, idiomatic English, nor ever had ideas
enough to fill a paragraph of any kind, whose opinion on a matter
of nice phraseology or even of disputed pronunciation would be of
use to no living being, fancies himself entitled to add after his
name "defender of the English language," because he is always
strict to write *honour* instead of *honor,* and *travelled* instead of
traveled, and never misses an opportunity, public or private, to
sneer at those who do otherwise.

[7]   In what we have said, we have been solicitous only to put
the defense of our present modes of spelling upon its true ground,
showing that it is a pure and simple conservatism, which by no
means founds itself upon useful principles, historical or other, but
only in certain cases hides itself behind them. We may next inquire
what reasons we have for finding fault with this conservatism and
its results, and for wishing and attempting to overthrow them.

In the first place, English orthography violates the true ideal of the relation of written language to spoken, and of an alphabetic mode of writing. To those who have never looked into the subject, it may seem that a phonetic spelling, giving one sign to every sound and one sound to every sign, is a rude and simple device, which an enlightened ingenuity might well enough be tempted to enrich and adorn by mixing it with elements of higher significance. But the student of language knows that the case is far otherwise: that an alphabet is the final result of centuries, even ages, of education and practice in the use of written characters. As a historical fact, writing began, not with representing spoken language, but with trying to do over again what language does—to put occurrences and ideas directly before the mind by intelligible symbols. Only later, and by an indirect process, were men brought to see that, having already produced one system of means, namely words, for bodying forth thought and knowledge, it was needless to devise another and independent one for the same purpose; that their written tongue might best undertake simply to place before the eye their spoken tongue. The great step toward the perfection of writing was taken when it was fully subordinated to speech, and made to represent the names of things instead of things themselves. But even this brought it out of the purely pictorial into a hieroglyphic stage, where it long continued, awkward and unmanageable; and another difficult and protracted process of development was necessary, in order to impart to it a phonetic character, so that it should signify words no longer by simple indivisible symbols, but by characters representing sounds. Our best illustration of the whole history is furnished in the Egyptian monuments, where we see signs of every kind—purely didactic pictures, figures of objects representing those objects themselves, other figures standing for the names of the objects they depict, others for some part, as the consonants, of those names, others, finally, as single letters for the initial sound of their names—all mingled together and exchanging with one another, making up a system of writing not less inconsistent than the English, and infinitely more intricate and troublesome. The Egyptians were too conservative to seize upon the one practically valuable principle which their system contained, and to carry it out consistently, casting aside its inherited incumbrances. But what they could not do was within the power of another people. Every one knows that our own alphabet goes back, through the Latin and Greek, to the Phenician; and it is at least exceedingly probable, though far from admitting of demonstration, that the Phenicians learned to write of the Egyptians. Either of the Egyptian or of some other analogous history of alphabetic development the Phenicians inherited the results, and their alphabet was a simple scheme of twenty-two characters, the names of which (*aleph*, "bull," *beth*, "house," etc.; whence the Greek *alpha, beta,* etc.) began respectively with the sound which each represented. Yet this system, while it discarded everything but the purely phonetic part of the Egyptian, was no complete phonetic alphabet; it wrote the consonants alone, leaving the vowels to be supplied by the reader. It received its full perfection only upon passing into the keeping of the Greeks; they converted some of its superfluous characters into vowel-signs, added others, and produced at last an instrumentality which could and did set faithfully before the sight the whole structure of spoken speech. Among all the alphabets of the world, ancient and modern, there are few, excepting the Greek and its derivatives, which have attained this completeness—to which there does not cleave some taint of a pictorial or a syllabic character.

The Latin alphabet, taken from the Greek, fully accepted and carried out the phonetic principle, rejecting some of the Greek signs and devising new, so as to make an exact adaptation of its modes of writing to its modes of utterance. Nor have its descendants, in their turn, meant to do otherwise. But it is very difficult to maintain the principle in perfect purity, because the spoken forms of words change more insidiously than the written; all tongues which have had a long written history have become more or less "historic" in their spelling, change of orthography lagging ever behind the heels of change of pronunciation. And peculiarly unfavorable circumstances, which in no small part can be distinctly pointed out, have suffered to grow up a greater discordance between the written and the spoken speech among us than in any other community of equal enlightenment. This is the whole truth; and any attempt to make it appear otherwise savors only of the wisdom of the noted fox who lost his brush in a trap, and wanted to persuade himself and the world that the curtailment was a benefit and a decoration. Every departure from the rule that writing is the handmaid of speech is a dereliction of principle, and an abandonment of advantages which seemed to have been long ago as-

sured to us by the protracted labors of many generations of the
most gifted races known to history. The handmaid has no right to
set up to be wiser and better than her mistress in a single particular. That the written word in any case deviates from the spoken is
a fault; which may, indeed, admit of palliation, even amounting
to excuse, but which it is an offense against all true science and
sound sense to extol as a merit.

We have, of course, no intention of bringing forward the un-
faithfulness of our orthography to the highest ideal of a mode of
writing as a sufficient reason for an orthographic revolution. A
grand practical question, which touches so nearly the interests of
so many millions of writers and speakers, is not to be settled by
sentimental considerations—any more by this which we have adduced upon the one side, than, upon the other, by the gratification
of the small class of curious heads who may delight themselves
with seeing Greek and Latin and Old English utterances dimly
reflected in our modern spelling. But it was desirable, and even
necessary, to draw out the exposition, in order to show that the
phonetists have the advantage upon their side, not less in regard
to the principle involved in the cause they are defending than in
regard to the convenience and enlightenment of the historical student of language.

[8] It is upon practical grounds that our final judgment of the
value of English orthography must mainly rest. The written language is a universal possession, an instrument of communication
for the whole immense community of English speakers, and anything which impairs its convenience and manageableness as an
instrument is such a defect as demands active measures for removal. Now, no one can question that the practical use of our
tongue is rendered more difficult by the anomalies of its written
form. We do not, indeed, easily realize how much of the learning-
time of each rising generation is taken up with mastering orthographical intricacies; how much harder it is for us to learn to read
at all, and to read and write readily and correctly, than it would
be if we wrote as we speak. We accomplished the task so long ago,
most of us, that we have forgotten its severity, and decline to see
any reason why others should ask to be relieved from it. Teachers,
however, know what it is, as do those who for want of a sufficiently
severe early drilling, or from defect of native capacity, continue all
their lives to be inaccurate spellers. Such may fairly plead that

their orthographical sins are to be imputed, in great part, not to themselves, but to the community, which has established and sustains an institution so unnecessarily cumbrous. We may see yet more clearly the nature of the burden it imposes by considering what it is to foreigners. Our language, from the simplicity of its grammatical structure, would be one of the easiest in the world to learn if it were not loaded with its anomalous orthography. As the matter stands, a stranger may acquire the spoken tongue by training of the mouth and ear, or the written by help of grammar and dictionary, and in either case the other tongue will be nearly as strange to him as if it belonged to an unknown race. It is doubtless within bounds to say that the difficulty of his task is thus doubled. And this item must count for not a little in determining the currency which the English shall win as a world-language—a destiny for which it seems more decidedly marked out than any other cultivated speech. In view of what we expect and wish it to become, we have hardly the right to hand it down to posterity with such a millstone about its neck as its present orthography.

It is, moreover, to be noted that a phonetic spelling, far from contributing, as its enemies claim, to the alteration and decay of the language, would exercise an appreciable conserving influence, and make for uniformity and fixedness of pronunciation. So loose and indefinite is now the tie between writing and utterance, that existing differences of utterance hide themselves under cover of an orthography which fits them all equally well, while others spring up unchecked. No small part of the conservative force expends itself upon the visible form alone; whereas, if the visible and audible form were more strictly accordant, it would have its effect upon the latter also. The establishment of a phonetic orthography would imply the establishment and maintenance of a single authoritative and intelligible standard of pronunciation, the removal of the more marked differences of usage between the cultivated speakers of different localities, and the reduction of those of less account; and it would hold in check—though nothing can wholly restrain—those slow and insidious changes which creep unawares into the utterance of every tongue.

One more thing is worthy of at least a brief reference—namely, that a consistent spelling would awaken and educate the phonetic sense of the community. As things are now, the English speaker comes to the study of a foreign written language, and to the examination of phonetic questions generally, at a disadvantage when compared with those to whom other tongues are native. He has been accustomed to regard it as only natural and proper that any given sound should be written in a variety of different ways, that any given sign should possess a number of different values; and it requires a special education to give him an inkling of the truth that every letter of our alphabet had originally, and still preserves in the main, outside of his own language, a single unvarying sound. His ideas of the relations of the vowels are hopelessly awry; he sees nothing strange in the designation of the vowel-sounds of *pin* and *pine*, or of *pat* and *pate*, or of *pun* and *pure*, as corresponding short and long, although we might as well assert that *dog* and *cat*, or that *horse* and *cow*, or that *sun* and *moon*, are corresponding male and female. And he reads off his Latin and Greek in tones that would have driven frantic any Roman or Athenian who suspected it to be his own tongue that was so murdered, with un-suspecting complacency, even flattering himself that he appreci-ates their rhythm and melody. It is not the least telling of the indi-cations he furnishes of a sense for the fitness of things debauched by a vicious training, that he is capable of regarding a historical spelling as preferable to a phonetic—that is to say, of thinking it better to write our words as we imagine that some one else pro-nounced them a long time ago than as we pronounce them our-selves. A thoroughly consistent spelling would be a far more valu-able means of philological education than such a one as we now follow, were the latter twice as full as it is of etymological suggestiveness.

We are, then, clearly of opinion that a phonetic orthography is, of itself, in all respects desirable, and that there is no good reason against introducing it save the inconvenience of so great a change. Every theoretical and practical consideration makes in its favor. At the same time, our hope of a reform is exceedingly faint. No reform is possible until the community at large—or at least, the greater body of the learned and highly educated—shall see clearly that the advantage to be gained by it is worth the trouble it will entail: and whether and when they will be brought to do so is very doubtful. At present the public mind is in a most unnaturally sen-sitive condition upon the subject; it will listen to no suggestion of a change from any quarter, in any word or class of words. The great need now is to enlighten it, to show that its action is the result of a blind prejudice alone, and really founded on none of the reasons which are usually alleged in its support; that there is nothing sacred in the written word; that language is speech, not spelling; and that practical convenience is the only true test of the value of an orthographic system. Until this work is accomplished, all reformers will be likely to meet the fate of Noah Webster, one of the best-abused men of his generation, and for one of the most creditable of his deeds, the attempt to amend in a few particulars our English spelling—an attempt for which (however fragmentary it may have been, and ill-judged in some of its parts) we ourselves feel inclined to forgive him many of his false etymologies and defective definitions. We have read in the story-books that a certain Prince Nosey was condemned by a malevolent fairy to wear a portentously long nose until he should himself become convinced that it was too long, which salutary but unpalatable truth was kept indefinitely concealed from him by the flattery of his courtiers. The English-speaking people are in somewhat the same case; and though fairy days are now over, and we can no longer hope that our superfluous nasal inches will drop off the moment we recognize their superfluity, we know that at any rate we shall not lose them sooner, because we shall not sooner be willing to set about the work of ridding ourselves of them. Of course our words would look very oddly to us now in a phonetic dress; but that is merely because we are used to them in another. So our friends the ladies, if they should suddenly appear before our sight in the head-gear which they are going to wear five years hence, would shock us and provoke the cut direct; yet we shall by that time be looking back to the bonnets of this season as the height of absurdity. If once brought to the adoption of a consistent orthography, we should soon begin to regard with aversion our present ideographs and historiographs, and wonder that we could ever have preferred, or even tolerated them. It is easy now to raise a general laugh against the man who writes *news* "*nuz*"; but so the Englishman can count upon an admiring and sympathizing audience among his own countrymen when he turns against the Frenchman that crushing question, "What can you think of a man who calls a *hat* a '*shappo*'?"—and the appeal is really to the same narrow prejudice and vulgar ignorance in the one case as in the other.

The future is a very long period, and a great deal is possible in the course of it. There is no telling, spite of present appearances, that the public temper may not come to admit, some time, the introduction of improvements of one kind and another into our orthography which shall prepare the way for a more thorough reform. Meanwhile we look with interest and respect upon the effort of every one who is laboring toward that end, since however little he may seem to accomplish, he is at least contributing his mite toward the arousing of public attention to the subject, and helping perhaps to inaugurate a change of feeling.

SUMMARY

[1] Efforts at a spelling reform, which once seemed threatening, are now (1867) not so, though a few efforts are being made to simplify English orthography.

[2] A good reason for opposing a change in English spelling is that the present spelling is the one we know; but we should perhaps examine the advantages of keeping it.

[3] First, the advantage of our distinguishing homonyms (*to, too, two*) by spelling is a false one, for we need to distinguish them neither in writing nor systematically, as a matter of fact.

[4] Second, the claim that our spelling preserves the history of our words is also false, for English spelling has never been phonetic and present spellings do not preserve the earlier pronunciations very adequately. Besides, even if our spelling were "historical," it is absurd to suppose that simplified spelling would mean the end of English literature.

[5] Moreover, the contention that our spelling leads to an etymological interest in our vocabulary is not grounded in fact, for spelling is not a safe guide to our words' histories; very few people have etymological sensibilities; and we should re-do our spelling system if we wish it to be truly "historical." As it is, etymological spelling is a luxury of the learned, of little value to the general public.

[6] Finally, the only defense of our present spelling is that it is our present spelling. All defenses purportedly based upon "principle" or the preservation of linguistic purity are phoney, and the most vigorous defenders of the language are often most ignorant about the language.

[7] Next, we should examine reasons *for* changing our spelling. First, the whole development of the alphabet was designed to make writing a copy of speech and not *another* and a separate "language." The Greek alphabet finally got rid of the pictorial and syllabic taints of earlier writing systems. The Latin and subsequent European alphabets were intended to be phonetic in character. Whenever writing deviates from speech, it is faulty. In short, in principle the advocates of simplified spelling have everything on their side of the argument.

[8] It is, however, on practical grounds that we will or will not

change our spelling to a phonetic system. Having learned our present system, we resist changing it; but we should recognize that our spelling is a chief obstacle to the rise of English as a world-language. Moreover, simplified spelling would help stabilize the pronunciation of the tongue and tend to keep it from changing. And finally a phonetic spelling of English would somewhat aid us in the study of foreign languages.

[9]   Yet, though all theoretical and practical considerations argue for a phonetic spelling of English, hope for reform is small: the public at large is uninformed and uninterested; and a great job of education is needed before we can put up with the temporary inconvenience of a spelling reform.

PART FOUR   Grammar and Grammars

The Parts of Speech

L. M. MYERS

L. M. Myers is head of the Division of Language and Literature at Arizona State University, where he has been professor of English since 1937. Author of a number of books on American English, Professor Myers always manages to combine an elegant writing style with a practical approach to language study.

[1] Many grammars begin their discussion of word-forms by saying, "There are eight parts of speech in English: nouns, pronouns, verbs, adjectives, adverbs, prepositions, conjunctions, and interjections." We cannot afford to accept such a statement without asking two very important questions: (1) How do we know? and (2) Why? Neither of these questions is frivolous. In fact, the failure to ask them—and to insist on reasonable answers—has been responsible for a great deal of confusion.

Many people believe that the division into these parts of speech has been established as beyond question for centuries, and that ability to identify words as belonging to one or another of these parts is for some mysterious reason an important accomplishment in itself.

As to the first, all sorts of divisions have been used, and every number of parts of speech from zero to ten has been "proved" the right one; but grammarians are still arguing about how many categories there "really" are, and which words belong in each one. The two grammars most often referred to today as authori-

Pp. 45–52 from L. M. Myers, *American English* (Englewood Cliffs, N.J.: Prentice-Hall, 1952). Reprinted by permission of the author.

tative (those of Curme and Jespersen) differ widely and fundamentally. As to the second belief, the classification of words is
useful if, and only if, it enables us to handle them better.

The chief reason for this apparently hopeless disagreement and
all the trouble it has caused is a basic confusion between classification by *form* and classification by *function.* Of course both
kinds of classification are perfectly legitimate, but it does not help
to mix them.

To make a comparison, suppose we are going to build a group
of frame houses, using only a limited variety of lumber—two-by-
four scantling, one-by-six boards, shingles, clapboards, and laths.
We have exactly five kinds of materials, all easily distinguishable
as to form; and we need exactly five terms by which to refer to
them as materials, *regardless of the way they are used.*

When it comes to building the houses, we need another, and
rather more complicated, set of *structural* terms. An individual
two-by-four may be used as a *joist,* a *stud,* a *strut,* or a *rafter;* or
several may be bolted together to form a *beam* or a *post.* Likewise,
our boards may be used as *flooring, sheathing,* and so forth. We
shall probably use most of our shingles for *roofing,* and most of
our clapboards for *siding;* but if Smith wants a cottage with shin-
gled sides, and Jones wants a clapboard roof, we are prepared to
accommodate them. Not all of our materials are appropriate for
all purposes, but there is no absolute connection between form
and function. We never say that a certain piece of wood is a
joist *because* it is a two-by-four, or a two-by-four *because* it is a
joist. And we should certainly not run the two lists together and
say that "the parts of building are boards, rafters, shingles, siding,
clapboards, struts, laths, and roofing."

[2]   It may seem an open question whether the division into
parts of speech should be used basically as a list of materials or
as a list of functions; but since we have another set of terms to
describe functions (subject, complement, modifier, and so forth),
it seems more useful to use it as a list of materials, which is what
it was originally intended to be.

If we tentatively agree to use the parts of speech to designate
the "lumber" with which we build our sentences, we find that we
use *six physically different kinds of material,* which we may call
nouns, pronouns, verbs, adjectives, adverbs, and *connectives* or
invariables. These are neither as uniform among themselves nor

quite as easy to tell apart under all circumstances as boards, shingles, clapboards, and so forth; but they do have certain physical characteristics which must be recognized and studied. For instance, nouns change form in one way, verbs in another, and adverbs do not change form at all, but do have a characteristic form of their own. *The reason for dividing words into parts of speech is simply to make it possible to study these characteristics systematically.* It is obviously easier to say, "most nouns form their plurals by adding -*s* or -*es*"- than to say, "more than one *dog* is *dogs,* more than one *fox* is *foxes,*" and so on indefinitely.

Three of the parts of speech usually considered separately—prepositions, conjunctions, and interjections—are lumped together under one heading in this list. We shall consider later whether it is necessary to make functional distinctions between these three "kinds of words"; but there is no doubt that a single classification is adequate as far as their *form* is concerned. There is nothing to learn about their form-changes, because they never change form; and unlike adverbs, they have no characteristic forms of their own. If we described them physically as three different groups, the three descriptions would be exactly alike.

[3] If we turn now to consider the actual building of sentences, we find that we use our materials as *subjects, verbs, complements, modifiers, connectives,* and a few other things. Since some of them (like laths) show a rather close connection between form and function, we use the words *verb* and *connective* in both sets of terms. But others (like two-by-fours) may serve several very different purposes. Both nouns and adjectives, for instance, may be used as either subjects or modifiers.

For example, when we classify our materials, we find that *poor* is an adjective, having the typical adjective forms, *poor, poorer,* and *poorest,* and not having the typical noun forms, *poor's, poors,* and *poors'.* But in the sentence "The *poor* are suffering," we find that *poor* seems to be used as the subject. It is rather like finding a house with shingles on the sides instead of on the roof—slightly unusual, but not really disturbing. The advantage of keeping our categories of form and function distinct is that we do not have to devise an elaborate justification for the irregularity. We do not say, "*Poor* is a noun in this sentence, since it is used as the subject." This is too much like saying, "Those shingles are clapboards on that house, since they are used on the sides." Nor do we say,

"Since *poor* is an adjective, it cannot be the subject, but modifies the 'understood' subject, *people*." We simply say that the adjective *poor* is the subject—a secondary, but possible, function of an adjective.

[4]   So far our system seems to work very well; but before we decide on it definitely, we should see what happens if we adopt the opposite system, and consider the parts of speech as functional categories. Some grammars now announce sweepingly that "the part of speech to which a word belongs is determined by its use in the sentence." If we take this as the simple truth, *it would be totally impossible to misuse a part of speech.* A boy kept after school for his errors could tell his teacher: "I objection bitter to your punish. And don't tell me that *objection* isn't a verb, or *punish* a noun, or *bitter* an adverb. That is just what they are, because I am using them that way, and they depend entirely on the way I use them." Since most of us (presumably) agree that there is something wrong with the boy's sentence, we had better revise the basis for determining the parts of speech.

Of course there is some truth in the "use in the sentence" criterion. We have a verb with the forms *man, mans, manned, manning*, and a noun with the forms *man, man's, men, men's*. If we see the word *man* alone we cannot tell whether it is a form of the noun or a form of the verb. In the sentence, "The *man* died," we recognize it as a noun, and in the sentence, "They *man* the boats," we recognize it as a verb. But the "determination" is merely a matter of recognition, not of automatic conversion from one part of speech to another.

[5]   The reason that our grammatical theory is in such a peculiar state is that we have not yet completely broken away from the habit of trying to explain English constructions in terms originally devised to describe Latin. Latin is not only a highly inflected language, but one in which form and function are so closely tied together that the same classification can be used reasonably well to explain them both.

Chinese, on the other hand, is composed of unchanging words with *no* formal characteristics; and any word may be used in any way that makes sense. There is no basis for dividing Chinese words into parts of speech. We may say that a word is used here as a subject and there as a modifier; but it would be ridiculous to talk of nouns and adjectives, since these categories would be *indistinguishable in form and interchangeable in function.*

Since English has lost most of its endings, it now lies somewhere on the scale between Latin, which has a great many, and Chinese, which has none. The endings that remain have to be learned, and they impose certain limitations on the extent to which words can shift their functions. A division into parts of speech is still useful; but it should be based on the differences in current English, rather than on those in Latin, *or on definitions derived from the study of Latin.*

For instance, in both English and Latin there is enough difference between words like *body, ship,* and *honor* and words like *he, they,* and *who* to justify calling one group nouns and the other pronouns; but there is no reason to expect that the boundaries between the two groups will be parallel in the two languages, and a little investigation shows that they are not. Also, there were good reasons for classifying prepositions and conjunctions as separate parts of speech in Latin, but these reasons no longer exist in English, as will be explained later.

[6] No conceivable system of parts of speech could do away with all borderline cases; but if we base our division on the observable facts of the language as now used, we find that words fall into six reasonably distinct groups.

The inflected parts of speech: Four of the parts of speech have characteristic inflections.

Nouns. Nouns change form to show number and possession (*boy, boy's, boys, boys'*). They are used primarily as *substantives* —that is, words that designate persons, animals, places, things, and ideas.

Pronouns. The pronouns are *I, he, she, it, we, you, they,* and *who,* with their compounds. Pronouns are also used as substantives, and they might be considered a sub-class of nouns; but their inflections are quite different, and their uses do not exactly parallel those of nouns.***

Verbs. Verbs typically have four or five forms (*walk, walks, walked, walking; sing, sings, sang, sung, singing*), the functions of which are too complicated for a brief description. They are used primarily to make statements about nouns and pronouns.

Adjectives. Most short adjectives have three forms to show degree (*pretty, prettier, prettiest*). Such words as *beautiful* and *terrible* have no inflections; but even in a classification based on form it is advisable to call them adjectives, since we must discuss the differences between them and the parallel adverbs, *beautifully* and *terribly*. They are used primarily to modify (describe or limit) nouns and pronouns.

The uninflected parts of speech: The two remaining parts of speech have no inflections.

Adverbs. Adverbs do not change form, but have a characteristic form of their own—the *-ly* ending. They are used to modify anything but nouns and pronouns.

Connectives and miscellaneous invariables. These words neither change form nor have any characteristic form of their own. The group includes all the words usually classed as interjections, prepositions, and conjunctions, those "adverbs" which do not have an *-ly* ending, and a few words that originally belonged to other parts of speech, but which have now lost their inflections. Most of these words are used in a number of different ways; and in a classification based on function they have to be listed under two, three, or even more of the parts of speech. This is unfortunate, since there are no problems of form involved, and the problems of use are complicated rather than solved by a classification which involves so much overlapping. For convenience they will hereafter be called simply connectives. It is true that some of them do not connect; but then, some adverbs (*solely, consequently,* and so forth) are seldom used to modify verbs.

[7]   Three types of invariable words are excluded from this class:

1. The one-form verbs *must* and *ought*. (*Went* might be added; but it is usually, and sensibly, treated as the past tense of *go*.)
2. Such one-form nouns as *courage, measles,* and *mathematics*.
3. Such adjectives as are compared by *more* and *most* rather than *-er* and *-est*.

"Interjections" (*ouch, whoopee,* and so forth) may be considered either as belonging to this group, or as being completely outside the parts of speech. They cause no trouble.

Such exclusions may not be strictly logical, but they are convenient; and we should remember that the classification is designed as a matter of *convenience rather than doctrine*. It enables us to make a systematic study of all the inflections in the language, and to discuss the characteristic functions of the words in each class. When there is no question about what the proper form of a word is, or how the word should be used, it is a waste of time to argue about what it should be called. We can avoid many such arguments by calling *but* a connective whenever it appears, instead of a conjunction in one sentence, a preposition in another, and an adverb in a third.

A beginning student will probably accept this classification cheerfully enough, because it is obviously much easier to use than the conventional "eight parts." On the other hand, anybody who has had years of training in grammar is likely to regard it with suspicion. The very fact that it avoids so many difficulties suggests that it may be dangerously superficial. It is therefore up to the author to defend the following proposition:

> The difficulties eliminated by following this system are artificial and unnecessary; and the solution of them is of no value whatever except as an intellectual exercise.

Since the details of the defense are contained in the following chapters, only a sample illustration will be given here.

[8]   Webster's *New Collegiate Dictionary* lists the word *what* not only as belonging to six of the conventional eight parts of speech (noun, pronoun, adjective, adverb, conjunction, and interjection), but as a member of several different sub-classes under some of these (as a pronoun it is an "interrogative," a "compound relative," an "indefinite relative," and an "indefinite pronoun"). (We might argue that it should also be listed as a verb. "Those children *what* and *why* you to death" seems just as legitimate as the noun use, "He wanted to know the *what* and *why* of it.") The reason that it cannot be a preposition has nothing to do with any grammatical restriction—there just seems to be no possibility of using it in a way that could be called prepositional.

Unfortunately, even those grammarians who agree that *what* can be all these things do not agree about when it is which. *What* in a given sentence may be parsed several different ways in different grammars. An innocent schoolboy who is expected to "identify" it whenever it occurs has a hopeless task.

Now, just how much is accomplished by all this elaboration of theory? Since *what* has only one form, there is nothing to learn about its inflections. The only misuse that is at all probable is in such a sentence as "He is the man *what* I saw"; and there is nothing in the whole theory that is of the slightest help in teaching students to avoid such expressions. We can't tell them not to use a relative pronoun, because both *that* and *whom,* the two acceptable substitutes, are also called relative pronouns. And we can't tell them that *what* is not a relative pronoun, because it is called one in several admittedly legitimate constructions. The only simple and honest thing to do is to tell them that in standard English *what* is not used in such constructions, and nobody really knows why.

As for its legitimate uses, we may have occasion to point out that *what* serves as a subject in one sentence, a modifier in a second, an exclamation in a third, and so forth; but we gain nothing by insisting that it is either a noun or a pronoun when it is a subject, an adjective or an adverb when it is a modifier, and so forth.

The author has no desire to insist that his classification be accepted to the exclusion of all others as the one final expression of the truth. It makes little difference whether we call *what* a pronoun or a connective, as long as we don't bewilder the young by insisting on nebulous distinctions. It does no harm for a carpenter to say "Hand me that stud," instead of "Hand me that two-by-four (which I intend to use as a stud)"—especially if he points to the thing he wants. But it would be decidedly confusing if he should say:

A timber is either a two-by-four or a one-by-six, whereas a board is either a one-by-six or a two-by-four. Whether a piece of wood is a timber or a board is determined by its use in the house. You must learn to distinguish between them carefully, and remember never to use one when the other is required.

So far as I know, carpenters never say things like this; but grammarians have gotten into the habit of making fairly comparable statements.

NOTES

Though Professor Myers' presentation is beautifully lucid, it may be helpful to add some background:

"TRADITIONAL" PARTS OF SPEECH

A *noun* is a word by which a person, place, or thing is named.

A *verb* is a word that asserts action or state of being.

An *adjective* is a word that modifies a noun or pronoun.

An *adverb* is a word that modifies a verb, adjective, or other adverb.

A *pronoun* is a word used in place of a noun.

A *preposition* is a word that connects a noun to the rest of the sentence and indicates the noun's relationship to the other words.

A *conjunction* is a word used to join words, phrases, or clauses.

An *interjection* is a word used to express emotion or high feelings.

The definitions for noun and verb square with neither of Professor Myers' bases, of form and function. These definitions suggest neither the forms of the words nor their function in sentences. Instead, they suggest the relationship between the word and the world we live in. They are what grammarians usually call "logical" or "notional" definitions, for they indicate the nature of the word's *meaning* in isolation from other words. In a sense, the definition for pronouns above is also a "logical" one, too, for it depends upon meaning, again. (A pronoun must *mean* the same as the noun it substitutes for; it must, we say, refer to the same person, place, or thing.)

The only real attempt in English grammar at a "logical" grammar was that of Sir Henry Sweet, which you may study on pages 254–264 (sections [5] to [24]); as you will see, Sweet soon threw over the idea that a "logical" grammar was satisfactory. Meanwhile, it might be interesting to suggest the definitions that a thoroughgoing "logical" grammarian would give for the traditional eight parts of speech. They might go something like this:

"LOGICAL" PARTS OF SPEECH

A *noun* is a word that names a person, place, or thing.

(A *pronoun* is also a word that names a person, place, or thing, and hence falls in the noun class.)

A *verb* is a word that asserts action or state of being.

An *adjective* is a word that indicates qualities and quantities.

An *adverb* is a word that indicates time, place, degree, manner, means, negation, etc.

A *preposition* is a word that indicates relationships in time and space.

A *conjunction* is a word that indicates relationships between ideas.

An *interjection* is a word that indicates states of emotion.

Clearly, the "logical" grammarian faces a number of difficulties. *Somebody* could be called a noun, because it stands for some person, presumably. But *nobody* is not a noun, for it does not stand for anybody or anything; it would have to be called an adverb (it indicates negation). Similar trouble would be given by such words as *absence* and *disappear*. *Swims, swimming,* and a *swim* would all have to be called verbs, for all assert action. But *swam* would be both verb and adverb, because it also indicates time. And similar confusions are posed by *home* (a place as well as a thing), *partner* (a person, but also a relationship) and *hysteria* (a "thing" in the wide sense, but also a quality and hence adjective, as well as a state of emotion and hence interjection!).

It is little wonder that English grammarians have not taken this point of view very seriously or that the one grammarian who tried a logical system soon abandoned it.

As Professor Myers suggests, a "functional" grammarian comes out with a rather different set of parts of speech. A simple functional grammar, *A New Plan for English Grammar* (New York: Holt, 1933) by Mrs. Janet R. Aiken, suggests such a list as Professor Myers has hinted at: subjects, verbs, objects or complements, modifiers, connectives, and absolutes. I hesitate to list definitions, for, though this seems a very simple system, the definitions of these parts of speech are very difficult, indeed. Take, for instance, "modifier." In a sentence like this:

The young woman sang a Mozart aria.

—obviously *young* modifies *woman;* but do not *sang, aria,* and *Mozart* also? They modify our concept of the woman, for a woman who sings, who sings an aria, who sings Mozart is a sort of woman, after all! And, for that matter, don't all these words also modify *sang* (*woman, young, aria,* and *Mozart* all qualify the sort of singing, surely)? In short, doesn't everything seem to modify everything else? And, if so, what about the other "parts of speech"?

In choosing the "formal" position, Professor Myers is on safer grounds than he boasts, for certainly we can easily test whether a word may take an -*s* to mean "more than one" or an -*ed* to mean "in the past" or an -*er* to mean "more." So it is perhaps no accident that English grammars of recent times have taken the "formal" line predominantly. This does not mean, of course, that this is the "best" line in any ultimate sense. As Professor Myers wisely observes, the choice is one of convenience and not necessarily one of doctrine.

Defining Parts of Speech in English

SUMNER IVES

Professor of English at Syracuse University, Sumner Ives is known for his work in applying linguistic knowledge to the practical problems of teaching English and composition, as A New Handbook for Writers *(1960) illustrates. This article, which first appeared in* College English, *outlines a modern structuralist's approach to the English parts of speech.*

[1]   To a person whose habits of thought have been developed in the intellectual climate of Western culture, a division of the words in his vocabulary into the traditional eight parts of speech makes a kind of sense. These categories seem to have a kind of logical validity arising from the nature of human thought. And in Latin these "logical" categories are very nearly formal grammatical categories. A word, simply as an isolated, cited item in a list, can ordinarily be identified as a member of a grammatical category; that is, it has "part of speech" as an inherent and immediately recognizable grammatical property before it is used in a sentence. Even the most diverse category, the pronouns, are marked by a distinctive dative singular form or by a genitive singular with *-ius*. Prepositions and conjunctions have neither inflections nor special endings, but this fact sets them apart from other classes of words. Then, since prepositions combine rather freely with verbs to make other verbs, they are clearly a distinct category from conjunctions.

This is one of the characteristics of Latin as a language—one of the ways in which its grammar differs from that of English. One can cite an English word like *rule,* and nothing about the single word itself shows whether it is a noun or a verb. As a verb, it can be a finite verb by itself or a part of a finite phrase which is introduced by a modal auxiliary, *shall, will, can,* or some other. Its form alone does not tell us fully its person, number, or mood. An

Reprinted from *College English* (April 1957) with the permission of the National Council of Teachers of English and Sumner Ives.

equivalent Latin word, on the other hand, must be cited in a nearly specific grammatical form. Thus, *regula* is a noun, nominative singular; *regunt* is a verb, third person plural, present indicative. This basic difference between English and Latin makes the classification of words into parts of speech in one language something quite different from such a classification in the other.

If we use exactly the same list of categories for the words of English as are used for those of Latin, we get some groupings which work out very well, but we get others which include words about which the same general statements do not apply. For example, the grammatical properties of *very* differ considerably from those of *soon,* yet both are called adverbs in traditional grammar. English simply has a short list of words, one of which is *very,* which modify modifiers but never verbs. The inclusion of both *very* and *soon* in the same class ruins both the logical and the grammatical validity of the category. Putting both *that* and *few* in the same class is just as bad.

If we classify the words of English by inflectional criteria, we get a list of parts of speech which is not particularly useful in a description of syntax. For one thing, the endings *-er* and *-est* are used with words that should, on a basis of their total properties, be divided into two classes, and they are not used with all members of these two classes. The inflections for plurality and the genitive case could mark another category, but it is doubtful that *empathy* and *indecisiveness,* which should go into this category, ever appear with these endings. The nearest correspondence there is between an inflectional distinction and a grammatically valid part of speech is the occurrence of *-ing* as a mark of verbs. But some words which are not verbs have this ending ("the listing is . . ."), and not all verbs do have it. Moreover, there is a great residue of English words which have different functions in the syntax but which have no inflectional peculiarities that serve to divide them into form-classes. One must accept a somewhat different concept of "part of speech"—as well as a different list of categories—if he is to use a classification of this general type for the vocabulary items of English.

[2] Grammarians who have accepted, even as a temporary expedient, the eight Latin categories as appropriate to English, have tried solutions of three basic types. One type of solution is to regard the eight categories as logical categories and give defini-

tions for them which are based on meaning. However, in addition to the fact that this classification is not fully satisfactory for English structure, no one has been able to word these definitions in a clear manner. Differentiation on this basis between prepositions and conjunctions has been especially difficult, yet their distinction is essential to a statement of English syntax.

But the most serious fault in this solution is the way it inhibits one's understanding of how languages work as symbolic systems. It implies a correlation between the structural forms of a particular language and the "laws of human thought" which simply does not exist. What appears to be a logical division, one that is true *ex natura,* may be a grammatical division which is found with greater or less clarity in the Indo-European languages (of which English is one) but which is quite foreign to the grammars of some other languages. For example, even a basic concept like "thingness" may include different natural phenomena in different languages. In some languages the symbol for "fist" is a verb; one "fists."

To a native speaker of English, a statement like "a noun is a name of a person, place, or thing" may be of some use, for he gets his idea of "thingness" from the grammatical structure of English. But if he studies another language, or tries to understand how languages work as symbolic systems representing meaning according to different "structurings" of meaning, he must learn that another language may ascribe "thingness" to different concepts. The statement is not a reliable correlation between language and logic; it is a circular pointing device, not a definition. This comment is likewise true for all the meaning-based, or "logical" definitions for such matters as case and tense. They may be represented by quite different grammatical devices in different languages, even within the Indo-European family. To try to settle arguments in philosophy or pedagogy by appeal to the grammatical structure of a language or to teach the forms of a language through "logical" categories is to misunderstand how languages work, and to pass this misunderstanding on to others.

A second common solution is to regard classification into parts of speech as entirely a matter of syntax. The parts of speech derived by this approach are not form-classes in the morphology; they are function-classes in the syntax. For example, a single citation like *shelter* is simply an unclassified word. It becomes a noun in "under the shelter" and a verb in "shelter the horse." However, when using this approach, we find that the term noun may apply, at one time or another, to words with such diverse morphological and syntactic properties as *they, brave, whoever, enough, most, five, swimming,* and some others, and to constructions like "history teaching," "over the fence," and "whatever comes." We must recognize that some nouns (gerunds) may have a complement like verbs and that some (as in "the bravest will win") can be compared like adjectives. Our statements about the properties of elements in the various function-classes become extremely complex.

A more practicable solution is to keep "part of speech" on the word level and to use different types of definitions for the separate classes. Thus one can define nearly all verbs by their inflectional characteristics and conjunctions by how they join words and larger structures. If the properties which are selected as definitive are matters of form or of context, the eight categories can be isolated with reasonable clarity. This is essentially what has been done by Paul Roberts (*Understanding Grammar*). So long as the available textbooks on composition and communication and the books on grammar which are used in the lower grades retain the traditional classification, one should probably select one of the books recently published by these scholars and see that all prospective teachers of English understand it. This does not mean, however, that we should continue to accept this classification any longer than we must. It is not a fact of nature, or even of language, and it should be replaced as soon as possible.

[3] Meanwhile, several people with training in descriptive linguistics are working on alternative classifications for the elements in English. Essentially they are trying to do for English what was done for Greek, and later for Latin, hundreds of years ago. They are looking for ways to classify the linguistic items, on the various levels of complexity, so that better and more specific statements can be made about items as members of classes. This involves grouping them so that all the items in the same class will have a common, or nearly common, set of properties and so that there is some formal or contextual sign by which each member of the class can be identified. It may be possible to make more than one such classification for English; it may be necessary to make classifications on different structural levels. However, the only way to make one that is consistent with modern principles of language study is to rely wholly on the physical signs which are used in

English—whether they appear in some other language, whether they have the same value in other languages, or whether the classification agrees with one made for another language are all quite irrelevant. The first problem, therefore, is the identification of the ways by which English grammatical categories are isolated—that is, the symbols in English which have grammatical significance.

The first step in doing this is the identification of all the phonetic values which serve to differentiate one linguistic item from another. In English these consist of at least two types of acoustic values. One type is called the segmental phonemes: vowels, semi-vowels, and consonants; the other type is called the supra-segmental phonemes: contrasting differences in relative pitch and relative stress. Something of the grammatical relevance of stress differences can be perceived by comparing different readings of "what are you waiting for?" One reading will mean "what do you expect?" The other reading will mean "why are you waiting?" The meanings are differentiated, in part, by the difference in stress on *for*. The relevance of pitch differences can be learned by pronouncing "that is a ladder" in different ways to make the sequence of words into statements and questions with different over-all meanings. When analyzing the grammar of English, one must also consider the juncture features which separate elements on different levels of complexity. How relevant this is can be seen by reading the following aloud: "if the dog would tree the 'possum" and "if the dogwood tree would blossom."

The linguistic items which are differentiated by the phonemes are called morphemes. These are the basic linguistic elements to which some fragment of "message," or item of linguistic value, is attached. Grammar is the body of conventions according to which these morphemes are combined into larger structures. One must note that some of the morphemes are patterns of stress, contours of pitch, and types of juncture as well as sequences of vowels, semi-vowels, and consonants. Therefore, a grammar of English, to be exhaustive and definitive, must state the rules pertaining to stress, pitch, and juncture as well as those pertaining to morphemes made by the other type of phoneme, morphemes which we ordinarily call words or affixes. One must also realize that morphemes carry not only the kinds of meaning which are given in dictionary definitions but the grammatical meanings like "subject," "past tense," "infinitive," and so on. Thus, the stress pattern which makes *brick yard* (place where bricks are kept) a compound is a morpheme, and so is the -*ize* which makes the verb *civilize* from the adjective *civil*. George L. Trager and Henry Lee Smith, Jr., have done a great deal of research on the phonological elements in grammar, but much of their work has not been published.

[4]   Some descriptive linguists think that grammatical analysis should proceed as a matter of "pure" research, that a complete and tested description of English structure should be developed before serious attempts are made to get it into the academic program. There is much to be said for this view. However, the defects of traditional grammar and the limits on its value as a prelude to composition have been so well publicized that the need for something better seems to be immediate. Progress is a matter of trying for limited objectives. Each advance becomes a point for a further advance. Each new proposal must be within the reach of the current teaching force; hence, changes can proceed no faster than the re-education of the teaching force. The rest of this discussion will be consistent with this program of limited objectives; it will not be an attempt at a final and definitive statement.

[5]   Before giving a tentative classification of the elements in English, I shall sketch the devices and patterns according to which these elements are made. Between the morpheme and the sentence, English has at least two structural levels. One is the word level. These are either combinations of morphemes or single morphemes. A morpheme which has the freedom of occurrence that a word has is called a free form; one that must be joined to a free form or to another which is not free is called a bound form. The bound forms which are most relevant to grammatical meaning are inflections, suffixes which indicate grammatical functions, and superfixes—stress morphemes which make compounds out of otherwise free forms. Thus, *landing-place, horse race, used to,* and *give out* (when meaning "distribute") are single words with superfixes, regardless of the spelling. A special type of element in English which is neither clearly a free form or a bound form is the marker, specifically the articles and the *to* which is the sign of the marked infinitive. Other elements can act as markers, but these other elements are free forms.

The basic structures in English are listed below. These are not all on the same level of analysis. An MH structure which is introduced by a noun marker can be the S in an SV structure or the C in a VC structure; a PH structure can be the M of an MH structure, and so on.

1. SV (subject-verb) structures.
2. VC (verb-complement) structures.
3. MH (modifier-head) structures.
4. HH (head-head) structures. These include coordinates like "ham and eggs" and "you and I" and appositions like "we men" and "the composer Bach."
5. PH (preposition-head) structures.
6. AV (auxiliary-verb) structures. These are the phrases which begin with some auxiliary verb or "phrase-making" verb like "keeps (on)" and end with a non-finite form of a full verb. "Is about to leave," "has been sleeping," etc.

[6] The elements which are used in the making of sentences can be classified according to the types of bound morphemes in them, according to the inflections which can be added to them, according to the "normally" associated marker words, and/or according to the limitations on their use as constituents of the various structures.

[7] As indicated earlier, the internal structure of English words, including their inflections, is not always definitive. The distinction between morphology and syntax which is clear in Latin does not appear on the same analytical level in English. The level in English which is most nearly congruent with the morphological level in Latin includes both the morphemic composition of words and their association with the markers. Something of how this works can be shown by comparison with French and German. When memorizing nouns of those languages, we learn the definite articles which go with them so as to remember their grammatical gender. English does not have grammatical gender as a regular characteristic of common nouns, but they are divided into three grammatically different sub-classes by their use with markers. Thus: *a cat, the water,* and *empathy* (no marker). Also, in a full classification of all the words, one needs to rely, to a limited extent, on the capacity of the words to enter specific lower level structures, the MH, PH, and AV. Thus, what is here called the "form-class" level in English is not truly a level on which words are distinguished by their forms alone; it includes some part of what is traditionally called syntax.

[8]   Also, these "form-classes" of English, even when defined on a basis of the criteria suggested in the preceding paragraph, do not correlate consistently with specific uses in English sentences. For example, *brick* can be in "a red brick" or "a brick house"; *tall* can be in "a taller man" or "the tall will have to stoop." At least two descriptive procedures are possible. The grammarian can describe a pattern of "functional shifts." He can say that some nouns, e.g., *brick*, can act as an adjective; some adjectives, e.g., *tall*, can act as a noun. However, when doing this, he is using the same terms with different meanings and on different levels of the same analysis. This can be confusing in many ways.

An alternative solution is the use of two correlating sets of terms. Some descriptive linguists are already using correlating sets of terms, but they differentiate between the sets in a somewhat different way from that which is being suggested here. For the "form-class" level, the traditional terms may be used—re-defined and supplemented by a few others; for the "function-class" level, new terms can be made with an *-al* suffix. Thus, the "form-class" *adjective* correlates with the "function-class" *adjectival*. It seems to me that the use of these two correlating sets of terms, or classes, is methodologically better and that it permits a more efficient description of the syntax.

[9]   Now for the classification of English words into "form-classes."

This is a tentative classification made, so far as possible, on the representation of the language which appears in writing. However, even in an analysis based on this limited evidence, one must keep the supra-segmental features of the language in mind. When comparing two forms to see if they are in the same class, the total context in which they are being compared must be kept constant. One cannot change the stress, pitch, or juncture characteristics of the context or the segmental characteristics. And words must be defined on a phonological basis. Thus, in "every once in a while," *every* is an adjectival modifying the nominal *once in a while,* which has an identifying superfix.

No attempt will be made to describe all the analytical steps which are preliminary to this classification, nor should one think that the statements are complete or that they are true definitions. Also, in making or using a classification, one should remember that some grammatical information is given in a variety of ways, sometimes simultaneously. There are various amounts of redundancy in the representation of grammatical meaning. Thus, in "they civilized the tribe," the second word is identifiable as to category by at least three signs: its position in respect to *they* and *the tribe,* the suffix *-ize,* and the inflection *-ed.* Also a morpheme like *-ly* may indicate one thing when attached to one word and something different when attached to another, e.g., *manly* and *quickly.* The values of some grammatical signals are in part derived from the context and in part inherent.

A full analysis of English morphemes and words shows that there are a great many stem-forming suffixes. These can be divided into four groups. English has correlating sets of words like *legislate, legislation, legislative, legislatively; arrive, arrival; season, seasonal; hope, hopeful, hopefully; satire, satirize, satirical, satirically;* and so on. The facts that there are just four sets of these suffixes and that the words on which they appear can be divided into four groups with different syntactic properties makes these morphemes be part-of-speech indicators. They do not, of course, appear on all English words which have these syntactic properties. But they suggest that four is the right number of divisions and that these four classes constitute a single category on a different level of the analysis. This single category is congruent with what C. C. Fries calls "open-class" words and with what Harold Whitehall and some earlier grammarians call "full" words. The four classes in the category are noun, verb, adjective, and adverb.

Nouns are indicated in English by one of the noun-indicator morphemes, by the possibility of inflections for plurality and the genitive case, and/or by a noun marker. The noun markers are the articles and the genitive case forms of pronouns or of other nouns. Of these identification signs, possibility of use with a prepositive genitive is probably the most nearly definitive. Proper nouns have a similar but not identical set of properties.

Verbs are indicated by one of the verb-indicator morphemes, by having at least three inflections, and/or by forming, with other verbs, AV structures.

Adjectives are indicated by one of the adjective-indicator morphemes, by the fact that they may come between a noun marker and a noun, and/or by the fact that they may appear with a prepositive intensifier. (Note: the second word in "the running boy" is not an adjective because it cannot be modified by *very,* a typical intensifier.)

Adverbs are indicated by one of the adverb-indicator morphemes, by the fact that they may be in sentence final position after a verb or a VC structure, and/or by the relative freedom with which they may be moved to specific places in the total clause. There are several subclasses of adverbs which are defined by the limitations on their freedom of movement. (Note that this eliminates two types of words from this category, those which behave like *very*, and those which behave like *almost*.)

Adjectives and adverbs have in common the property of taking the *-er* and *-est* suffixes or of making equivalent structures with prepositive *more* and *most*.

All these "form-classes" may appear as heads in MH structures.

Words which fall in the preceding categories include those words of the vocabulary which have the greatest freedom of substitution in the general patterns of the syntax. That is, one member of a class can be substituted for another member of the class without destroying the grammatical integrity of the context, although the resulting expression may not be true by reference to experience. The trick to writing jabberwocky consists of substituting nonsense "words" for members of these classes. The rest of the vocabulary is divided into classes on a basis of syntactic properties, although pronouns do indeed have inflections. These classes are congruent with what Fries calls "closed-classes" and some other grammarians call "empty" words. They are primarily part of the grammatical machinery of English rather than part of its lexical symbolization.

Pronouns have three-case sets of forms and/or three-person sets of forms. They act as substitutes for some previously used nominal or as identifiers of the encoder (speaker) or decoder (hearer) in a message transfer. This class thus includes only the personal pronouns, the compound personal pronouns, and the reciprocal pronouns of traditional grammar.

Demonstratives include a short list of words which have no case forms but which may act as nominals or as adjectivals. These are *that, those, this, these, such,* and *so.*

Indefinites do not have the case or person forms of pronouns nor do they require a specific antecedent. Their integrity as a class is indicated by the fact that they may be followed immediately by an *of* phrase, even when they are not preceded by an article. Compare: "some of the people" and "the apathy of these people." This class is not as homogeneous as some others, and some subdivisions can be set up.

Intensifiers form MH structures with many adjectives and adverbs but never with nouns or verbs. The typical intensifier is *very*. (Note that *very* has an adjective homonym—the very man.)

Qualifiers form MH structures with at least one sub-class of adverbs (*home, here*, etc.), with adjectives like *ready*, and with many verbs. The typical qualifier is *almost*.

These two classes are, of course, placed with adverbs in traditional grammar, but their total lists of properties are such that it is best to consider them apart from adverbs and from each other.

Prepositions are parts of PH structures. These must have, as minimal forms, an initial preposition and a final nominal. The PH structure may, nevertheless, act as an adjectival or as an adverbial, whereas MH and HH structures must, as structures, act in the same functions as their heads.

Interrogatives are words which typically introduce questions which invite more than a "yes" or "no" response. There are two types of these: those which may be nominals or adjectivals and those which may be neither.

Connectives join the basic types of structures. There are four types. Coordinating connectives consist of a list of seven: *and, but, or, nor, yet, for,* and *so*. These have somewhat different properties, but they have enough in common to be listed together.

Correlative connectives are those that operate as pairs, like *neither . . . nor*.

Subordinating connectives are those which introduce an SV structure which is part of another like or different structure. There are three types: those which introduce structures which may be moved; those which introduce structures that are fixed in postpositive position after a nominal or pronominal; and those which introduce structures that may be the S of an SV structure or the C of a VC structure.

Transitional connectives are those which typically join sentences into sequences of sentences. They usually, but not necessarily, stand between the structures they join.

Pattern words are those like *there* in "there are . . ." and *it* in "it is raining." They are used as fillers in normal structural patterns but have no referential or other grammatical value.

Markers are words which give an identification to some following word. The articles indicate and differentiate between nouns, and they sometimes indicate that a word from another "form-class" is being used as a nominal. The marker *to* indicates what is called a marked infinitive. Compare: "a run is necessary" with "to run is necessary."

Interjections are words which do not ordinarily combine with other words in the formation of structures. There are four types: those which call attention, either politely or abruptly; those which provide a carrier for a superfix or a continuation of noise while one is thinking; explosions like *ouch;* and profanity.

There is a considerable amount of overlapping in some of the categories. For example, some prepositions may be adverbials and some subordinating connectives may be prepositionals. In dealing with this situation, one can either decide arbitrarily to assign every orthographic symbol to some "form-class" and treat other uses as "function-class" uses, or one can regard the orthographic symbols as homonyms and list the form in each "form-class" which is appropriate. It is probably best to treat a word like *since* as a member of the "form-class" subordinating connective and note that it can also act as a prepositional. On the other hand, words like *so* and *that* should probably be given multiple listing on the "form-class" level. Questions like this are best left to trial in the marketplace.

It is obvious to the thoughtful reader that the criteria of identification which have been given do not give all the properties or the uses of the classes which have been listed. The only claims which are made for this classification are that it is based on characteristics within the structural patterns of English and that it provides a set of categories about which a great many more statements can be made than are possible if the traditional calssification is used. That is, a more detailed syntax and a more useful rhetoric can be made with this classification than can possibly be made on a basis of traditional grammar.

SUMMARY

[1]   Whereas in Latin we can usually tell the sort of word a word is by the forms it takes, in English we can not. Hence Latin parts of speech, when imposed upon the English language, pose problems for the grammarian.

[2]   English grammarians who have accepted the Latin terms for parts of speech have tried three solutions to the problems raised. Some have used the Latin terms for categories of meaning, but this ignores basic differences. Others have considered the parts of speech syntactical (functional) categories, but this leads to a complete separation of form and function. Still others have used different types of definitions for separate classes, and this has worked reasonably well, though it does not offer a permanent solution to the problem of English grammar.

[3]   Meanwhile descriptive linguists have been working on another system of classification for English, based on the concept of the various levels of English structure, beginning with the level of the phoneme and the level of the morpheme.

[4]   Though some think a linguistic grammar should wait until research is complete, a tentative grammar is possible at present, and one is badly needed.

[5]   Between the morpheme and the sentence, at least two linguistic levels may be seen: the word level (in which are found single morphemes or combinations of morphemes) and the phrase level, which has six basic structures: (1) subject-verb, (2) verb-complement, (3) modifier-head, (4) head-head, (5) preposition-head, and (6) auxiliary-verb.

[6]   Parts of speech may be classified according to some or all of these criteria: (a) the types of bound morphemes in them, or added to them (inflections); (b) the marker words normally associated with them; and (c) the limitations on their use as parts of various structures.

[7]   The forms of morphemes or words are not always a dependable criterion; morphemic composition and association with markers, together, are more dependable. A full classification, however, also must take into consideration the possible syntactic relations of words.

[8]   The "form classes" in English, even when so determined, are not always consistent, and the grammarian must either resort to "functional shifts" or use two sets of terms ("adjective" for form class, "adjectival" for function class); the latter seems a preferable alternative.

[9]   The parts of speech, then, may be separated upon three bases: the form of the word, its accompanying markers, and its position in structures. The stem-forming suffixes suggest four basic form-classes, and so do other grammatical observations: (1) nouns, (2) verbs, (3) adjectives, and (4) adverbs. Other word-classes are divided by syntactic properties: (5) pronouns, (6) demonstratives, (7) indefinites, (8) intensifiers, (9) qualifiers, (10) prepositions, (11) interrogatives, (12–15) connectives of four types, (16) pattern words, (17) markers, and (18) interjections. The first four classes grammatically allow free substitution within classes, are "open" classes, and are comparatively "full" of meaning; the last fourteen are "closed" classes and are comparatively "empty" of meaning.

NOTES

This is a difficult essay, largely because it is "packed" in meaning. Because it is packed, however, it will repay several re-readings. The essay is difficult also because it assumes a knowledge of various terms, some of which are explained in this short glossary:

Categories. A category is a class of persons, things, events, or ideas, a class set off from others by a principle or set of principles of division. For instance, college students are categorized as freshmen, sophomores, juniors, and seniors on the basis of the number of credits they have earned in the college. Grammatical categories are classes formed by some grammatical principle. For instance, there are a large number of words in English which have plural forms in -*s:*

> (*a*)   rock, rocks; desk, desks; cigarette, cigarettes.

And a large number of words have past-tense forms in -*ed:*

> (*b*)   help, helped; tease, teased; look, looked.

These are called *formal categories* in English grammar, because they are classes of words set off by the *forms* they take. They are also called *form classes.*

Upon another principle, the principle of distribution, we find that a number of words in our language will fit into this structure "frame":

> (*A*)   The _____ was good.   (cake, boy, swimming, etc.)

Another group will fit this "frame":

> (*B*)   The boys _____ the girls.   (like, kiss, hit, etc.)

These are called *functional* or *syntactical categories,* because they are classes of words set off by the functions or positions they can take in English sentence patterns. They are also called *function classes.*

As Professor Ives points out, form classes and function classes in English are not exactly the same. For the most part words in form-class (*a*) will fit into function-class (*A*):

> The _____ was good.   (rock, desk, cigarette)

But not all the words which fit into category (*A*) will fit category (*a*): we have *cake* and *cakes, boy* and *boys,* but not *swimming* and *swimmings.* Likewise, most of the words in form-class (*b*) will fit into function-class (*B*), but not all:

> The boys _____ the girls.   (help, teach, but not look)

And some words in function-class (*B*) will not fit form class (*b*): we have *like* and *liked, kiss* and *kissed,* but not *hit* and *hitted.*

Finite verbs. A finite verb is a form limited by person and number. Thus the form *am* is limited to the first person and singular number (I); *likes* is limited to third person and singular number (he, she, it). These are finite forms. On the other hand, *being* and *been, liking* are not so limited; they are called non-finite forms.

Functional shift is the term used to describe the fact that in modern English the same word can be found in positions usually associated with different parts of speech, without any change in the form of the word. For example:

The *garden* is pretty.   ["noun" or nominal position]
The *garden* tools are here.   ["adjectival" position]
We *garden* each summer.   ["verbal" position]

"Headed" constructions. Word-groups in English may be divided into headed ("endocentric" is Bloomfield's term) and non-headed ("exocentric") groups. A headed group is one which contains one element which might grammatically suffice for the whole group:

(a)   *The naughty little boys* teased the girls.
      (*Boys* teased the girls.)
(b)   The man *could have sought* his own wife.
      (The man *sought* his own wife.)
(c)   Oscar, *confounded by all the noise,* ran.
      (Oscar, *confounded,* ran.)
(d)   The answer was *easy to figure out.*
      (The answer was *easy.*)

In these examples, the italicized word-groups in (a) and (b) are sometimes called "tail-head" groups, because the "head word" comes last in the group; those in (c) and (d) are called "head-tail" groups because the head comes first in the group.

Other groups are not "headed"; that is, no one element in the group can stand alone, grammatically:

(e)   *We swam.*   [Both words are necessary.]
(f)   The list *of boys* was long.   [Both words are necessary.]

Inflection is the systematic changing of form of some words in a language to indicate some grammatical idea or ideas. The chief inflectional patterns in modern English are shown in these examples (called "paradigms"):

boy	help	tall
boy's	helps	taller
boys	helping	tallest
boys'	helped	

Inflectional changes are usually made by suffix—that is, by adding on to the end of the word, as the examples above show. These additions are not considered fundamental changes of the words: *boy, help* and *tall* are the "stems" and remain unchanged.

Another sort of suffix, which Ives mentions as the "stem-forming suffix," changes the basic word. The examples below, with suffixes italicized, illustrate this sort, which changes the part of speech of the word to which it is added (as inflectional suffixes do not):

boy*ish*   [from noun to adjective]
help*ful*   [from verb or noun to adjective]

homely   [from noun to adjective]
roundly   [from adjective to adverb]
beautify   [from noun to verb]

Phonetic. Traditionally, grammar has been divided into phonology (the study of sounds of language), morphology (the study of forms of language), and syntax (the study of relationships between forms). Phonology embraces phonetics and phonemics. Phonetics is the study of all sounds in a language, whether the sounds are linguistically significant or not. For instance, if you listen carefully when you say "Daddy'd not like that" rapidly, you will hear that the three *d* sounds in "Daddy'd" are different: the first is rather loudly exploded, the second is less so, and the third barely is said at all. *Phonetically* these sounds are different; but speakers of English take them all for the same sound. *Phonemics,* concerning itself with only linguistically significant differences, considers these three *d*'s as variants of the same sound (or, as the phonemicist would say, "as allophones of the phoneme /d/," an allophone being a "variant of a sound").

The phonemes of modern English are divided into "segmental" and "suprasegmental" ones. The consonant and vowel sounds constitute the "segmentals"; the phonemes of stress, pitch, and juncture constitute the "suprasegmentals"—features of sound over and above, as it were, the fundamental segments. Perhaps an illustration will clarify this. Listen to yourself as you read these sentences:

The play was good.
Oh, you're just saying that to make me feel happy.
I'm doing nothing of the kind. The play *was* good.

Now both sentences "The play was good" consist of these consonant and vowel (segmental) phonemes: /ðə pley wəz gud/. But the two sentences were differently said, with a difference in intended meaning. The difference in sound is one of stress and pitch. The first time the sentence is said, one stresses *play* and *good* and the pitch of the voice rises at the beginning of *good* and then quickly falls off. The second time the sentence is said, one stresses *was* most significantly, and the pitch of the voice rises at that word and begins trailing off before one says *good*. If we are to transcribe these sentences as they are spoken, then, we must assign some sort of "superfixes" or marks of the differences in the suprasegmental features of the two sentences.

Syntax. As noted above, syntax is the part of grammar which deals with the relations of words in sentences—in modern English largely the order of certain sorts of words in the various patterns ("syntactic structures") which we use. In Latin most grammatical information was given by the forms of the words (that is, morphologically); in English, most grammatical information is given by the order of words (syntactically). A sentence will illustrate this. In the Latin sentence *Malus puer vidit bellam puellam* ("The bad boy saw the pretty girl."), the forms of the words tell us everything we need to know to understand the sentence.

The form of *puer* tells us it is the subject of the verb. The form of *malus* tells us that it modifies *puer* ("the boy is bad"). The form of *vidit* tells us it is the verb. The form of *puellam* tells us it is the object of the verb ("it got seen"). The form of *bellam* tells us that it modifies *puellam* ("the girl is pretty").

Hence we can scramble the order of the words however we please:

> *Bellam puellam vidit malus puer.*
> *Bellam puer vidit malus puellam.*
> *Vidit puer malus puellam bellam.*   Etc.

All of these, though not equally excellent Latin, say the same thing. In the English counterpart, however, we depend almost entirely on word order to know the "grammar" of the sentence. We know that the boy is bad because *bad* precedes *boy;* that the boy did the looking because *boy* precedes *saw;* that the girl is pretty because *pretty* precedes *girl;* that the girl was seen because *girl* follows *saw.* If we scramble the word-order (syntax) of the English sentence, the result is chaos.

Understandably a Latin grammar is devoted largely to word forms. When English grammar is patterned after Latin grammar—as all early grammars were—it concentrates on word forms, even though they are not very important in English. The study of English syntax has been slow to develop. As Professor Ives suggests, it is the chief interest, and properly so, of modern English grammarians; but it is not completely worked out at present.

A Syntactic Approach to Part-of-Speech Categories

*Ralph B. Long is chairman of the English Department at the
University of Puerto Rico. This essay, which first appeared in
College English, suggests the approach to English taken in Professor Long's* The Sentence and Its Parts *(1961), a remarkably
rich and stimulating grammar from a functional point of view.*

[1] What our school grammars and handbooks have to say
about part-of-speech categories in modern English seems unsatisfactory to practically all specialists in English language now. In
the present decade we have had new formulations avowedly
representing decisive breaks with what has been taught as English grammar heretofore. The present paper outlines a less revolutionary formulation. It is assumed here that both the procedures
and the conclusions of the standard grammarians of English have
been essentially right, and that their terminology is fairly usable.
But it is also assumed that nothing is really worked out perfectly
once and for all, and that constant effort to improve even the best
formulations available is desirable for grammar as for other
studies.

[2] It is hard to see any real possibility of part-of-speech
classifications based in phonology or in morphology. Differences
in stress patterns within words and in vowel and consonant
sounds accompany part-of-speech distinctions we will want to
recognize in pairs such as *permít* and *pérmit, sing* and *song,
grieve* and *grief.* Some noninflectional suffixes such as the *-ize* of
pasteurize and the *-less* of *careless* correlate fairly well with part-
of-speech classifications. The inflectional patterns followed by
almost every verb correlate perfectly with part-of-speech classi-

---

Reprinted from *College English* (April 1957) with the permission of the
National Council of Teachers of English and Ralph B. Long.

fication: almost every verb has an -s form used (in the indicative present) when the subject is *he, she,* or *it,* and an -ing form used in phrasal progressives; and every word that has -s and -ing forms used in these ways is a verb. But criterions such as these do not carry us far enough. There are entirely too many words that cannot be classified on any of these bases. Examples are *fun, extinct, now, ouch, each,* and the *must* of *you must be tired.*

It is hard to see any real possibility of part-of-speech classifications based directly on the meaning expressed by the words which are to be classified. Ties with meaning are obviously the most important aspect of language. A schematically neat grammar would result if the grammarian could begin with categories of meaning: words applied to "things," places, and people are nouns; words applied to actions, events, and states of affairs are verbs; words applied to qualities are adjectives; and so on. But *death* is used of an event as truly as *die* is, and *honesty* and *honestly* are used of a "quality" as truly as *honest* is.

[3] Our generally useful criterions are two purely syntactic ones: (1) syntactic functions characteristically performed, and (2) kinds of prepositive modifiers characteristically accepted. The second criterion requires us to describe the parts of speech in terms of complex interrelationships. The first requires that we work out an analysis of the structure of clauses and clause equivalents along with our description of parts-of-speech categories. We can do this. The key to our analysis is known words employed in known combinations. Our analysis will be "mentalist," not mechanist: we will not need to begin with accurate descriptions of vowel and consonant sounds, stresses, pitches, and junctures in particular spoken versions of our examples. We need not hesitate to note both meanings and inflections where they seem to furnish useful supplementary criterions, but our basic criterions will be syntactic.

[4] We had better begin by making a clear distinction between syntactic functions performed in particular sentences and part-of-speech classifications. When we say of the word *furniture* in *but, George, furniture is expensive now* that it is a subject, we say one thing about it; when we say that it is a noun, we say another. When we say of *expensive* that it is a complement, we say one thing; and when we say that it is an adjective, we say another. We can speak similarly of *is* as a predicator in function and a verb

in part of speech.

Our list of major syntactic functions will have to include predicators, which we can regard as heads in their clauses; subjects, which we can regard as modifiers expressed or implied with all predicators and able to determine the form of many predicators (as when *go* becomes *goes* if the subject is *he*); complements, which we can regard as modifiers required by some predicators but not by others; and adjuncts, which we can regard as modifiers of predicators lying, in terms of layers, outside the clause nucleuses in which predicators, subjects, and complements are contained. *But, George,* and *now* can all be classified as adjuncts in the statement *but, George, furniture is expensive now.*

We will have to accept the reality of constant syntactic ellipsis. Thus when *Tuesday* is made a reply to *when did you see George?* the single word is a statement made up of an adjunct alone; as a reply to *what day is today?* the same word is a statement made up of a complement alone. What we can call isolates used in clause equivalents are another matter. *Ouch!* can be called an isolate given sentence status alone as a clause equivalent. In *good morning, George* the segment *good morning* can be described as an isolate modified by the adjunct *George: good morning* looks like a reduction of a clausal sentence, but in contemporary use we cannot fill out a nucleus we feel confidence in.

We will need to recognize contained functions too, and collateral ones. In *good furniture is expensive* the subject is the segment *good furniture:* it is made up of a contained head and a contained modifier. If *George my boy* is added as an adjunct of direct address, we will have two other contained functions represented: that of principal (*George*) and that of appositive (*my boy*). If *at present* is added as an adjunct of time, two other functions are illustrated: that of preposition and that of object. If *here and elsewhere* is added as an adjunct of place, the function of coordinate within multiple segments is illustrated by *here* and *and elsewhere.* Our contained functions will be contained head and contained modifier, principal and appositive, preposition and object, and coordinate. A full treatment of syntactic functions within clauses and clause equivalents would give attention to several collateral functions performed only by words or segments which also perform basic or contained functions. Here we need note only one: that of clause marker. When we analyze subordinate clauses such as *when it's over* in *call me when it's over* and questions such as *what does George mean?* we will want to note that *when, what,* and *does* all function as clause markers besides functioning as *then, that,* and *does* function in *then it's over* and *George does mean that.*

[5]   We can describe the syntactic functioning of everything put into English in these terms. The unnormalized English of comfortable speech will often present problems; so will such unnormalized written English as the unpunctuated twenty-five-thousand-word reverie at the end of Joyce's *Ulysses.* Both the grammarian and the phonemicist tend to avoid unnormalized English. There is no possibility of eliminating all problems in classification, just as there is no possibility of eliminating all ambiguity. But with our list of functions agreed on, we can go on to describe our part-of-speech categories. When we assign part-of-speech classification to a word, we should look beyond the sentence in which the word occurs and ask ourselves questions about the word's characteristic behavior when it expresses the meaning in point in other sentences too. In essence our part-of-speech classifications will be statements about characteristic syntactic functioning.

We can give first place to the verbs. These are the words which function characteristically as predicators. In statements they accept nominative or common-case forms of personal pronouns as their most distinctive prepositive modifiers—that is, as their subjects. All but a very few defectives (*can, may, must, ought, shall, should, will*) follow unmistakable patterns of inflection. We cannot refuse verb classification to the defectives: if we do, we will not be able to deal with the contrasts seen in *he must be French* and *he probably is French.*

We can give second place to the nouns. The syntactic function of greatest significance for the assignment of part-of-speech classification as a noun is that of subject. Almost all nouns are usable as subjects. Other functions that we can describe as nounal, meaning that they are most characteristically performed by nouns and nounlike pronouns, are those of complement of certain ("transitive") verbs and of object of prepositions. The most distinctive prepositive modifiers of nouns are adjectives, as in *pleasant houses,* and determiners such as articles and possessives, as in *a house* and *Jack's house.* The characteristic inflections of nouns are inflection for plural number and for possessive case.

But our category of nouns will contain three rather sharply distinct subcategories. There are the pluralizers, such as *house* and (in the plural only) *trousers*. Singular forms of pluralizers are rarely used alone as subjects in normalized modern English: *house is pleasant* simply will not do. There are the quantifiables, such as *furniture* and *milk* and *news* and *honesty* and *fun*. Quantifiables have no plurals, though it is true that many words have both quantifiable and pluralizer status—so that, for example, *too much fear* and *too many fears* exist side by side though *too much furniture* contrasts clearly with *too many chairs*. Finally, there are the proper nouns, such as *George* and *Mexico*. True proper nouns have no plurals, almost never take prepositive modifiers of determiner type, and take adjective modifiers (as in *poor George*) only in a very limited way. The effective meaning of the proper noun *George* in *George met us at the airport* is wholly individual, perhaps accumulated through many years of acquaintance; the *George* of *there are three Georges in the class* has become a pluralizer not wholly unlike the pluralizer *boys* in meaning, not a true proper noun. As for inflection for the possessive, on the one hand the use of the possessive is limited sharply in modern English, and on the other hand the inflection has become in effect a kind of postpositive equivalent of a preposition and attaches to words of varied types, as in *someone else's* turn and in such perhaps-nonstandard sequences as *the boy she goes with's car*. Finally, it must be noted that some words which are used in only one or two nounal ways require classification as functionally limited nouns. This is true, for example, of *behalf, sake,* and *stead*.

The adjectives will constitute a third part of speech. Our adjectives will be words which most characteristically perform the functions (1) of prepositive modifiers of nouns and (2) of complements of *be* with collateral relationships to the subjects of *be*. Thus *pleasant* is usable both as in *Jack's pleasant house* and as in *Jack's house is pleasant*. The most distinctive prepositive modifiers of adjectives are adverbs, as in *Jack's house is very pleasant* and as in *Jack's manner was deceptively pleasant*. The only inflection adjectives ever have is that for comparison, as when *old* becomes *older* and *oldest*. Not all adjectives inflect for comparison: *extinct,* for example, does not. Some words that are used in only one of the two characteristically adjectival functions will have to be classified as functionally limited adjectives. This is true

of the *mere* of *a mere child,* the *lone* of *a lone child,* and the
desirous of *they were desirous of prolonging the negotiations.*

We will need to recognize a category of adverbs as our fourth
part of speech. The functions most characteristically performed
will be (1) that of adjuncts to predicators, (2) that of prepositive
modifiers of adjectives, other adverbs, and prepositional segments,
(3) that of prepositions, and (4) that of postpositive contained
modifiers. Though most nouns and adjectives are usable in all
the characteristically nounal and adjectival ways, probably no
adverb is used in all the characteristically adverbial ways. Thus
here is most characteristically used as an adjunct as in *we're
happy here,* and *very* is most characteristically used as a prepositive modifier of an adjective or another adverb, and *of* is characteristically used as a preposition, and *percent, o'clock,* and
galore are characteristically used as postpositive contained modifiers as in *five percent* and *flowers galore. Here* is used as a complement in *he isn't here,* as a postpositive modifier in *the weather
here is almost perfect,* and as object of a preposition in *I'm sure
they'll start from here;* such words as *of* and *percent* are much
more limited in use. The distinctive prepositive modifiers of
adverbs are other adverbs, in which respect adverbs and adjectives are of course indistinguishable. A few words we will want
to classify as adverbs form comparatives and superlatives with
-er and *-est:* this is notably true of *often* and *soon.*

Several rather distinct subcategories of adverbs should be
noted. Adjective-like words in *-ly* form one: *badly, hardly, lately,
merely, mistakenly, seemingly, gently, partly,* and *mostly* can
serve as examples. Such words as *lonely* and *manly* must of
course be classified as adjectives, not as adverbs. Adverbs in *-ly*
function most characteristically as adjuncts, but they are also
given frequent use as contained modifiers, as in *absolutely impossible, curiously silent, easily obtainable, numerically equal,
practically there, desperately in love,* and *hardly anyone.* Clause-
marker adverbs form a second subcategory. Except for *that* and
such words as *before* and *since,* the words which are called subordinating conjunctions in the school grammars and handbooks
can more conveniently be classified as adverbs which commonly
perform both basic or contained syntactic functions and also
collateral clause-marker functions. Thus in *can you tell me where
the post-office is?* the word *where* can be said to function both as

the complement in the subordinate clause, exactly as *there* does in *the post-office is there,* and as a clause marker. *Where* obviously functions quite similarly in the main question *where is the post-office?* In *I'll go if I can* the word *if* can be said to function both as an adjunct in its clause, as *perhaps* does in the statement *perhaps I can,* and as a clause marker. The four coordinators *and, but, or,* and *nor* can be said to constitute a third subcategory among the adverbs: we will not need a part-of-speech category called "conjunctions." Simple conjunctive adverbs such as *also, therefore, yet, nevertheless,* and *else* perhaps deserve a subcategory of their own among the adverbs. Prepositional adverbs certainly deserve a subcategory. There are two reasons for not letting them stand as a separate part of speech. First, the terms *preposition* and *object* are useful as names of companion functions, and function and part of speech must be distinguished. Second, the behavior of the words which function as prepositions makes it simplest to regard them as transitive adverbs. There is no more reason to assign the *in* of *the Dean isn't in his office* to a different part-of-speech category from that of the *in* of *the Dean isn't in* than there is to assign the *play* of *Helen doesn't play bridge* to a different part-of-speech category from that of the *play* of *Helen doesn't play.* Nor is there any reason to assign *before* to different part-of-speech categories on the basis of its uses in *he'd been there before,* in *he'd been there before that,* and in *he got there before we did* (where the prepositional adverb *before* has a clausal object). Other adverbs of miscellaneous types remain. *Rather, quite, soon, doubtless* (in syntax quite unlike *fearless,* for example), *well, sometime, anyhow, now, twice, seldom, anew, apiece,* and *ago* show something of the variety that exists. *Ago* even has nouns and nounal segments as its characteristic prepositive modifiers, as in *years ago.* Our adverb category is an exceptionally miscellaneous one, but it would be hard to break it up into smaller categories that were both well unified in syntax and reasonably large in size.

We will need a fifth part-of-speech category for the words which most characteristically function as isolates, with the syntactic value of whole nucleuses. We can call these words absolutes. They will include such "interjections" of the school grammars as *ouch, wow, zowie,* and *hello,* and the substitute words *yes* and *no.* Many isolates are not absolutes. Thus the emo-

tional clause equivalents *gracious! well!* and *my!* have isolates as
their sole components, but in terms of part-of-speech classifications these words are best regarded as adjective, adverb, and
pronoun respectively.

Finally, we had better recognize the pronouns as a sixth part
of speech distinct from the other five (though not from such subcategories as the coordinating adverbs) in that it is closed. It will
be both desirable and relatively easy to list the words to be
placed in the category of the pronouns. The words for which
such classification seems desirable are of two kinds, which can
be called determinative and nounal.

Determinative pronouns include, first of all, the full determinatives of identification: *this, that, the, a, some, any, either, every,
each, no, neither, what, which, whatever, whichever.* These are
the words which, along with possessives and the numeral *one,*
can determine the singular forms of pluralizer nouns and so produce units which are usable as subjects, as undetermined singular
pluralizers usually are not. "*A house* is being built across the
street." "*Which house* is the larger?" Some full determinatives of
identification can modify plurals and quantifiables, some cannot.
Partial determinatives of identification will require recognition
too: *same* and *selfsame, such, other,* the ordinal numerals, *last,
next, former, latter, own. Last* and *next* are sometimes full determinatives, as in *next week will be very busy.* Determinatives of
number and quantity will include the cardinal numerals, *few,
little, several, enough, many, much* and *overmuch, all,* and *both.*
Determinatives of number and quantity are characteristically
used to modify (1) plural forms of pluralizer nouns and (2) quantifiable nouns. Except for the cardinal numeral *one,* they modify
singular forms of pluralizers only very exceptionally. *Some, any,*
and *no* often pattern as determinatives of number and quantity,
it should be said; and there is a frequent mixing of interest in
identification with interest in quantity and number.

The most characteristic use of determinative pronouns of all
three types is the use as determiners with noun heads. But almost
all determinative pronouns are also usable rather freely in nounal
functions. In nounal uses they are best regarded as what we can
call accretional forms, having assimilated both the meanings and
the functions of what would be their heads in non-elliptical construction. "Most tourists are interested in the life of the people,

but *some* are interested only in nightclubs." "*Three* of the students are from Japan." Here *some* has the value of *some tourists* and *three* has the value of *three students,* which is undesirably complete before *of the students.* Sometimes no very precise unstated head is really thought of when determinative pronouns are used like nouns. "*This* is my friend Jack Harrar." "She's on her *own* now." Nevertheless it remains true that such determinatives as *this* and *own* are syntactically unlike both such words as *he* and the adjectives. Among the determinative pronouns only *the, a,* and *every* do not occur in accretional nounal uses. *No* has a long variant *none* in accretional uses, and *other* has an *-s* plural in accretional uses. "The work requires patience, and I have *none.*" "Some old friends write oftener than *others.*" Such numerals as *hundred* have *-s* plurals used in curiously limited ways. *This* and *that* show plural number in both determiner uses and accretional nounal ones. *Few, little, much,* and *many* compare, like many adjectives and a few adverbs; *much* and *many* have their comparative and superlative forms in common.

The nounal pronouns can be listed as follows:

1. The personals *I, you, he, she, it, we, they.*
2. The reciprocal *each other.*
3. The expletive *there.*
4. General *one* ("a person").
5. Substitute *one* (as in a *new car and an old one*).
6. The compounds in *-one, -body,* and *-thing.*
7. The clause markers *that, who,* and *whoever.*

In general, the nounal pronouns are not distinguishable from the nouns in syntactic functions characteristically performed. Expletive *there* is of course quite limited in syntactic functioning, but so is such a noun as *behalf.* Except for substitute *one,* the nounal pronouns are rarely modified by prepositive adjectives or determiners. In this respect they are like the proper nouns, and exceptional *dear me* is comparable to exceptional *poor George.* In the matter of inflections the nounal pronouns behave quite individually. Some do not inflect. Others, notably the personals, have remarkably complex inflections. *I,* for example, has a nominative and an objective, two possessives (*my* and *mine,* syntactically a pair like *no* and *none*), and the compounded form *myself. It* is more like the nouns: it has only a common-case form, one possessive, and the compounded form *itself*. In complexity (and archaism) of inflection *I* is to *boy* and *sheep* somewhat as *be* is to *play* and *put*. (For syntax, "inflected" forms need not be etymologically related: *went* is now an inflected form of *go*, not of *wend*.) It is noteworthy, incidentally, that an -*s* plural turns up in substitute *one*. The -*s* plurals of such compounds as the pronoun *ourselves* and the adverb *indoors* really belong to the noun components within the compounds.

The nounal pronouns do have enough in common with the determinatives to warrant putting them in the same part-of-speech category as the determinatives. *Who's he?* is syntactically more like *who's that man?* than like *who's that?* since *he* always has the value of determinative and head together; but the element of identification in terms of situation or context is very strong indeed in *he*. In such compounds as *something* the determinative element is even more obvious. Even substitute *one* still deals with identification in terms of situation or context. It seems wise to keep a small closed category of pronouns and to include both the words which normally function as determiner modifiers of nouns and the words here listed as nounal pronouns.

[6]   Our part-of-speech categories, then, include verbs, nouns, adjectives, adverbs, absolutes, and pronouns. Some words will require classification now in one part of speech, now in another. A word which accepts distinctive modifiers of two different types will require two classifications. Thus *conservative* is an adjective in *he is very conservative* and in *they are very conservative*, but a noun in *he is a true conservative* and in *they are true conservatives*. Where sharp distinctions in meaning correlate with significant distinctions in syntactic function, two classifications seem desirable. Thus *little* is a pronoun in *a little fun*, where an indefinite article which cannot modify quantifiable *fun* modifies it, and an adjective in *a little boy*, where it is a size word like *small*. *There* is an adverb in *there it is* but a pronoun in *there isn't time*. *Still* is an adjective in *the still figure* but an adverb in *I still like it*. *Pretty* is an adjective in *pretty girls* but an adverb in *pretty bad*. Some words require several part-of-speech classifications: *round* is an example.

Performance of untypical functions must not be regarded as in itself a basis for multiple part-of-speech classifications. *Hours* is a noun in *hours later*. *Toy* is a noun in *tóy cupboard*, meaning a cupboard for toys, and also in *toy cúpboard,* meaning a cupboard which is itself a toy. *Long* is an adjective in *he hasn't lived here long,* in *that happened long ago,* and in *he'll be back before long. Hard* is an adjective in *he works hard. Easy* is an adjective in *easy does it* and in *take it easy. Recently* is an adverb in *until recently. Yes* is an absolute in *a yes man. No* is a pronoun in *no better,* and *much* in *much worse* and in *I didn't like it much.* The *poor* of *the poor suffered most* and the *know* of *he's in the know* present special problems, since they have articles modifying them as determiners just as articles modify nouns. But *poor* is usable in this nounal fashion only when it has plural force, and neither *poor* nor *know* accepts other determiners, or adjectives, freely. We had better call *poor* an adjective and *know* a verb even when they are used with determiner *the.*

Inflected forms should be classified with their basic forms as much as possible. Thus though possessives function much more like determinative pronouns than like their own common-case forms, they should be classified with their common-case forms. But many words of gerundial and participial origin require noun and adjective classifications in some of their uses. Thus *singing* had better be called a noun when adjectives and/or determiners precede it or could easily be placed before it. In *window washing is exciting up here* the word *washing* had better be called a noun, since *window washing* is not clausal in structure. In *washing windows is exciting up here,* the same word had better be called a verb form functioning as predicator in a gerundial clause without expressed subject but with implied general subject. In *Spanish-speaking students* the word *speaking* is best called an adjective; in *they ended the year speaking Spanish* it had better be called a verb form functioning as predicator in a clause whose subject is suggested by the main subject.

Simple definitions of the names of the parts of speech can obviously be useful. Those which we all learned from the school grammars and handbooks have now been demolished, and we have nothing to take their place. Perhaps, as Jespersen thought, we cannot make simple definitions which are also accurate, just as we cannot make a simple definition of the word *dog* which is also accurate. But we can formulate fairly compact statements of the characteristic syntactic behavior of our verbs, nouns, adjectives, adverbs, absolutes, and pronouns.

SUMMARY

[1] Although nearly everybody agrees that the parts-of-speech categories in grammars texts are unsatisfactory, this approach is less revolutionary than many being offered.

[2] Parts-of-speech categories based in phonology, morphology, or the meanings of words are not satisfactory.

[3] Two functional criteria are useful as bases for judging parts of speech: functions which words characteristically perform and kinds of modifiers characteristically placed before words.

[4] We must then at the beginning distinguish between functions and parts of speech. Major functions are: predicators, subjects, complements, and adjuncts. We must accept the reality of syntactic ellipsis. We must recognize the following "contained" functions: heads and modifiers, principals and appositives, prepositions and objects, and coordinates; and also such "collateral" functions as that of clause markers.

[5] With these assumptions we can satisfactorily describe the parts of speech of all normal English. Our parts of speech are:

1. *Verbs,* which function as predicators, accept "subjects" as prepositive modifiers, and with few exceptions follow patterns of inflection.

2. *Nouns,* which function as subjects, complements, and objects; take "adjectives" and "determiners" as prepositive modifiers; and usually inflect for plural number and possessive case; with three subcategories:
   (a) pluralizers, like *house, boy*
   (b) quantifiables, like *furniture, sugar*
   (c) proper nouns, like *Chicago, George*

3. *Adjectives,* which function as prepositive modifiers of nouns and as complements of *be,* and take adverbs as prepositive modifiers (some inflect for comparison).

4. *Adverbs,* which function as adjuncts to predicators, as prepositive modifiers of adjectives, adverbs, and prepositional phrases, as prepositions, and as post-positive contained modifiers; and take other adverbs as prepositive modifiers (a few inflect for comparison); with six or more subcategories:
   (a) adjective-like words in *-ly,* like *badly, totally*
   (b) clause markers, like *where, because*
   (c) coordinates, like *and, but*
   (d) conjunctives, like *therefore, yet*
   (e) prepositionals, like *of, with*
   (f) miscellaneous, like *rather, soon, well,* and *ago*

5. *Absolutes,* which function as isolates with syntactic value of whole nucleuses; with two subcategories:
   (a) interjections, like *ouch* and *wow*
   (b) substitute words, like *yes* and *no*

6. *Pronouns,* a closed group of words whose functions vary from

determining nouns as subjects to assimilating both the meanings and functions of what would be their head nouns; of two sorts:
(a) determiners of three sorts
(b) nounals of seven sorts

[6]   Some words will be classified at times as different parts of speech, but untypical function itself is not a basis for different classification. Inflected forms should be classified with their basic forms, though their functions may change, unless the attendant syntactical features make reclassification more sensible.

NOTES

Professor Long calls his recent grammar, *The Sentence and Its Parts* (Chicago, 1961), a "traditional" grammar, because his method is like that of such great English grammarians as Sweet, Curme, and Jespersen, who packed their grammars with ideas and illustrations. This essay excellently illustrates that method: a full outline of the essay would amount to the essay itself!

Long's approach is basically functional, and as it has already been pointed out (p. 144), functional concepts in grammar are the most difficult to pin down. "Subject," "modifier," "complement," "predicator" are all concepts with which grammarians have long wrestled without achieving completely satisfactory results. If you find yourself a bit unsure of the meaning of these terms, you may derive some consolation from the fact that a host of distinguished grammarians have also found themselves rather befuddled about them. But if you will study the numerous examples given by Professor Long, you may be pleasantly surprised to find how much they help bring into focus the terms they are illustrating. Again, if you suspect that at times Professor Long is arbitrary in his pronouncements (*e.g.*, the subject is a modifier of the predicator; why not the other way around?), you will be in more or less respectable company. But if you think about these matters, you will realize that seemingly arbitrary statements have not been made thoughtlessly.

In short, this essay is tough going. But it is correspondingly rewarding to those who will study it to winnow out its complexities. Perhaps a word or so will start you in the right direction in your understanding of this essay.

In section [3] we get the two main bases upon which Professor Long proceeds: (1) syntactic functions and (2) prepositive modifiers. A word about each may help you.

The chief syntactical functions are the three which combine to form the "clause nucleus": subject, predicator, and complement. A few short sentences will illustrate these three:

SUBJECT	PREDICATOR	COMPLEMENT
Boys	like	girls
Mary	could be	jealous

Mothers	hate	violence
Dancing	is	fun
Men	are	deceivers
We	are going	—

This is what you have probably long since learned as subject, verb, and complement; as Professor Long promised, his grammar is not "revolutionary." By "adjuncts" he means the various modifiers lying "outside" these basic three elements—not literally outside, as the first example below shows, but "outside" in the sense of "less immediate grammatical importance."

Boys *usually* like girls.
Men are deceivers *ever*.
Mary could be jealous, *Henry*.

Prepositive modifiers are modifiers "placed before" other words. Here are some examples of various sorts:

PREPOSITIVE MODIFIER	NOUN
honest	work
big	boy
easy	lesson

PREPOSITIVE MODIFIER	ADJECTIVE
very	honest
extremely	honest
too	easy

PREPOSITIVE MODIFIER	VERB
smoothly	paddled
barely	seen
completely	painted

These are the basic ideas upon which Long's analysis operates, and both are "syntactical" ideas—ideas having to do with the relationships between words. Very likely you have already met them, though perhaps under different names, in your study of grammar. This fact may help you understand the essay.

Section [5], in which Professor Long outlines his part-of-speech categories, is by far the longest section of this essay. The sections preceding it are crucial to our understanding of it, and they should be studied with care. Long keeps the functions which words perform and their part-of-speech classes separate. "Subject" is a function; "noun" is a part of speech. Subjects are often nouns and nouns are often subjects, but not always in either case. Besides, nouns have other characteristics in addition to their functional ones, most notably characteristics of form. Long, though he takes function as the most important criterion in grammatical analysis, realizes that other observations must be made. He sees that no *one* basis for analysis will fully explain so complicated a language as ours.

Grammarians who follow the "formal" or "structural" approaches to our langauge have the real and immediate advantages of clarity and coherence of grammatical theory. It is not hard to see why they have achieved such success in recent years. The most persuasive criticism of their grammars, however, has been that they do not explain very satisfactorily the range, richness, and complexity of modern English: their approaches suggest that the language is simpler than it really is. Professor Long's approach leaves no question of the complexity of our language. But some feel that his description, relying as it does upon difficult and rather slippery basic concepts, is in its own way deceptive, too: the basic ideas of a functional grammar are not immediately clear or simple. Unhappily, no English grammarian has been able to combine the qualities of simplicity and clarity with those of richness and complexity.

The ideal English grammar is yet to be written. Meanwhile, it does us little good to complain that grammars are different, and quite fundamentally so. Some of us may wish that the prose writings of Jonathan Swift matched those of John Milton in richness, complexity, and imagination. We may complain, with Samuel Johnson, that Swift "never hazards a metaphor." On the other hand, we may wish that Milton's writings shared Swift's directness, lucidity, and precision. But our wishes are nugatory. And it may be that we really shouldn't want things otherwise. In any event, it is from the merits of writers that we learn.

From the merits of various grammarians we may learn much about our language. From a listing of their shortcomings we can hope to gain little beyond self-congratulation and complacency, questionable acquisitions at best. Certainly no college or university was ever founded to seek for them.

Transformations[1]

PAUL A. OLSON

A medievalist and professor of English at the University of Nebraska, Paul A. Olson has become a leader in the nation-wide movement to build an articulated English curriculum for American schools through his work with the Nebraska Curriculum Development Center. This short selection from A Curriculum for English, *the preparation of which Mr. Olson directed and edited, shows his ability to translate abstract linguistic and literary concepts into terms which teachers and students can readily grasp.*

[1] If we imagine language as a kind of game we play with words, sounds, and strings of words and sounds, we shall perhaps gain a certain insight into parts of its working. That is, we can think of words, sounds, and strings of words and sounds as pieces in, say, such a game as chess. The pieces in such a game can be moved about to form a variety of patterns, but the patterns which can be formed are determined by something we call "the rules of the game." Thus, in chess, we can move a knight out of the back row without moving any pawns in front of it, but, before we can move the bishop out of the same row, we must move one of the pawns which sit on a diagonal in front of it. When we begin the game, we know that our pieces can be moved from "starting position" according to prescribed rules and thus we have a certain number of likely opening gambits open to us. After the game gets

---

1. The present discussion is not intended as a contribution to transformation theory; it is intended as a precis of Noam Chomsky's *Syntactic Structures* (The Hague, 1957) and is directed toward giving elementary and secondary school teachers a rough understanding of Mr. Chomsky's approach as described in *Syntactic Structures*. I have simplified Chomsky's discussion, removed the apparatus which he takes over from symbolic logic, and given a very truncated description of the so-called morphophonemic aspects of Chomsky's procedure; I have done this in the interests of accessibility. The student should be encouraged to consult Mr. Chomsky's own work.

From Paul A. Olson, *A Curriculum for English* (Nebraska Council of English, 1961). Reprinted by courtesy of the council.

going, though we may feel that we can move our pieces a good deal more freely, particularly after our "strong" pieces have got free of the pawns, though the configurations which we can devise at such stages in the game are almost infinitely various and complicated, yet we know that every move that we make must obey a rule. We cannot "remake the board" to our tastes and still be playing chess; we can't move the bishop in an L pattern, however handy that might be for the purposes of defeating our opponent.

Now if we keep this idea in mind as a kind of general analogy, it may help us to understand what linguistics speak of as transformations. There are certain kinds of moves that we can make with certain words in relation to their sentence in the same way that there are certain moves that we can make with a chess piece in relation to its board. There are other moves which are not allowed to the English speaker, for, if he makes them, he will cease to be speaking English.

Let us take a simple sentence:

The farmer brought in the chickens.

Now one of the moves that one can make with this sentence is:

The farmer brought the chickens in.

However, other moves or series of moves do not seem so allowable:

In the chickens the farmer brought.
The farmer the chickens in brought.
Chickens the the farmer in brought.

We are inclined to say, of the last sentence, "But that isn't English," and we would be right.

[2]   Let us take a fairly simple sentence and see what kinds of moves we can make with it: Let us take the sentence, *The boy pets the dog.* We can divide it into two parts, a noun phrase, *the boy* and a verb phrase *pets the dog.* The noun phrase divides into two parts, *the* and *boy,* an article and a noun. The verb phrase can be divided into two parts, a verb, *pets,* and another noun phrase, *the dog.* If we were describing how to put together a sentence of this kind, we might say, "You are trying to make a sentence which consists of a noun phrase and a verb phrase. The noun phrase contains an article and a noun, the verb phrase a

verb and a second noun phrase which can also be broken into an article and a noun." One might diagram the process in this way:

Noun phrase	Verb phrase
Article-Noun	Verb phrase
Article-Noun	Verb-Noun phrase
The Noun	Verb-Noun phrase
The boy	Verb-Noun phrase
The boy	*pets* Article-Noun
The boy	*pets the* Noun
The boy	*pets the dog.*

Now it is clear that this series of steps, however artificial it may seem, will work for a great many English sentences. I can put in different verbs, different nouns, different articles according to the pattern suggested by the formula, and each sentence that I manufacture according to the formula will be, grammatically speaking, an English sentence though I should write *A dinosaur squeezes the syllogism,* or some such nonsense. I have, in short, constructed "rules" for what the transformationists call the "phrase structure" part of grammar, I have described the holes and pegs which go with very simple sentences.[2]

The sentence I have constructed is a simple sentence. It is as if I were placing pieces on a game board and had chess squares labelled Article-Noun-Verb-Article-Noun and had placed, on these squares, the pieces *The-boy-pets-the-dog.* I could have placed other pieces in the same squares just so that they were the kinds of pieces required by the squares. A *dinosaur squeezes the syllogism* is all right, but *Dinosaur a syllogism the squeezes* is no good because I haven't put the articles, nouns, and verbs where they belong. Now one might consider this the opening set up in a game; all the pieces are in their places, and, of course, I can expand the noun phrase and the verb phrase so that I will say *The pretty bright boy pets the big, brown collie dog.* I have here simply expanded the word groups, put several pieces on one square, and this is neither a complicated move nor the kind of

2. The phrase structure rules also include rules for the incorporation of the auxiliary verb into the verb phrase. The modal auxiliary allows one to substitute for the verb in the Article-Noun-Verb-Noun pattern (*The man pets the dog*) a modal auxiliary plus the verb (*will pet, can pet, may pet, shall pet, must pet*). The regular auxiliary patterns allow one to substitute for the verb the *have* and *be* forms of the auxiliary and combinations of these.—Noam Chomsky, *Syntactic Structures,* p. 39.

move with which the linguist interested in transformations much concerns himself.

[3]   We may speak of substitutions, situations in which we substitute new words in old patterns as we can put new chess pieces on old chess boards. However, we may also speak of transformations. A transformation is a shifting around of the pattern in which we place the words itself, as if we could move the queen's square, in a game of chess, over by a rook's square or put two black squares together. Transformation grammar is concerned with when we can move the squares of the Article-Noun-Verb-Article-Noun pattern (and similar simple ones) around, and it describes the rules of the game.[3]

I. For instance, the passive commonly moves the squares:

    The boy is petting the dog.
     1   2 3   4   5   6
    art. N aux V   art. N
    noun phrase verb phrase

The passive transformation changes this all around:

    The dog is being petted by the boy.
     5   6 3 New   4 New 1   2

II. The verb particle transformation moves as follows:

    The boy brushed down the dog.
     1   2   4   part. 5   6
    art. N   verb   part. art. N

One may say:

    The boy brushed the dog down.
     1   2   4   5   6 part.

When one substitutes the pronoun, *him,* for *dog,* one must use the latter construction:

    The boy brushed him down.
     1   2   4   5(6) part.

Not:

    The boy brushed down him.
     1   2   4   part. 5(6)

The latter sentence alters the meaning. The pronoun-particle

3. Cf. Noam Chomsky, *Syntactic Structures,* p. 43, rule 37.

transformation is obligatory.

III. For the verb-complement transformation, we begin with the passive set-up:

The dog was considered mad   by   the boy.
5   6   new   4   part. new 1   2

However, we cannot transform this construction into the normal active order without separating verb and complement. We do not say:

The boy considered mad the dog.
1   2   4   comp. 5   6

We say:

The boy considered the dog mad.
1   2   4   5   6 comp.

The backshifting of the complement part of the verb phrase is like the backshifting of the particle part of the verb phrase.

IV. The negative transformation is as follows: We have a "not" construction in a sentence using an auxiliary; we add the *not* to the auxiliary:

The boy can't pet the dog.
The boy won't pet the dog.
The boy hasn't petted the dog.
The boy isn't petting the dog.

However, where we have no auxiliary, we cannot add the *not* to the main verb:

The boy petsn't the dog.

We must add the affix bearer *do* and attach the affix *s* and the *not* to it:

The boy doesn't pet the dog.[4]
1   2   affix 4(3) 5   6

Do functions only as an affix bearer here.

V. Sometimes the word *do* functions as a stress bearer. Thus, we say:

The boy cán pet the dog.
1   2   3   4   5   6

4. Chomsky, p. 62, rules 37 ff.

/
The boy will pet the dog.
  1   2   3   4   5   6

But, where we have not such a "meaningful" auxiliary, and wish to stress the verb phrase, we introduce *do* as a stress bearer:

/
The boy does pet the dog.
  1   2 stress 4 5   6

Do functions only as a stress bearer.

VI. The question transformation. Examine the following sentences:

(a)   The boy pets the dog.
         1   2   4   5   6
(b)   The boy can pet the dog.
         1   2   3   4   5   6
(c)   The boy has petted the dog.
         1   2   3   4   5   6
(d)   The boy is petting the dog.
         1   2   3   4   5   6

The question transformation for (b), (c), (d) is identical:

(b)   Can the boy pet the dog?
         3   1   2   4   5   6
(c)   Has the boy petted the dog?
         3   1   2   4   5   6
(d)   Is the boy petting the dog?
         3 1   2   4   5   6

However, for (a) there are several possibilities:

(1)   Pets the boy the dog?   [a bit clumsy]
         4   1   2   5   6
(2)   Does the boy pet the dog?
        affix 1   2   4   5   6

Do fills the slot of the auxiliary but only as an affix bearer in the interrogative transformation. We also have the *what* transformation for questions:

The boy pets the dog.
The boy did pet the dog.
Did the boy pet the dog? (Did the boy pet what?)
What did the boy pet?

The *who* transformation simply substitutes *who* for the noun phrase:

The boy pets the dog.
Who pets the dog?

[4] Transformation grammars are synthetic rather than analytic. They begin with generalizations or rules about simple sentence patterns, about where the "squares" go in those patterns: Article-Noun-Verb-Article-Noun patterns; Articles-Noun-Verb-Article-Noun-Article-Noun patterns, etc. These are called *phrase structure* rules (noun phrase-verb phrase rules) and are similar to the syntactic rules of the older linguistic grammarians (the four basic syntactic patterns: N, V, N; N, V, N, N; etc.). Transformation grammars, second (and here they are new), go on to show how the "squares" or "notches" in the simple sentence patterns are moved about in variations of the simple patterns (or "transformations" generated by them). The examples given above are a simple version of a few of these transformation rules. Finally, these grammars show that such syntactic moves also affect the endings and sounds we assign to words; they affect phonology and morphology, and, for this, the transformation grammarians have a third set of rules, called "morphophonemic" rules. The older linguists tended to begin with the smallest unit, the sound, and to describe sounds, words, and syntax separately. The "transformation" grammarians began with the largest unit, the sentence and its variant patterns, and endeavor to show how the forms and sounds of words are determined by the larger pattern in which they are placed. They attempt to subsume the analysis of morphology and phonology in the analysis of syntax.

Transformation grammar is still young, and its more technical aspects are still too difficult for students. However, teachers should be aware of the new development, for it may become important in the teaching of language. Paul Roberts, for instance, is said to be writing a new grammar based less on the structural approach of his old book than the transformation approach; texts of this kind may become both standard and usable in the near future. For the time being, we suggest only that teachers exhibit the more common transformations according to the method suggested in the primary language section.

SUMMARY

[1] As in chess we may make only certain moves of pieces on the board, so in our language we may make only certain moves of words in sentences, if we are to remain within the "rules of the game" of our language.

[2] The phrase structure of modern English is the background

against which transformations work. This phrase structure may be thought of as a systematic series of divisions of the sentence-as-a-whole.

[3]   A transformation is a systematic shifting of the parts of the phrase-structure patterns. Examples are the transformations for passive voice, of verb particles, for negation, of stress-bearing auxiliary verbs, and for various questions.

[4]   Transformation grammars are synthetic, rather than analytic. They begin with generalizations about the language—about the phrase structure, possible transformations, and the effect of syntactical changes upon morphology and phonology.

NOTE

The chief text of the transformational or generative grammar is Noam Chomsky's *Syntactic Structures* (The Hague: Mouton, 1957). A very difficult book, it is in large part a criticism of the analytical "structural" grammars; it provides only the outline of the transformational or generative approach to modern English. No full transformational or generative grammar of English has yet appeared (1964); but some use has been made of the transformational ideas which Professor Olson here discusses, most notably by Paul Roberts in his text for secondary schools, *English Sentences* (New York: Harcourt, Brace and World, 1961).

Two Approaches to Languages

"Transformational" or "generative" grammar has caused a great stir in linguistic circles since the appearance of Noam Chomsky's Syntactic Structures *in 1957. In this essay, which first appeared in* PMLA, *Professor Myers, of Arizona State University, places the new ideas in a historical and theoretical framework.*

[1] We all know that *linguist* has lately become a magic word. Men who used to be merely English or Spanish professors find that when they are called by this term they are welcomed almost as equals by ecologists and astrophysicists; and scientifically trained administrators on public platforms, anxious to show the breadth of their interests but not feeling quite up to coming out in favor of poetry, are happy to be able to bow in the direction of departments that once seemed hopeless. For the first time within living memory there is even a good deal of money and patronage available for language students—as long as they are labeled linguists.

It would take a wretch lost to all proper feeling to rock a boat as lovely as this, and I am none such. I enjoy being a linguist, if only because fewer people now start looking for an exit when introduced to me. But if our serene voyage is to continue much longer there are a few precautions we ought to take. There is an old saying about how many people you can fool for how long. If we don't want the tide of opinion to become uncomfortably choppy, we had better start talking a little less complacently about the state of our discipline.

[2] We might begin by outlawing the rather pathetic slogan that "linguistics is a rigorous science," since its obvious inaccuracy alienates many competent observers at once. Then we can con-

Reprinted from *Publications of the Modern Language Association*, Supplement to Vol. 77 (September 1962), with the permission of the Modern Language Association of America.

sider the implications of Gleason's more moderate estimate of the situation: ". . . in some places, linguistics has achieved an appreciable measure of scientific rigor and has the foundations for further development in this regard." [1] He does not here specify the places, but he provides a useful clue:

Descriptive linguistics is concerned with two very different but intimately related tasks. The first is to describe individual languages or dialects in terms of their own characteristic structure. For each of the numerous speech forms this is a separate task; the structure of no other language is directly relevant. . . .
The second task of descriptive linguistics is to develop a general theory of language structure—that is, to set up a conceptual framework within which an investigator can work as he seeks to understand a specific language. This theory must be sufficiently general and flexible to provide for any type of language structure that may be encountered, but also sufficiently precise and systematic to give real help. [2]

It seems to me that Gleason exaggerates the intimacy of the relation between these two tasks. Something over fifty years ago Saussure made an illuminating (though not precisely demonstrable) division of speech into langue and parole. Langue is a social institution, a set of conventions that each speaker must (more or less) master; parole is actual speaking. Any act of parole would be utterly meaningless if it were not a reflection of an underlying langue, but it can only be a reflection, and may involve a very considerable distortion. American linguists, following Bloomfield, [3] have usually approached through parole and concentrated on Gleason's first task. Most European linguists have followed Saussure, who declared that linguistics is properly concerned with langue alone. [4] The typical American position, certainly influenced by the availability of hitherto undescribed Indian languages to direct observation, will here be called anthro-

1. H. A. Gleason, *An Introduction to Descriptive Linguistics,* rev. ed. (New York, 1961), p. 12. [In this text on p. 11—Ed.]
2. *Ibid.,* p. 440.
3. "The only useful generalizations about language are inductive generalizations. Features which we think ought to be universal may be absent from the very next language that becomes accessible." Leonard Bloomfield, *Language* (New York, 1933), p. 20.
4. Ferdinand de Saussure, *Cours de Linguistique Générale* (Paris, 1916), p. 40. The book was not actually written by Saussure, but compiled, from notes on his lectures, by two of his students, Charles Bally and Albert Sechehaye. It has been translated into English by Wade Baskin as *Course in General Linguistics* (New York, 1959).

pological; and the European one, with its emphasis on underlying abstract relations, mathematical. There are linguists on both sides who dislike this terminology, since they prefer to call their own approach simply scientific, and the opposite one worthless.

[3] The anthropological linguists, studying each language on its own merits and in its own time, feel that the investigator should make his description directly from the immediate evidence. Resemblance to any other language should be regarded as no more than a coincidence, and any theory of historical development should at least be postponed until there is an ample supply of synchronic descriptions. Linguists using this approach may be careful, methodical, able, and generally admirable; but they can't very well be rigorous, because their job is not of a kind in which rigor is possible.

The mathematical linguists are basically interested in abstract relations and only secondarily concerned with physical phenomena of any sort. They do not regard the parole of native informants as the inviolable raw data from which inductive generalizations must be drawn, but rather as a sort of haze they must see through in order to get at the real organization of the underlying langue. Starting with postulates and proceeding by deduction, they want to work out the basic general laws of linguistic structure in such a comprehensive way that the structure of any given language will appear as a special case. In such work rigor is perfectly possible, but of course it applies only to the internal consistency of the theoretical system. The question of how accurately this system describes the actual phenomena of human communication is quite another matter.

To summarize the differences, anthropological linguists are concerned with the practical task of making useful descriptions of such languages as they encounter, while mathematical linguists are concerned with investigating the underlying structure of "language itself." It is of course possible for a man to be (at different times) both a geometer and a practical surveyor. But the two tasks remain fundamentally different; and though the findings of each may prove helpful to the other, we cannot simply add them together without getting most peculiar results. The second paragraph quoted from Gleason provides an example. If each language must be examined for itself, and the structure of no other language is directly relevant (anthropological), a general theory of language structure (mathematical) seems quite as likely to be an obstacle as an aid to accurate investigation. When this idea first occurred to them the anthropological linguists threw out (quite noisily) the old concept of universal grammar. To reintroduce the concept one level higher under the guise of universal analysis seems dubious progress.

It would certainly be convenient to find a general theory both sufficiently flexible to apply to any language and sufficiently precise and systematic to give real help in analyzing each one; but no evidence has yet been produced to indicate that any such theory is possible. We simply do not know that, either by common origin or by coincidence, all languages have enough in common to permit any one linguistic theory to provide for grammars that will usefully describe them all. It is of course clear that *some* languages have enough in common to be susceptible to compatible, though not identical, treatments, and that there would be decided advantages in having adequate grammars of these languages based on a common linguistic theory. But what is clearly true of some is not necessarily true of all, and the search for a universal theory may turn out to be as hopeless as the search for the Northwest Passage. Meanwhile it is using up a lot of valuable time, for many problems that could be handled quite simply by special theories are being complicated considerably in the hope that their treatment will fit in with the universal picture when it finally emerges.

[4]   Perhaps the best way to illustrate this point is to consider certain aspects of, and reactions to, Chomsky's *Syntactic Structures,* which for the past few years has been causing both excitement and confusion in linguistic circles. This is by our definition a completely mathematical treatment, though Chomsky prefers to call it Saussurean. As such it seems to me extremely interesting and definitely valuable. I am not surprised that it has converted some linguists from the anthropological to the mathematical approach. What does surprise me is that a good many linguists who continue to proclaim the anthropological faith seem to be rather placidly trying to fit Chomsky into it, with no awareness of the fundamental conflict.

Chomsky not only avoids phonetics but barely touches on phonemics. He says specifically that his monograph forms part of an attempt to construct a formalized theory of linguistic structure in which the descriptive devices utilized in particular grammars are presented and studied abstractly, with no specific references to particular languages. His investigations convince him that grammars have a naturally tripartite arrangement. Specifically:

> A grammar has a sequence of rules from which phrase structure can be reconstructed and a sequence of morphophonemic rules that convert strings of morphemes into strings of phonemes. Connecting these sequences, there is a sequence of transformational rules that carry strings with a phrase structure into new strings to which the morphophonemic rules apply.[5]

As an illustration he develops a tentative and partial grammar of English containing eleven rules of phrase structure, two morphophonemic rules (with a few others suggested), and sixteen transformational rules. It is clear that he has limited the sections on phrase structure and morphophonemics (which would be extremely large in a full grammar of this type) to the minimum required to provide him with material for developing the section on transformations, which is the really new and interesting part of the work.

The phrase-structure section is a kind of constituent analysis with such rules as "*Sentence→NP+VP*," "*NP→T+N*," and "*N→ man, ball*, etc." [Here *NP* stands for *noun phrase, VP* for *verb phrase, T* for *the*, and *N* for *noun*.] Each rule of the form "*X→Y*" is to be interpreted as "rewrite *X* as *Y*." And each *Y* is either an analysis of the corresponding *X* into smaller parts or the substitution of a specific example for the symbol of a type. The morphophonemic section has rules of a similar form, such as "*walk→* /wɔk/" and "*take+past→*/tuk/." Obviously in a full grammar of this type each of these sections must include the whole lexicon— the phrase-structure section by listing all the members of each of the categories (which will apparently be considerably more numerous than the traditional parts of speech), and the morphophonemic section as a sort of pronouncing dictionary (though I am sure Chomsky would never call it that).

Chomsky says that a grammar of English could conceivably consist of these parts alone; but:

> We can greatly simplify the description of English and gain new and important insight into its formal structure if we limit the direct descrip-

5. Noam Chomsky, *Syntactic Structures* (The Hague, 1957), p. 107.

tion in terms of phrase structure to a kernel of basic sentences (simple declarative, active, with no complex verb or noun phrases), deriving all other sentences from these (more properly, from the strings that underlie them) by transformation, possibly repeated. (pp. 106–107)

The "strings that underlie them" are the sequences of symbols that represent the order of morphemic elements in legitimate English sentences.

[5] When Chomsky says that we can "greatly simplify the description" by the use of transformations he is speaking from the somewhat specialized viewpoint of a mathematical linguist. I know English students, and even instructors, who would not regard the following rule as a particularly simple way of indicating where to put *not* or *n't* into a sentence to make it negative:

T_{not}—optional
Structural analysis:
$$\begin{cases} NP-C-V \cdots \\ NP-C+M- \cdots \\ NP-C+have- \cdots \\ NP-C+be- \cdots \end{cases}$$
Structural change: $X_1-X_2-X_3 \rightarrow X_1-X_2+n't-X_3$ (p. 112)

They might even be upset to find that many of the sentences derived by application of this transformation would be utterly impossible until they were corrected by another transformation of which this one contains no hint.

I do not wish to imply that the transformational theory is silly. On the contrary, it is extremely illuminating, particularly as it shows that certain aspects of English structure that have hitherto appeared anomalous are perfectly regular if we dig deep enough for the underlying pattern. There is no doubt whatever that *Syntactic Structures* makes some important contributions to our knowledge of English.

It does not, however, show much promise of leading to a comprehensive description of the ways that people, with all their inconsistencies, actually talk; rather it is a step in the development of a program by means of which machines (probably electronic, though a few flesh-and-blood ones might qualify) may some day be able to communicate. Though it is based on habits that happen to have developed, it in effect prescribes these habits (or rather a systematic selection from them) for future use, and demands that they be followed with a rigidity of which no considerable speech community has yet proved capable. For example, failure to make a verb-form agree with a remote subject is not merely a slip, but "the result will simply not be a sentence" (p. 45). In fact, except for the recognition that *not* may appear as *n't*, there is scarcely a mention of any possible human variation—nothing on dialects, only a very little on intonation (and that little very tentative), and nothing about the interaction of sounds as they occur in the flow of speech. Instead the whole analysis is of rigid, unvarying elements.

This is of course natural—in fact, inevitable—in a formal and rigorous system. We cannot reliably make even such a simple transformation as *x–y–z* into *x–z–y* if the elements blend with and influence each other; if significant contrasts are only relative; or if one man's *x* is another man's *y*, as it often is in ordinary speech. But when such a system completely ignores irregularities that are well known to exist it follows that there are some limitations to the ways in which it can be usefully applied.

Consider, for instance, the passive transformation:

> *Passive*—optional:
> Structural analysis: *NP–Aux–V–NP*
> Structural change: $X_1–X_2–X_3–X_4$
> $\rightarrow X_4–X_2–+be+en$
> $–X_3–by+X_1$ (p. 112)

This says in effect that if any utterance of the form "The dog bit the boy" is a grammatical sentence, then "The boy was bitten by the dog," derived by applying the transformation, is also a grammatical sentence.

At first glance this may seem like a mouse from a laboring mountain. We all know that most active sentences can be shifted into the passive, and can say so in a way that seems simpler than this. But our first reaction is unfair. Chomsky's mathematical statement is both more precise and more compatible with statements about other transformations than any that we should be likely to make, so that it will work out better in really complicated situations. Moreover, unlike ours, it has no exceptions whatever. To clarify this point I wrote him to ask what he would do about such sentences as "This room seats thirty people," "The dress becomes Mary," and "The climate suits his health." He answered: "As to rule (34), the examples that you mentioned, and similar ones, I think can best be regarded as showing that *becomes, seats, suits, weighs,* etc. are not transitive verbs, in line with the reasoning on pp. 83, 84."

Here once again we must be careful of our reactions. It is natural enough to think: "That's ridiculous. In the sentence given, *becomes* is exactly parallel to *adorns*, and everybody knows that *adorns* is a transitive verb, so of course becomes is too." But *becomes* is not parallel to *adorns* in its reaction to this particular transformation, and Chomsky has the mathematician's right to refine his definition in order to avoid a contradiction. He is in quite a different position from an experimental scientist, who has no right whatever to disregard a piece of physical evidence because it happens to conflict with his theory.

[6] It seems probable that Chomsky's work will be of considerable importance in machine translation and in such other machine communication as may be developed. Here the reordering of the elements in many of the formulas, which would be very difficult for most people to grasp, will cause no trouble; nor will the proper sequence in the application of the various transformations, which would put an intolerable burden on most human memories. And of course machine translation positively demands that the grammars of the languages involved in any one operation be based on the same underlying linguistic theory. This theory need not, however, be universal.

It might well prove better to have two quite different machine grammars of English, one compatible with Russian and another compatible with Chinese. Such grammars may be complete in the sense that they will do all that is required of them, but it seems likely that the lexicon will be reduced to a manageable figure and that the rules of phrase structure and transformation will somewhat limit the range of stylistic variation. It is now possible to envision the routine electronic translation of scientific papers and other factual discourse, but hardly of poetry or some other kinds of imaginative work.

Chomsky himself, however, tells me that he has no interest at all in machine translation or any other machine use of language. What does interest him is "a precise description of a set of abilities possessed by humans" which play a role in speaking and perceiving of sentences. The representation of this set of abilities is, he says, the grammar of the language. If the description is really precise it can be regarded as a set of instructions for an abstract machine, but he considers it a matter of no importance whether such a machine, or computer program, is actually constructed.[6]

The phrase "a precise description of a set of abilities possessed by humans" seems to imply that humans are a good deal more regular—more machinelike—in their linguistic reactions than my own experience would indicate. It would be silly for me to attempt a public argument with Chomsky on this point, since neither one of us claims any special competence in psychology or neurology; but it does seem to me that anyone who has spent much time trying to weed out some of the more conspicuous irregularities that crop up in a batch of themes would be likely to take my side. Altogether I am considerably puzzled to find that some of my friends who used to call themselves anthropological linguists now (a) don't seem to notice that this grammar is completely prescriptive, and (b) do seem to think that *these* prescriptions can be developed and applied, to the great benefit of all concerned. I do not, myself, regard *prescriptive* as a nasty word in all contexts; but, like most of us, I feel that any set of prescriptions for people who want to use standard English should be based on a very careful and accurate description of the habits of people who already use it, with no gross oversimplification of the very considerable variety that such people exhibit.

[7]   For this reason the expansion of Chomsky's sketch into a fairly complete description of human habits in the use of standard English appears impracticable. With no arbitrary limit on either the lexicon or the variety permissible in the syntax it seems likely that both the size and the complexity of the product would put it beyond the range of human usefulness. Moreover, it would necessarily depart so far from the simplicity and elegance that attract Chomsky that it is hard to see how anybody capable of compiling it would be interested in doing so.

I do not of course mean that there can be no further interesting developments. There have already been a number, by Chomsky himself and others, which we needn't go into here, and there are bound to be more. But quite aside from the prohibitive size of a complete grammar of this sort, I simply cannot find out what it is to be about. Chomsky says: "The grammar of L [a given language] will thus be a device that generates all of the grammatical

6. I sent Chomsky a draft of this paper, got a rather extensive criticism in reply, and have made some modifications as a result, though not as many as he suggested.

sequences of L and none of the ungrammatical ones" (p. 13). I can see, if rather dimly, how this might work out in a machine; and I think I can see quite well how it could work out in an elementary language class, with a carefully selected list of words and a limited number of rules for arranging them. But when I think of the language at large the phrase "all the grammatical sequences of L" becomes completely unreal. I am forced to conclude that Chomsky has taken a very illuminating, but dangerous, remark of Saussure's as the literal truth.

Saussure says: "La langue existe dans la collectivité sous la forme d'une sommes d'empreintes déposées dans chaque cerveau, à peu près comme un dictionnaire dont tous les exemplaires, identiques, seraient répartis entre les individus" (p. 39).* Of course it might be objected that what we all have in our heads that makes it possible for us to talk to each other is more like a grammar than a dictionary, but that is quibbling. The real flaw is that the word *identiques,* placed so emphatically between commas, is false. Our copies are not from a single press run; in spite of all our attempts to make them uniform, they are much more like individual manuscripts—and anybody who doesn't know how much they can vary is invited to examine a page or so of the six-text edition of Chaucer. To collate a few million copies would be a task of some magnitude, though of course it would only be a preliminary step in devising a grammar that would generate all the grammatical sequences of a language, and only those.

There remains the possibility that particular developments of Chomsky's may be incorporated in grammars of a very different kind. Certainly his discussion of transformations is too illuminating to be disregarded, particularly that part of it which is based on section (37), since he proves an underlying regularity in such apparently different types of sentences as yes-or-no questions, negations, stressed statements, and statements after *so,* as well as some apparent anomalies in the use of *have* and *be.* His demonstration here is as fascinating and unexpected as Grimm's Law. However, like Grimm's Law, it is neither comprehensible nor useful to everybody, and it may not prove to be particularly important in grammars designed for general instruction.

* [Baskin's translation of this passage is as follows: "Language exists in the form of a sum of impressions deposited in the brain of each member of a community, almost like a dictionary of which identical copies have been distributed to each individual." (p. 19)—EDITOR'S NOTE.]

Two other aspects of his work may well turn out to be of more significance in the development of improved English grammars. One is his rather casual demonstration that the theory of unmixable levels is unsound. The other is the unintentionally convincing evidence that a rigorous treatment of a language must be both selective and prescriptive. It may therefore be appropriate as a grammar of a rather artificial dialect of written English designed to meet specific editorial standards, but it cannot be an accurate description of speech as it happens. Thus an anthropological linguist who wishes to attempt a purely descriptive grammar can stop bothering about either mathematical rigor or final truth, and concentrate on making an analysis that is reasonably consistent and understandable from a given point of view.

SUMMARY

[1]   Linguists are now respected and popular; if they are to remain so, they must look critically at the state of their discipline.

[2]   Linguists seem interested in two quite different things: on the one hand, descriptions of individual languages in terms of their own structures; on the other hand, a general theory of language structure applicable to all languages. These two interests roughly reflect Saussure's division of speech into *parole* and *langue* and the division between American and European linguists, who might be called, respectively, anthropological and mathematical linguists.

[3]   Anthropological linguists, studying each language inductively, can be methodical, but they cannot hope for logical rigor in their approach. Mathematical linguists, working for a coherent theory of language, can expect logical rigor in their approach, but they cannot be sure that their rigorous theory accurately fits any given language. Though some languages are sufficiently similar to admit of a common grammar, we do not yet know if all languages can be fitted into a single grammatical theory.

[4]   This problem is illustrated in some aspects of and response to Chomsky's *Syntactic Structures*, which attempts to construct a theory of linguistic structure pertinent to all languages. Chomsky maintains that all grammars consist of a triple arrangement: (1) a series of rules for phrase structure, (2) a sequence of morphophonemic rules, and (3) a sequence of transformational rules. To illustrate, Chomsky gives a partial grammar of English, containing eleven rules of phrase structure, two morphophonemic rules (plus others, perhaps), and sixteen transformational rules, only the last of which are worked out reasonably fully. Obviously, a full grammar of this sort would be extremely long and complicated.

[5]   When Chomsky claims that his grammar can "greatly simplify" our grammar, he is speaking as a mathematical linguist and means that his grammar is logically more simple than others. His system offers important insights into the nature of English; but it is more rigorous than the language itself. Being a mathematical linguist, he can rule out whatever in the language fails to fit his theory.

[6]   Chomsky's work will probably be of importance in machine translations of one language into another, though Chomsky protests no interest in such uses of his theory. But as "a precise description of a set of abilities possessed by humans," his theory implies that humans are much more logically consistent in their language than in fact they are.

[7]   Not only would a full grammar following Chomsky's theories be extremely long and complex, but the fundamental assumption that his grammar would be able to "generate" or predict all the "grammatical" sequences possible in a language and none of the "ungrammatical" ones is completely unreal; for human language is individual, not uniform. Some of Chomsky's observations, however, are brilliant and useful for all grammarians.

The Classification of Languages

FREDERICK BODMER

At one time a member of the staff of the University of Cape Town, Frederick Bodmer planned and wrote The Loom of Language, *in collaboration with Lancelot Hogben, as a book to bring the findings of linguistic scientists to the general public.*

[1]   Before there were comparative linguists, practical men already knew that some European languages resemble one another noticeably. The English sailor whose ship brought him for the first time to Amsterdam, to Hamburg, and to Copenhagen was bound to notice that many Dutch, German, and Danish words are the same, or almost the same, as their equivalents in his own tongue. Where he would have said *thirst, come, good,* the Dutchman used the words *dorst, komen, goed;* the German *Durst, kommen, gut;* and the Dane, *Tørst, kom, god.* The Frenchman calling on Lisbon, on Barcelona, and on Genoa discovered to his delight that *aimer* (to love), *nuit* (night), *dix* (ten) differ very little from the corresponding Portuguese words *amar, noute, dez;* Spanish *amar, noche, diez;* or Italian *amare, notte, dieci.* In fact, the difference is so small that use of the French words alone would often produce the desired result. Because of such resemblances, people spoke of *related* languages. By the sixteenth century, three units which we now call the *Teutonic,* the *Romance* or

Chapter 5 from *The Loom of Language* by Frederick Bodmer, and Lancelot Hogben, editor. Reprinted by permission of W. W. Norton & Company, Inc. Copyright 1944 by W. W. Norton & Company, Inc. Published in Canada by George Allen & Unwin Ltd.

Latin, and the *Slavonic* groups were widely recognized. If you know one language in any of these three groups, you will have little difficulty in learning a second one. So it is eminently a practical division.

When the modern linguist still calls English, Dutch, German, Danish, Norwegian, Swedish *related* languages, he means more than this. We now use the term in an evolutionary sense. Languages are *related,* if the many features of vocabulary, structure, and phonetics which they share are due to gradual differentiation of what was once a single tongue. Sometimes we have to infer what the common parent was like; but we have firsthand knowledge of the origin of one language group. The deeper we delve into the past, the more French, Spanish, Italian, etc., converge. Finally they become one in Latin, or, to be more accurate, in *Vulgar* Latin as spoken by the common people in the various parts of the Western Roman Empire.

Like the doctrine of organic evolution, this attitude to the study of languages is a comparatively recent innovation. It was wholly alien to European thought before the French Revolution. For more than two thousand years before that time, grammatical scholarship had existed as a learned profession. During the whole of this period scholars had accepted the fact that languages exist without probing into the origins of their diversity. In Greece the growth of a more adventurous spirit was checked by the prevailing social outlook of a slave civilization. When Christianity became the predominant creed of the Western world, Hebrew cosmogony stifled evolutionary speculation in every field of inquiry.

Investigations of Greek philosophers and grammarians suffered at all times from one fundamental weakness. They were strictly confined to the homemade idiom. This was the inevitable consequence of a cultural conceit which divided the world into Greeks and Barbarians. The same social forces which held back the progress of mechanics and of medicine in the slave civilizations of the Mediterranean world held up the study of grammar. To bother about the *taal* of inferior people was not the proper concern of an Athenian or of a Roman gentleman. Even Herodotus, who had toured Egypt and had written on its quaint customs, nowhere indicates that he had acquired much knowledge of the language.

The Alexandrian conquest brought about little change of mind when Greek traders and travelers were roaming far beyond the Mediterranean basin, establishing intimate contact with Bactrians, Iranians, and even with India. Both Greek and Roman civilization had unrivaled opportunities for getting acquainted with changing phases in the idioms of peoples who spoke and wrote widely diverse tongues. They had unrivaled, and long since lost, opportunities to get some light on the mysteries of ancient scripts such as hieroglyphics and cuneiform. They never exploited their opportunities. The Egyptian hieroglyphic writing was a sealed book till the second decade of the nineteenth century. The decoding of cuneiform inscriptions is a work of the last hundred years.

Christianity performed one genuine service to the study of language, as it performed a genuine service to medicine by promoting hospitals. It threw the opprobrious term *Barbarian* overboard, and thus paved the way for the study of all tongues on their own merits. Before it had come to terms with the ruling class, Christianity was truly the faith of the weary and heavy laden, of the proletarian and the slave without property, without fatherland. In Christ there was "neither Scythian, barbarian, bond nor free, but a new creation." Accordingly the early church ignored social rank and cultural frontiers. All idioms of the globe enjoyed equal rights, and the gift of tongues was in high esteem among the miracles of the apostolic age.

Christian salvation was an act of faith. To understand the new religion the heathen must needs hear the gospel in their own vernaculars. So proselytizing went hand in hand with translating. At an early date, Christian scholars translated the Gospels into Syriac, Coptic, and Armenian. The Bible is the beginning of Slavonic literature, and the translation of the New Testament by the West Gothic Bishop, Ulfilas, is the oldest Germanic document extant. Even today the Christian impulse to translate remains unabated. Our Bible societies have carried out pioneer work in the study of African and Polynesian dialects.

The historical balance sheet of Christian teaching and language study also carries a weighty item on the debit side. The story of the Tower of Babel was sacrosanct, and with it, as a corollary, the belief that Hebrew was the original language of mankind. So the emergence and spread of Christianity was not followed by any deeper understanding of the natural history of language. Throughout the Middle Ages the path trod by the Christian scholar was one already beaten by his pagan forerunner. There was no significant progress in the comparative study of languages, but mercantile venture and missionary enterprise during the age of the Great Navigations made a wealth of fresh material accessible through the new medium of the printed page, and encouraged European scholars to break away from exclusive preoccupation with dead languages. For the first time, they began to recognize that some languages are more alike than others.

Joseph Justus Scaliger (1540–1609), variously recognized as *the phoenix of Europe, the light of the world, the bottomless pit of knowledge*, saw as much, and a little more, when he wrote his treatise on the languages of Europe. He arranged them all in eleven main classes, which fall again into four major and seven minor ones. The four major classes he based on their words for *god*, into *deus-, theos-, gott-*, and *bog-* languages, or, as we should say, into Latin (Romance) languages, Greek, Germanic, and Slavonic. The remaining seven classes are made up of Epirotic or Albanian, Tartar, Hungarian, Finnic, Irish (*that part of it which today is spoken in the mountainous regions of Scotland*, i.e., Gaelic), Old British, as spoken in Wales and Brittany, and finally Cantabrian or Basque.

During the seventeenth century many miscellanies of foreign languages, like the herbals and bestiaries of the time, came off the printing presses of European countries. The most ambitious of them all was the outcome of a project of Leibniz, the mathematician, who was assisted by Catherine II of Russia. The material was handed over to the German traveler, Pallas, for classification. The results of his labor appeared in 1787 under the title, *Linguarum Totius Orbis Vocabularia Comparativa* ("Comparative Vocabularies of All the Languages of the World"). The number of words on the list circulated was 285, and the number of languages covered was 200, of which 149 were Asiatic and 51 European. In a later edition, this number was considerably increased by the addition of African and of Amerindian dialects from the New World. Pallas' compilation was of little use. He had put it together hastily on the basis of superficial study of his materials. Its merit was that it stimulated others to undertake something more ambitious and more reliable. One of them was the Spaniard,

Hervas; another the German, Adelung. Leibniz's suggestions influenced both of them.

Lorenzo Hervas (1735–1809) had lived for many years among the American Indians, and published the enormous number of forty grammars, based upon his contact with their languages. Between 1800 and 1805 he also published a collected work with the title: *Catálogo de las lenguas de las naciones conocidas y numeracion, division y clases de estas segun la diversidad de sus idiomas y dialectos* ("Catalog of the languages of all the known nations with the enumeration, division, and classes of these nations according to their languages and dialects"). This linguistic museum contained three hundred exhibits. It would have been more useful if the author's arrangement of the specimens had not been based on the delusion that there is a necessary connection between race and language. A second encyclopedic attempt to bring all languages together, as duly labeled exhibits, was that of the German grammarian and popular philosopher, Adelung. It bears the title, *Mithridates, or General Science of Languages, with the Lord's Prayer in nearly 500 Languages and Dialects,* published in four volumes between 1806 and 1817. When the fourth volume appeared, Adelung's compilation had become entirely obsolete. In the meantime, Bopp had published his revolutionary treatise on the conjugational system of Sanskrit, Greek, Latin, Persian, and German.

[2]   Previously, there had been little curiosity about the way in which language grows. In the introduction to *Mithridates* Adelung makes a suggestion, put forward earlier by Horne Tooke, without any attempt to check or explore its implications. This remarkable Englishman was one of the first Europeans to conceive a plausible hypothesis to account for the origin of flexion. In a book called *Diversions of Purley,* published in 1786, Tooke anticipates the central theme of the task which Bopp carried out with greater knowledge and success during the first half of the nineteenth century. Thus he writes:

All those common terminations, in any language, of which all Nouns or Verbs in that language equally partake (under the notion of declension or conjugation) are themselves separate words with distinct meanings . . . these terminations are explicable, and ought to be explained.

The work of Bopp and other pioneers of comparative grammar

received a powerful impetus from the study of Sanskrit. Though Sassetti, an Italian of the sixteenth century, had called Sanskrit a *pleasant, musical* language, and had united *Dio* (God) with *Deva*, it had remained a sealed book for almost two hundred years. Now and then some missionary, like Robertus Nobilibus, or Heinrich Roth, a German who was anxious to be able to dispute with Brahmanic priests, made himself acquainted with it, but this did not touch the world at large. After Sassetti, the first European to point out the staggering similarities between Sanskrit and the European languages was the German missionary, Benjamin Schultze. For years he had preached the Gospel to the Indian heathen, and had helped in the translation of the Bible into Tamil. On August 19, 1725, he sent to Professor Franken an interesting letter in which he emphasized the similarity between the numerals of Sanskrit, German, and Latin.

When English mercantile imperialism was firmly grounded in India, civil servants began to establish contact with the present and past of the country. An Asiatic Society got started at Calcutta in 1784. Four years later, a much-quoted letter of William Jones, Chief-justice at Fort William in Bengal, was made public. In it the author demonstrated the genealogical connection between Sanskrit, Greek, and Latin, between Sanskrit and German, and between Sanskrit, Celtic, and Persian:

> The Sanskrit language, whatever be its antiquity, is of a wonderful structure; more perfect than the Greek, more copious than the Latin, and more exquisitely refined than either; yet bearing to both of them a stronger affinity, both in the roots of verbs and in the forms of grammar, than could have been produced by accident; so strong indeed, that no philologer could possibly examine all the three without believing them to have sprung from some common source which, perhaps, no longer exists. There is a similar reason, though not quite so forcible, for supposing that both the Gothic and Celtic, though blended with a different idiom, had the same origin with the Sanskrit.

This happened within a few years of the publication of Hutton's *Theory of the Earth,* a book which challenged the Mosaic account of the creation. Custodians of the Pentateuch were alarmed by the prospect that Sanskrit would bring down the Tower of Babel. To anticipate the danger, they pilloried Sanskrit as a priestly fraud, a kind of pidgin classic concocted by Brahmins from Greek and Latin elements. William Jones, himself a scholar of unimpeachable piety, had to make the secular confession:

I can only declare my belief that the language of Noah is irretrievably lost. After diligent search I cannot find a single word used in common by the Arabian, Indian, and Tartar families, before the admixture of these dialects occasioned by the Mahommedan conquests.

Together with tea and coffee, Napoleon's blockade of England withheld from the Continent Sanskrit grammars and dictionaries which English scholars were now busy turning out. Fortunately the Bibliothèque Nationale in Paris possessed Sanskrit texts. Paris had in custody Hamilton, an Englishman who enlivened his involuntary sojourn in the French capital by giving private lessons in Sanskrit. One of his pupils was a brilliant young German, Friedrich Schlegel. In 1808, Schlegel published a little book, *Über die Sprache und Weisheit der Inder* ("On the Language and Philosophy of the Indians"). This put Sanskrit on the Continental map. Much that is in Schlegel's book makes us smile today, perhaps most of all the author's dictum that Sanskrit is the mother of all languages. None the less, it was a turning point in the scientific study of language. In a single sentence which boldly prospects the field of future research, Schlegel exposes the new impetus which came from contemporary progress of naturalistic studies:

Comparative grammar will give us entirely new information on the *genealogy* of langauge, in exactly the same way in which comparative anatomy has thrown light upon the natural history.

The study of Latin in the Middle Ages had preserved a secure basis for this evolutionary approach to the study of other languages, because the Latin parentage of modern French, Spanish, Portuguese, Italian, and Rumanian is an historically verifiable fact. Unfortunately, history has not been so obliging as to preserve the parent of the Teutonic and the Slavonic groups. To be sure, the present differences between Dutch, German, and the Scandinavian languages diminish as we go back in time. Still, differences remain when we have retraced our steps to the oldest records available. At that point we have to replace the *historical* by the *comparative* method, and to try to obtain by inference what history has failed to rescue. We are in much the same position as the biologist, who can trace the record of vertebrate evolution from bony remains in the rocks, till he reaches the point when vertebrates had not acquired a hard skeleton. Beyond this, anything we can know or plausibly surmise about their origin must be based upon a comparison between the characteristic features of the vertebrate body and the characteristic features of bodily organization among the various classes of invertebrates.

THE BASIS OF EVOLUTIONARY CLASSIFICATION

[3] Biologists who classify animals from an evolutionary point of view make the assumption that characteristics common to all—or to nearly all—members of a group are also characteristic of their common ancestor. Similar reasoning is implicit in the comparative method of studying languages; and those who study the evolution of languages enjoy an advantage which the evolutionary biologist does not share. No large-scale changes in the diversity of animal life on our planet have occurred during the period of the written record, but distinct languages have come into being during comparatively recent times. We can check the value of clues which suggest common parentage of related languages by an almost continuous historical record of what has happened to Latin.

Word similarity is one of the three most important of these clues. It stands to reason that two closely related languages must have a *large* number of recognizably similar words. Comparison of the members of the Romance group shows that this is so. Such resemblance does not signify identity, which may be due to borrowing. Evidence for kinship is strongest if words which are alike are words which are not likely to have passed from one language to the other, or to have been assimilated by both from a third. Such *conservative* words include personal pronouns; verbs expressing *basic* activities or states, such as *come* and *go, give* and *take, eat,* and *drink, live* and *die;* adjectives denoting elementary qualities such as *young* and *old, big* and *small, high* and *deep;* or names which stand for universally distributed objects, such as *earth, dog, stone, water, fire,* for parts of the body such as *head, ear, eye, nose, mouth,* or for blood relationship such as *father, mother, sister, brother.*

If the number of words which two languages share is small, and confined to a special aspect of cultural life, it is almost certain that one is indebted to the other. This applies to word similarities which the Celtic and Teutonic groups do not share with other Aryan languages. The common words of this class are all nouns, some of which are names for metals, tools and vehicles. This does

TENSES OF THE VERB *BE* IN ROMANCE LANGUAGES
(pronouns only used for emphasis in parentheses)

	ENGLISH	FRENCH	SPANISH	LATIN	ITALIAN
Present	I am	je suis	(yo) soy	(ego) sum	(io) sono
	thou art	tu es	(tú) eres	(tu) es	(tu) sei
	he is	il est	(él) es	(ille) est	(egli) è
	we are	nous sommes	(nosotros) somos	(nos) sumus	(noi) siamo
	you are	vous êtes	(vosotros) sois	(vos) estis	(voi) siete
	they are	ils sont	(ellos) son	(illi) sunt	(essi) sono
Past Imperfect	I was (used to be)	*j'étais*	era	eram	ero
	thou wert	*tu étais*	eras	eras	eri
	he was	*il était*	era	erat	
	we were	*nous étions*	éramos	eramus	eravamo
	you were	*vous étiez*	erais	eratis	eravate
	they were	*ils étaient*	eran	erant	erano
Past Definite	I was	je fus	fuí	fui	fui
	thou wert	tu fus	fuiste	fuisti	fosti
	he was	il fut	fué	fuit	fu
	we were	nous fûmes	fuimos	fuimus	fummo
	you were	vous fûtes	fuisteis	fuistis	foste
	they were	ils furent	fueron	fuerunt	furono
Future	I shall be	je serai	seré	*ero*	sarò
	thou wilt be	tu seras	serás	*eris*	sarai
	he will be	il sera	será	*erit*	sarà
	we shall be	nous serons	seremos	*erimus*	saremo
	you will be	vous serez	seréis	*eritis*	sarete
	they will be	ils seront	serán	*erunt*	saranno
	to be	être	ser	esse	essere

not indicate that there is a particularly close evolutionary relationship between Celtic and Teutonic in the sense defined above. Other features show that a wide gulf separates them. Archaeological evidence suggests that the Teutons took over words with the arts they assimilated from Celtic communities at a higher cultural level.

Through such culture contacts words have wandered from one language to another of a totally different origin. The modern word *bicycle* pedals over linguistic frontiers as the machine used to pedal over national boundaries before passports were obligatory. The word material of all, or nearly all, languages is more or less mongrel. Even in the more exclusive members of the Teutonic group the number of intruders is many times larger than the number of words which the linguist thinks he can trace back to the hypothetical common idiom called primitive Teutonic. When dealing with words for numbers, or weights and measures, we have always to reckon with the possibility of cultural, and therefore *word*, diffusion. If vocabulary is the only clue available, we have to give due consideration to geographical situation. If two languages which share a considerable portion of conservative root words are not geographically contiguous, it is highly probable that they are related.

Word similarity is a good clue. A second is agreement with respect to *grammatical behavior*. French, Spanish and Italian, which we may use as our control group, have a host of common grammatical features such as:

1. A future tense which is a combination of the infinitive and the auxiliary *to have*, (Fr. *aimer-ai, aimer-as;* Ital. *amar-ò, amar-ai;* Span. *amar-é, amar-ás.*)

2. The definite article (Fr. masc. *le,* fem. *la,* Span. *el* or *la,* Ital. *il* or *la*), and pronouns of the third person (Fr. *il* or *elle,* Span. *él* or *ella,* Ital. *egli* or *ella*) all derived from the Latin demonstrative *ille, illa.*

3. A twofold gender system in which the masculine noun generally takes the place of the Latin neuter (Fr. *le vin,* the wine; Span. *el vino;* Ital. *il vino;* Latin *vinum*).

Grammatical peculiarities, like words, may be more or less conservative. In the widest sense of the term, grammar includes the study of idiom and sentence construction, or *syntax,* in contradistinction to *accidence,* which deals with the modification of individual words by flexion or root-vowel changes. The syntax of a language is much less conservative than its accidence. When we meet with resemblances of the latter type, it would be far-fetched to attribute them to chance or to borrowing. All the evidence available tends to show that, while words and idioms diffuse freely, peculiarities of *accidence* do not. Now and then a language may borrow a prefix or a suffix, together with a foreign word, and subsequently tack one or the other on to indigenous words, as

German did with *-ei* (*Liebelei,* "flirtation"), which is the French *-ie* (as in *la vilenie,* "villainy"); but we know of no language which has incorporated a whole set of alien endings like those of the Latin verb.

Absence of grammatical resemblance does not invariably mean that two or more languages are unrelated. Once a parent language has split into several new species, the different fragments may move more or less swiftly along similar or different paths. For example, French has discarded more of the luxuriant system of Latin verb flexions than its Italian sister. English has experienced catastrophic denudation of its Teutonic flexions. Consequently its grammar is now more like that of Chinese than like that of Sanskrit. Grammatical comparison may therefore mislead us, and when the evidence of word similarity does not point to the same conclusion as the evidence from grammatical peculiarities, the latter is of little value.

A third clue which reinforces the testimony of recognizable word similarities arises from *consistent differences* between words of corresponding meaning. We can easily spot such a consistent difference by comparing the English words *to, tongue,* and *tin* with their German equivalents *zu, Zunge* and *Zinn.* The resemblance between members of the same pair is not striking if we confine our attention to one pair at a time, but when we look at the very large number of such pairs in which the initial German Z (pronounced *ts*) takes the place of our English T, we discover an immense stock of new word similarities. The fact that changes affecting most words with a particular sound have taken place in one or both of two languages since they began to diverge conceals many word similarities from immediate recognition. This inference is not mere speculation. It is directly supported by what has happened in the recorded history of the Romance group, as illustrated in the following examples showing a vowel and a consonant shift characteristic of French, Spanish and Italian.

LATIN	FRENCH	SPANISH	ITALIAN
*o*vum (egg)	œ*uf*	h*u*evo	*uo*vo
n*o*vum (new)	n*eu*f	n*u*evo	n*uo*vo
m*o*rit (he dies)	m*eu*rt	m*u*ere	m*uo*re
fa*ct*um (fact)	fa*it*	he*ch*o	fa*tt*o
lac(*-tis*) (milk)	la*it*	le*ch*e	la*tt*e
o*ct*o (eight)	hu*it*	o*ch*o	o*tt*o

If we observe correspondence of this type when we investigate two other languages, such as Finnish and Magyar (Hungarian), we have to conclude that each pair of words has been derived from a single and earlier one. If we notice several types of sound replacement, each supported by a large number of examples, we can regard relationship as certain. This conclusion is of great practical value to anyone who is learning a language. Sound transformations between related languages such as English and German, or French and Spanish, are not mere historical curios, like the sound changes in the earlier history of the Indo-European group. How to recognize them should take its place in the technique of learning a foreign language, because knowledge of them is an aid to memory, and often helps us to spot the familiar equivalent of an unfamiliar word.

❖   ❖   ❖

One of the words in the preceding lists illustrates this forcibly. At first sight there is no resemblance between the Spanish word *hecho* and the Latin-English word *fact* or its French equivalent *fait*. Anyone who has been initiated into the sound shifts of the Romance languages recognizes two trademarks of Spanish. One is the *CH* which corresponds to *IT* in words of Old French origin, or *CT* in modern French and English words of Latin descent. The other is the initial silent *H* which often replaces *f*, as illustrated by the Spanish (*hava*) and Italian (*fava*) words for *bean*. If an American or British student of German knows that the initial German *D* replaces our *TH*, there is no need to consult a dictionary for the meaning of *Ding* and *Durst*.

[4]   If we apply our three tests—community of basic vocabulary, similarity of grammatical structure, and regularity of sound correspondence—to English, Dutch, German and the Scandinavian languages, all the findings suggest unity of origin. Naturally, it is not possible to exhibit the full extent of world community within the limits of this book. ❖ ❖ ❖ Here we must content ourselves with the illustration already given on page 7, where a request contained in the Lord's Prayer is printed in five Teutonic and in five Romance languages.❖ The reader may also refer to the tables of personal pronouns printed on pages 218 and 219.†

❖ [In Notes.—EDITOR'S NOTE.]
† [In Notes.—EDITOR'S NOTE.]

The grammatical apparatus of the Teutonic languages points to the same conclusion, as the reader may see by comparing the forms of the verb *to have* displayed in tabular form below. Three of the most characteristic grammatical features of the Teutonic group are the following:

1. Throughout the Teutonic languages, there is the same type (see table on p. [213]) of comparison (English *thin, thinner, thinnest;* German *dünn, dünner, dünnst;* Swedish *tunn, tunnare, tunnaste*).

2. All members of the group form the past tense and past participle of the verb in two ways: (*a*) by modifying the root vowel (English *sing, sang, sung;* German *singen, sang, gesungen;* Danish *synge, sang, sungen*); (*b*) by adding *d* or *t* to the stem (English *punish, punished;* German *strafen, strafte, gestraft;* Danish *straffe, straffede, straffet*).

3. The typical genitive singular case mark is */-s*, as in English *day's,* Swedish *dags,* Danish *Dags,* German *Tages*.

If we follow out our third clue, we find a very striking series of sound shifts characteristic of each language. We have had one example of consonant equivalence in the Teutonic group. Below is a single example of vowel equivalence:

ENGLISH	SWEDISH	GERMAN
bone	ben	Bein
goat	get	Geiss
oak	ek	Eiche
stone	sten	Stein
whole	hel	heil

THE INDO-EUROPEAN FAMILY

[5] Similarities are comparatively easy to trace in closely related languages such as Swedish and German or French and Italian. We can still detect some, when we compare individual members of these groups with those of others. Centuries back some people felt, though dimly, that the Teutonic group was not an isolated unit. In 1597, Bonaventura Vulcanius observed that twenty-two words are the same in German and Persian. Twenty years later, another scholar stressed the similarities between Lithuanian and Latin. Both were right, though both drew the

ENGLISH	SWEDISH		DANISH		DUTCH *		GERMAN *
I have	*Du*		*jeg*		*ik* heb		*ich* habe
thou hast	*han*	har	*Du*	har	*jij* hebt		*du* hast
he has	*de*		*han*		*hij* heeft		*er* hat
we	*jag*		*vi*		*(un)*		*wir* haben
you have	*vi*	hava	*De*		*jullie*	hebben	*ihr* habt
they	*Ni*		*de*		*(uz)*		*sie* haben
I had					*ik*		*ich* hatte
thou hadst	*jag,* etc., hade				*jij*	had	*du* hattest
he					*hij*		*er* hatte
we					*wij*		*wir* hatten
you had	*jag,* etc., hade		*jeg,* etc.,		*jullie*	hadden	*ihr* hattet
they			havde		*zij*		*sie* hatten
I have had	*jag* har haft		*jeg* har haft		*ik* heb gehad		*ich* habe gehabt
I shall have	*jag* skall hava		*jeg* skal have		*ik* zal hebben		*ich* werde haben

* For polite address German has *Sie* + third person plural; Dutch has U + third person singular.

wrong conclusions from their findings, the former that German had an admixture of Persian, the latter that the Lithuanians were of Roman stock.

Two hundred years later, in 1817, Rasmus Kristian Rask, a brilliant young Dane who had been investigating the origin of Old Norse in Iceland, first drew attention to sound correspondence between Greek and Latin on the one hand, and the Teutonic languages on the other. Textbooks usually refer to this discovery as Grimm's Law—after the German scholar who took up Rask's idea. One item of this most celebrated of all sound shifts is the change from the Latin *p* to the Teutonic *f*:

LATIN	ENGLISH	SWEDISH	GERMAN
*p*lenus	*f*ull	*f*ull	*v*oll *
*p*iscis	*f*ish	*f*isk	Fisch
*p*ed-is	*f*oot	*f*ot	Fuss
*p*ater	*f*ather	*f*ader	Vater

* The German V stands for the *f* sound in *far*.

A little later the German scholar Franz Bopp (1791–1867) showed that Sanskrit, Persian, Greek, Latin, and Teutonic in its earlier stages, have similar verb flexions. His studies led him to the conclusion that Aryan verb and case flexion have come about by the gluing on of what were once independent vocables such as pronouns and prepositions. It was a brilliant idea. Bopp's only weakness was that he tried to establish its validity when sufficient evidence was not available. Inevitably, like other pioneers, he made errors. His disciples grossly neglected the important part which *analogy* has played in the accretion of affixes to roots. Subsequently a strong reaction set in. Even now, many linguists approach Bopp's agglutination theory squeamishly, as if it dealt with the human pudenda. This attitude is none the less foolish when it affects scientific caution for its justification, because much valid historic evidence to suport Bopp's teaching is available from the relatively recent history of Indo-European languages.

The present tense of "to bear," "to carry," in the following table, where the Teutonic group is represented by Old High German, illustrates obvious affinities of conjugation in the Aryan family:

ENGLISH	SANSKRIT	GREEK (DORIC)	LATIN *	OLD HIGH GERMAN	OLD SLAVONIC
I bear	bharami	phero	fero	biru	bera
(thou bearest)	bharasi	phereis	fers	biris	beresi
he bears	bharati	pherei	fert	birit	beretu
we bear	bharamas	pheromes	ferimus	berames	beremu
you bear	bharata	pherete	fertis	beret	berete
they bear	bharanti	pheronti	ferunt	berant	beratu

* The initial *f* sound in many Latin words corresponds to *b* in Teutonic languages, cf. Latin *frater*, English *brother*.

The singular of the present *optative* of the verb *to be*, corresponding to the use of *be* in *if it be*, in three dead languages of the group is:

SANSKRIT	OLD LATIN	GOTHIC
syam	siem	sijau
syas	sies	sijais
syat	siet	sijai

From a mass of phonetic, morphological and word similarities, we thus recognize the unity of the well-defined family called *Aryan* by Anglo-American, *Indo-European* by French, and *Indo-Germanic* by German writers. The last of the three is a misnomer begotten of national conceit. Indeed the family does not keep within the limits indicated by the term *Indo-European*. It is spread out over an enormous belt that stretches almost without interruption from Central Asia to the fringes of westernmost Europe. On the European side the terminus is Celtic, and on the Asiatic, *Tokharian,* a tongue once spoken by the inhabitants of Eastern Turkestan and recently (1906) unearthed in documents written over a thousand years ago.

The undeniable similarities between these languages suggest that they are all representatives of a single earlier one which must have been spoken by some community, at some place and at some time in the prehistoric past. The idiom of the far-flung *Imperium Romanum* began as a rustic dialect of the province of Latium; but nobody can tell where the speakers of proto-Aryan lived, whether in Southern Russia, or on the Iranian plateau, or somewhere else. If, as some philologists believe, Old Indic and the Persian of the *Avesta* have the most archaic features of Aryan languages known to us, it is not necessarily true that the habitat of the early Aryan-speaking people was nearer to Asia than to Europe. The example of Icelandic shows that a language may stray far away from home and still preserve characteristics long ago discarded by those that stayed behind. Only one thing seems certain. When the recorded history of Aryan begins with the Vedic hymns, the dispersal of the Aryan-speaking tribes had already taken place.

From the writings of some German authors we might gain the baseless impression that we are almost as well-informed about the language and cultural life of the proto-Aryans as we are about Egyptian civilization. One German linguist has pushed audacity so far as to compile a dictionary of hypothetical primitive Aryan, and another has surpassed him by telling us a story in it. Others have asserted that the proto-Aryans were already tilling the soil with the ox and the yoke. The proof adduced is that the word for the *yoke* is common to all Aryan languages (Old Indian *yugam;* Greek *zygon;* Latin *jugum;* Gothic *yuk*). Hence the thing, as well as the name, must have been part of primitive Aryan culture. Arguments of this kind are not convincing. The fact that the word *yoke* occurs in all Aryan languages is explicable without burdening the primitive Aryan dictionary. There is no reason whatsoever why an Aryan-speaking tribe should not have borrowed the yoke from a non-Aryan-speaking community, and then passed it on to others. Though we know little about early culture contacts, com-

ANGLO-AMERICAN	SWEDISH	DANISH		DUTCH	GERMAN

a. Regular type

RICH	rik	rig		rijk	reich
RICHER than	rikare än	rigere end		rijker dan	reicher als
RICHEST	rikast	rigest		rijkst	reichst

b. Irregular forms

i)
GOOD		god(t) *		goed	gut
BETTER	bättre	bedre		beter	besser
BEST	bäst	bedst	best		

ii)
MUCH	mycken(t)	megen(t)		veel	viel
MORE	mera	mere		meer	mehr
MOST		mest		meest	meist

iii)
LITTLE	liten(t)	lille		weinig	wenig
	lilla (pl.)				weniger (minder)
LESS		mindre		minder	
LEAST	minst	mindst		minst	wenigst (mindest)

* The -t ending is that of the neuter form.

mon sense tells us that what has happened in historical times must also have happened before.

It has also been said that the primitive Aryan-speaking tribes could count at least as far as one hundred. This does not necessarily follow from the fact that names for 2 or for 3 or for 10, etc., are alike. You cannot exchange goods without being able to count. It is therefore quite possible [1] that Aryan-speaking tribes borrowed the art of counting from an outside source, or that it diffused from one branch of the family to its neighbors. Indeed, numerals are the most indefatigable wanderers among words, as indefatigable as alphabets. In the language of the Gypsies, an Indic tribe, the names for 7, 8, and 9 are modern Greek, whereas those for 5 and 10 are Indic. In the Finno-Ugrian group, the word for 100 is borrowed from Iranian; and Hebrew *schesh* (6) and *scheba* (7) are supposed to be derived from Aryan, while the Hebrew name for 8 is assumed to be Egyptian. But there is no need to go so far back. The English *dozen* and *million* have been taken over in comparatively recent times from the Romance languages.

1. Philologists sometimes justify emphasis on similarity of number words on the ground that they also share general phonetic features characteristic of a language as a whole. This is also true of words which have undoubtedly been borrowed, and is easily explained by the phonetic habits of a people.

THE TEUTONIC VERB

ANGLO-AMERICAN		SWEDISH	DANISH	DUTCH	GERMAN
		A. STRONG TYPE			
a. to give		att giva	at give	te geven	zu geben
given (part)		givit	givet	gegeven	gegeben
give(s)	(sing.)	giver	} giver	} geef(t)	gebe (gibt)
	(plur.)	giva		geeven	geben
gave	(sing.)	gav	} gav	} gaf	gab
	(plur.)	gavo		gaven	gaben
b. to come		att komma	at komme	te komen	zu kommen
come (part.)		kommit	kommet	gekomen	gekommen
come(s)	(sing.)	kommer	} kommer	} kom(t)	komme(t)
	(plur.)	komma		komen	kommen
came	(sing.)	kom	} kom	} kwam	kam
	(plur.)	komme		kwamen	kamen
		B. WEAK TYPE			
a. to work		att arbeta	at arbejde	te arbeiden	zu arbeiten
worked	(part.)	arbetat	arbejdet	gearbeid	gearbeitet
work(s)	(sing.)	arbetar	} arbejder	} arbeide(t)	arbeite(t)
	(plur.)	arbeta		arbeiden	arbeiten
worked	(sing.)	} arbetade	arbejdede {	arbeid*d*e {	arbeitete
	(plur.)			arbeid*d*en	arbeiteten
b. to hear		att höra	at høre	te hooren	zu hören
heard	(part.)	hört	hørt	gehoord	gehört
hear(s)	(sing.)	hör	} hører	} hoor(t)	höre(*t*)
	(plur.)	höra		hooren	hören
heard	(sing.)	} hörde	hørte {	hoorde {	hörte
	(plur.)			hoorden	hörten

German philologists have not been content to draw encouraging
conclusions from words which are alike and have the same meaning in all the Aryan languages. They have also speculated about
the significance of words which do not exist. Of itself, the fact that
the Aryan family has no common term for the tiger does not indicate that the proto-Aryans inhabited a region where there were
no tigers. Once the hypothetical *Urvolk* started to move, tribes
which went into colder regions would no longer need to preserve
the word for it. If we are entitled to deduce that the East did not
use salt because the Western Aryan word for the mineral does not
occur in the Indo-Iranian tongues, the absence of a common
Aryan word for milk must force us to conclude that proto-Aryan
babies used to feed on something else.

LANGUAGE FAMILIES OF THE WORLD

[6] In a modern classification of the animal kingdom taxono-
mists unite many small groups, such as fishes, birds and mammals,
or crustacea, insects and arachnida (spiders and scorpions) in
larger ones such as vertebrates and arthropods. Beyond that point
we can only speculate with little plausibility about their evolutionary past. Besides about ten great groups, such as vertebrates
and arthropods, embracing the majority of animal species, there
are many small ones made up of few species, isolated from one
another and from the members of any of the larger divisions. So
it is with languages. Thus Japanese, Korean, Manchu, Mongolian,
each stand outside any recognized families as isolated units.

We have seen that most of the inhabitants of Europe speak
languages with common features. These common features justify
the recognition of a single great *Indo-European family*. Besides
the Romance or Latin and the Teutonic languages mentioned in
the preceding pages, the Indo-European family includes several
other well-defined groups, such as the Celtic (Scots Gaelic, Erse,
Welsh, Breton) in the West, and the Slavonic (Russian, Polish,
Czech and Slovak, Bulgarian and Serbo-Croatian) in the East of
Europe, together with the Indo-Iranian languages spoken by the
inhabitants of Persia and a large part of India. Lithuanian (with
its sister dialect, Latvian), Greek, Albanian, and Armenian are
isolated members of the same family.

The Indo-European or Aryan group does not include all existing European languages. Finnish, Magyar, Esthonian and Lappish have common features which have led linguists to place them
in a separate group called the *Finno-Ugrian* family. So far as we
can judge at present, Turkish, which resembles several Central
Asiatic languages (Tartar, Uzbeg, Kirghiz), belongs to neither of
the two families mentioned; and Basque, still spoken on the
French and Spanish sides of the Pyrenees, has no clear affinities
with any other language in the world.

Long before modern language research established the unity of
the Aryan family, Jewish scholars recognized the similarities of
Arabic, Hebrew and Aramaic which are representatives of a
Semitic family. The Semitic family also includes the fossil languages of the Phoenicians and Assyro-Babylonians. The languages of China, Tibet, Burma and Siam constitute a fourth great

language family. Like the Semitic, the *Indo-Chinese* family has an indigenous literature. In Central and Southern Africa other languages such as Luganda, Swahili, Kafir, Zulu, have been associated in a *Bantu* unit which does *not* include those of the Bushmen and Hottentots. In Northern Africa Somali, Galla and Berber show similarities which have forced linguists to recognize a *Hamitic* family. To this group ancient Egyptian also belongs. A *Dravidian* family includes Southern Indian languages, which have no relation to the Aryan vernaculars of India. Yet another major family with clear-cut features is the *Malayo-Polynesian,* which includes Malay and the tongues of most of the islands in the Indian and Pacific Oceans.

Something like a hundred language groups, including the Papuan, Australian and Amerindian (e.g. Mexican and Greenlandic) vernaculars, Japanese, Basque, Manchu, Georgian, and Korean, still remain to be connected in larger units. This has not been possible so far, either because they have not yet been properly studied, or because their past phases are not on record. Below is a list of families which are well-defined:

I. INDO-EUROPEAN
(a) *Teutonic* (German, Dutch, Scandinavian, English)
(b) *Celtic* (Erse, Gaelic, Welsh, Breton)
(c) *Romance* (French, Spanish, Catalan, Portuguese, Italian, Rumanian)
(d) *Slavonic* (Russian, Polish, Czech, Slovakian, Bulgarian, Serbo-Croatian, and Slovene)

(e) *Baltic* (Lithuanian, Lettish)   (h) *Armenian*
(f) *Greek*   (i) *Persian*
(g) *Albanian*   (j) *Modern Indic dialects*

II. FINNO-UGRIAN
(a) *Lappish*   (d) *Cheremessian,*
(b) *Finnish*   *Mordvinian*
(c) *Esthonian*   (e) *Magyar (Hungarian)*

III. SEMITIC
(a) *Arabic*   (c) *Hebrew*
(b) *Ethiopian*   (d) *Maltese*

IV. HAMITIC
(a) *Cushite (Somali, Galla)*
(b) *Berber* languages

V. INDO-CHINESE
(a) *Chinese*   (c) *Siamese*
(b) *Tibetan*   (d) *Burmese*

VI. MALAYO-POLYNESIAN

(a) *Malay*   (c) *Tahitian*
(b) *Fijian*   (d) *Maori*

VII. TURCO-TARTAR

(a) *Turkish*   (c) *Kirghiz*
(b) *Tartar*

VIII. DRAVIDIAN

(a) *Tamil*   (c) *Canarese*
(b) *Telugu*

IX. BANTU

Kafir, Zulu, Bechuana, Sesuto, Herero, Congo, Duala, etc.

SUMMARY

[1]   Though people have known for ages that some languages resemble one another, the acceptance of the idea of the organic evolution of language families was delayed—by the indifference of Mediterranean cultures to "barbarian" languages and by the Christian beliefs in the Tower of Babel story and the primacy of the Hebrew language—until the late eighteenth or early nineteenth century.

[2]   The idea that languages grow and develop, though anticipated by Tooke and Adelung, gained chief impetus from the discovery and study of Sanskrit, the comparative grammar of Bopp, and the revolution in geological thought which cast doubt upon the Biblical story of the Creation. Schlegel's study of Sanskrit (1808) may be considered to be the turning point in the study of language. The preservation of Latin provides an example of historical linguistic development.

[3]   The assumption that there is a similarity among languages presupposes a common ancestor; this assumption underlies the evolutionary theory of languages. There are three types of evidence of similarity: (1) word similarity (especially of conservative and basic words); (2) grammatical behavior (tense forms, articles, gender—morphological features primarily, for they are more conservative features of a language than syntactical ones); and (3) consistent differences among words of corresponding meanings (especially in pronunciations).

[4]   These three tests, when applied to English, German, Dutch, and Scandinavian, suggest that these languages stem from a common source. Words are similar, grammatical features are alike, and consistent differences may be found in pronunciation.

[5]   The idea of a more comprehensive language family than the Teutonic (or Germanic) group resulted from Rask's and Grimm's observations of systematic sound shifts between Latin and Teutonic languages and from Bopp's discovery of the similarity of verb inflections in a wide variety of languages. This language family, called Aryan or Indo-European or Indo-Germanic, seems to have evolved from one parent tongue, spoken at some place and at some time by some community. But explanations of the locale or culture of the original language are not very convincing.

[6]   Most modern languages fall into nine large families, but there
are major languages which do not fall in any of the large families.

NOTES

The "discovery" of the Indo-European family of languages is, of
course, the discovery not of a *fact* but rather of a *hypothesis*. Given the
evidence accumulated by a long list of comparative linguists, the
assumption of an original Indo-European parent language seems the
best explanation for many of the facts of the various languages considered members of the language family. Certainly the existence of such
a parent language has not been "proved" beyond doubt. But the pre-
ponderance of evidence which supports the hypothesis is so great that
no linguistic scholar doubts the validity of the assumption.

All this is to say, simply, that we must not confuse matters of fact
with matters of theory; and no scientist, in language as in other studies,
wishes to confuse the two. The theory of biological evolution is still a
theory, and so is the atomic theory. Both are hypotheses or "guesses"
offered to explain a large body of observable facts. As more facts which
support a hypothesis are turned up, the credibility of the "guess" grows.
When the evidence becomes sufficiently great, the hypothesis gains
general acceptance.

You are not forced to accept the hypothesis of a parent Indo-

PERSONAL PRONOUNS

ENGLISH	SWEDISH		DANISH	DUTCH	GERMAN
I	jag		jeg	ik	ich
me		mig		mij	mich, mir
(thou)		Du		jij	du
(thee)		Dig		jou	dich, dir
we		vi		wij	wir
us	oss		os	ons	uns
you	Ni		De		Sie
(subject)				U	
you	Er		Dem		Sie, Ihnen
(oblique)					
he		han		hij	er
him	honom		ham	hem	ihn, ihm
she	hon		hun	zij	sie
her	henne		hende	haar	ihr
it		den, det		het	es
(subject)					
it		den, det			es, ihm
(oblique)					
they		de		zij	sie
them		dem		hen, hun	sie, ihnen

TEUTONIC POSSESSIVES

ENGLISH	DANISH	SWEDISH	DUTCH	GERMAN
my	*min* (etc.)		*mijn* †	mein (etc.)
(thy)	*Din* (etc.)		*jovw*	dein (etc.)
our	*vår* (etc.)	*vor* (etc.)	*onze, ons*	unser (etc.)
your	*Er* (etc.)	*Deres*	*Uw*	Ihr (etc.)
his		hans	*zijn*	sein (etc.)
her	hennes	hendes	*haar*	ihr (etc.)
its	dess	dens	zijn	sein (etc.)
their	deras	deres	*hun*	ihr (etc.)

Those italicized have neuter singular and plural forms *mitt-mina* or *mit-mine, vart-vara* or *vort-vore*. The form given is the common singular. *Din* and *Er* behave like *min* and *var* respectively.

† Like other adjectives take *-e* in plural

These have case as well as gender and number forms and are declined like *ein*, e.g. unser, unsere, unser. The form given is the masc. nomin. sing.

European language, and you are not forced to accept any grammatical theory, any more than you are forced to accept the theory of biological evolution or of economic supply and demand. But rational people in your civilization do accept these theories, and they are likely to consider you irrational if you do not.

The "request" referred to on p. 208 is "Give us this day our daily bread":

Gib uns heute unser täglich Brot (German)
Geef ons heden ons dagelijksch brood (Dutch)
Giv os i Dag vort daglige Brød (Danish)
Giv oss i dag vårt dagliga bröd (Swedish)
Gef oss i dag vort daglegt brauð (Icelandic)
Da nobis hodie panem nostrum quotidianum (Latin)
Donne-nous aujourd'hui notre pain quotidien (French)
Danos hoy nuestro pan cotidiano (Spanish)
Dacci oggi il nostro pane cotidiano (Italian)
O pão nosso de cada dia dai-nos hoje (Portuguese)

Why Study Other Languages?

WILLIAM DWIGHT WHITNEY

One of the most learned of nineteenth-century American lin-
guists, William Dwight Whitney takes in this essay a suprisingly
radical view of the study of foreign languages, but it is "radical"
in the original sense of the word; he attempts to get at the root
of the problem.

[1]   We are not prepared to inquire what the study of foreign
languages is to do for us, until we have seen clearly what our
own is worth to us, and how; for the learning of a foreign tongue
is but the repetition, under other circumstances, of the learning
of our own; and what fruit the one yields is of the same kind with
that derived from the other. Great as is the difference of the two
cases (consisting chiefly in the fact that that training of the consciousness and reasoning powers which is involved in learning to
speak at all is done once for all, in the main, and does not admit
of being repeated), it is one of degree and circumstance only. One
language is in itself as much extraneous to our mental acts as
another. As a part of acquired and acquirable culture, our speech
is determined by the particular advantages which we enjoy. With
a change of surroundings during childhood, we should have
made French, or Turkish, or Chinese, or Dakota, our "mother
tongue," and looked upon English as the strange jargon which we
must acquire artificially. We may even now, if we choose, and if
our present habits of thought and of articulation are not too firmly
fixed upon us, make ourselves so at home in any one of the
tongues just mentioned, that it shall become to us more native
than English. There can be, therefore, no peculiar and magical
effect derived from the addition to the body of signs for thought
with which we are already familiar of another body of signs, used
now or in the past by some other community; it is simply a continuing and supplementing of the possession we already enjoy—

wealth added to wealth.

How far it is desirable or necessary thus to continue and supplement one's natively acquired possession will naturally depend,
in no small measure, upon the amount of wealth gained with the
latter. The Polynesian or African, for example, who should wish
to rise to the level of the best culture of the day, could climb but
a very little way by the help of his own dialect. When this had
done its utmost for him, he would, though raised greatly above
what he could have been without it, still be far down in the scale
of human development, and with a sadly limited space for further
growth opened to him. Let him add English to his possessions,
and his horizon would be inconceivably expanded; his way would
be clear to more than he could ever hope to gain, though he devoted to study all the energies of a long life. What was thus made
accessible to him by a secondary process, by education in the
narrower sense, is made accessible to us by a first process, the
natural learning of our mother tongue. All that English could do
for him it can do for us. It were vain to deny that true and high
culture is within reach of him who rightly studies the English
language alone, knowing naught of any other. More of the fruits
of knowledge are deposited in it and in its literature than one man
can make his own. History affords at least one illustrious example,
within our own near view, of a people that has risen to the loftiest
pinnacle of culture with no aid from linguistic or philological
study: it is the Greek people. The elements, the undeveloped
germs of the Greek civilization, did indeed in part come from foreign sources: but they did not come through literature; they were
gained by personal intercourse. To the true Greek, from the beginning to the end of Grecian history, every tongue save his own
was barbarous, and unworthy of his attention; he learned such,
if he learned them at all, only for the simplest and most practical ends of communication with their speakers. No trace of
Latin, or Hebrew, or Egyptian, or Assyrian, or Sanskrit, or Chinese was to be found in the curriculum of the Athenian student,
though dim intimations of valuable knowledge reached by some
of those nations, of noble works produced by them, had reached
his ear. What the ancient Greek could do, let it not be said that
the modern speaker of English, with a tongue into which have
been poured the treasures of all literature and science, from every
part of the world, and from times far beyond the dawn of Grecian

history, cannot accomplish.

[2] We must be careful, however, not to hurry from this to the conclusion that there is no longer good ground for our studying any language save our own. We have, rather, only to draw one or two negative inferences. In the first place, that we must not contemn the man who knows no other language than his own as lacking the essentials of culture, since he may have derived from his English what is an equivalent, or more than an equivalent, for all the strange tongues we have at command. In the second place, that our inducement to study Latin and Greek, or any other such tongue, is very different from that which should lead our imagined Polynesian or African to study English. At the revival of letters, indeed, the classical tongues stood toward those of modern Europe in something such a position as one of the latter now to the Polynesian or African dialects; they contained the treasures of knowledge and culture, which were only attainable through them; hence, they were the almost exclusive means of discipline; to study them was to learn what was known, and to lay the necessary foundation for further productiveness in every department. The process of change from that condition of things to the present, when the best and most cultivated modern languages are far richer in collected wealth than ever was either the Greek or the Latin, has been a gradual one, accompanying the slow transfusion of the old knowledge into new forms, and its increase by the results of the best thought, the deepest wisdom, and the most penetrating investigation of the past six or eight centuries.

[3] The reasons why we may not imitate the ancient Greek contempt and neglect of foreign tongues are many and various, and sufficiently evident. In brief, our culture has a far wider and stronger basis than that of the Greek, including numerous departments of knowledge of which he had no conception; history, and antiquity, and literature, and language itself, are subjects of study to us in a sense altogether different from what they were to any ancient people; we have learned, moreover, that the roundabout course, through other tongues, to the comprehension and mastery of our own, is the shortest; and we recognize other communities besides ourselves as engaged in the same rapid career of advancement of knowledge, and constantly setting us lessons which we cannot afford to leave unread.

Of these reasons, the last is the most obvious and elementary.

Language is primarily a means of communication; and as the possession of our native tongue gives us access to other minds, so the acquisition of more languages widens our sphere of intercourse, lays open additional sources of enlightenment, and increases the number of our instructors. Even were it possible that everything valuable that was produced abroad should find its way into English, it would yet be more promptly and better studied in the form in which it originally appeared. No one can claim to have ready access to the fountains of knowledge nowadays who has it only by the channel of his native speech.

The important bearing of the study of foreign languages and literatures upon that of our own is also universally recognized. It has become a trite remark, that no one knows his own tongue who knows no other beside it. Our native language is too much a matter of unreflective habit with us for us to be able to set it in the full light of an objective study. Something of the same difficulty is felt in relation also to our native literature; we hardly know what it is and what it is worth, until we come to compare it with another. No doubt this difficulty admits of being measurably removed by other means; but the easiest and most effective means is philological study. This supplies us the needed ground of comparison, and brings characteristic qualities to our conscious apprehension; nothing else so develops the faculty of literary criticism, and leads to that skilled and artistic handling of our mother tongue which is the highest adornment of a natural aptitude, and is able even in no small degree to supply the place of this. He whose object it is to wield effectively the resources of his own vernacular can account no time lost which he spends, under proper direction, in the acquisition of other tongues. Nothing else, again, so trains the capacity to penetrate into the minds and hearts of men, to read aright the records of their opinion and action, to get off one's own point of view and see and estimate things as others see them. Those who would understand and influence their fellows, those who deal with dogma and precedent, with the interpretation and application of principles that affect man most nearly, must give themselves to studies of which philology is a chief means and aid.

When it comes, however, to the question of deeper investigations into human history, in all its branches, then the necessity of a philology that reaches far beyond the boundaries of English becomes at every turn most clearly apparent. No part of our modern culture—language, literature, or anything else—has its roots in itself, or is to be comprehended without following it up through the records of its former phases. The study of history, as accessible especially in languages and literatures (in a far less degree in art and antiquities), has become one of the principal divisions of human labor. No small part of our most precious knowledge has been won in it, and has been deposited in our own tongue, even entering to a certain extent into that unconscious culture which we gain we hardly know whence or how. But while its results are thus accessible even in English, so far as may serve the purposes of general culture to one whose special activity is to be exerted in a different direction, that kind of thorough mastery which has been described above as needed to make knowledge disciplinary is not to be won in this manner. How tame and lifeless, for example, is his apprehension of the history of English words who looks out their etymologies in a dictionary, however skillfully constructed, compared with his who reads it in the documents in which it is contained! Again, the general truths of linguistic science, having been once wrought out by the study and comparison of many tongues, are capable of being so distinctly stated, and so clearly illustrated out of the resources of English, as to be made patent to the sense of every intelligent and well-instructed English scholar; yet only he can be said to have fully mastered them who can bring to them independent and varied illustration from the same data which led to their establishment. And the case is the same with all the elements that make up our civilization; while there is a primitive darkness into which we cannot follow them, they have a long history of development which must be read where it is found written, in the records of the many races through whose hands they have passed on their way to us. The work is far from being yet completely done; an inexhaustible mass of materials still remains to be explored and elaborated; and men have to be trained for the task, not less than for the investigation of material nature.

PART SIX   Language and Literature

Language and Literature

*Edward Sapir was Sterling Professor of Anthropology and Lin-
guistics at Yale from 1931 until his death in 1939. An authority
on the Indo-European languages, ancient and modern, and on
American Indian, African, Hebrew, Semitic, and Sinitic languages as well, he was also interested in many other things, as
this selection from his* Language *(1921), one of the earliest and
best written books on the subject, clearly shows.*

Languages are more to us than systems of thought-transference.
They are invisible garments that drape themselves about our
spirit and give a predetermined form to all its symbolic expression.
When the expression is of unusual significance, we call it literature.[1] Art is so personal an expression that we do not like to feel
that it is bound to predetermined form of any sort. The possibilities of individual expression are infinite, language in particular is
the most fluid of mediums. Yet some limitation there must be to
this freedom, some resistance of the medium. In great art there
is the illusion of absolute freedom. The formal restraints imposed
by the material—paint, black and white, marble, piano tones, or
whatever it may be—are not perceived; it is as though there were
a limitless margin of elbow-room between the artist's fullest utili-

1. I can hardly stop to define just what kind of expression is "significant"
enough to be called art or literature. Besides, I do not exactly know. We
shall have to take literature for granted.

Chapter XI from *Language* by Edward Sapir, copyright, 1921, by Harcourt, Brace and World, Inc.; renewed, 1949, by Jean V. Sapir. Reprinted
by permission of the publisher.

lization of form and the most that the material is innately capable of. The artist has intuitively surrendered to the inescapable tyranny of the material, made its brute nature fuse easily with his conception.[2] The material "disappears" precisely because there is nothing in the artist's conception to indicate that any other material exists. For the time being, he, and we with him, move in the artistic medium as a fish moves in the water, oblivious of the existence of an alien atmosphere. No sooner, however, does the artist transgress the law of his medium than we realize with a start that there is a medium to obey.

Language is the medium of literature as marble or bronze or clay are the materials of the sculptor. Since every language has its distinctive peculiarities, the innate formal limitations—and possibilities—of one literature are never quite the same as those of another. The literature fashioned out of the form and substance of a language has the color and the texture of its matrix. The literary artist may never be conscious of just how he is hindered or helped or otherwise guided by the matrix, but when it is a question of translating his work into another language, the nature of the original matrix manifests itself at once. All his effects have been calculated, or intuitively felt, with reference to the formal "genius" of his own language; they cannot be carried over without loss or modification. Croce [3] is therefore perfectly right in saying that a work of literary art can never be translated. Nevertheless literature does get itself translated, sometimes with astonishing adequacy. This brings up the question whether in the art of literature there are not intertwined two distinct kinds or levels of art—a generalized, non-linguistic art, which can be transferred without loss into an alien linguistic medium, and a specifically linguistic art that is not transferable.[4] I believe the distinction is entirely

2. This "intuitive surrender" has nothing to do with subservience to artistic convention. More than one revolt in modern art has been dominated by the desire to get out of the material just what it is really capable of. The impressionist wants light and color because paint can give him just these; "literature" in painting, the sentimental suggestion of a "story," is offensive to him because he does not want the virtue of his particular form to be dimmed by shadows from another medium. Similarly, the poet, as never before, insists that words mean just what they really mean.

3. See Benedetto Croce, Æsthetic.

4. The question of the transferability of art productions seems to me to be one of genuine theoretic interest. For all that we speak of the sacrosanct uniqueness of a given art work, we know very well, though we do not always

valid, though we never get the two levels pure in practice. Literature moves in language as a medium, but that medium comprises two layers, the latent content of language—our intuitive record of experience—and the particular conformation of a given language—the specific how of our record of experience. Literature that draws its sustenance mainly—never entirely—from the lower level, say a play of Shakespeare's, is translatable without too great a loss of character. If it moves in the upper rather than in the lower level—a fair example is a lyric of Swinburne's—it is as good as untranslatable. Both types of literary expression may be great or mediocre.

There is really no mystery in the distinction. It can be clarified a little by comparing literature with science. A scientific truth is impersonal, in its essence it is untinctured by the particular linguistic medium in which it finds expression. It can as readily deliver its message in Chinese [5] as in English. Nevertheless it must have some expression, and that expression must needs be a linguistic one. Indeed the apprehension of the scientific truth is itself a linguistic process, for thought is nothing but language denuded of its outward garb. The proper medium of scientific expression is therefore a generalized language that may be defined as a symbolic algebra of which all known languages are translations. One can adequately translate scientific literature because the original scientific expression is itself a translation. Literary expression is personal and concrete, but this does not mean that its significance is altogether bound up with the accidental qualities of the medium. A truly deep symbolism, for instance, does not depend on the verbal associations of a particular language but rests securely on an intuitive basis that underlies all linguistic expression. The artist's "intuition," to use Croce's term, is immediately fashioned out of a generalized human experience—thought and feeling—of which his own individual experience is a highly personalized

---

admit it, that not all productions are equally intractable to transference. A Chopin étude is inviolate; it moves altogether in the world of piano music. A Bach fugue is transferable into another set of musical timbres without serious loss of esthetic significance. Chopin plays with the language of the piano as though no other language existed (the medium "disappears"); Bach speaks the language of the piano as a handy means of giving outward expression to a conception wrought in the generalized language of tone.

5. Provided, of course, Chinese is careful to provide itself with the necessary scientific vocabulary. Like any other language, it can do so without serious difficulty if the need arises.

selection. The thought relations in this deeper level have no specific linguistic vesture; the rhythms are free, not bound, in the first instance, to the traditional rhythms of the artist's language. Certain artists whose spirit moves largely in the non-linguistic (better, in the generalized linguistic) layer even find a certain difficulty in getting themselves expressed in the rigidly set terms of their accepted idiom. One feels that they are unconsciously striving for a generalized art language, a literary algebra, that is related to the sum of all known languages as a perfect mathematical symbolism is related to all the roundabout reports of mathematical relations that normal speech is capable of conveying. Their art expression is frequently strained, it sound at times like a translation from an unknown original—which, indeed, is precisely what it is. These artists—Whitmans and Brownings—impress us rather by the greatness of their spirit than the felicity of their art. Their relative failure is of the greatest diagnostic value as an index of the pervasive presence in literature of a larger, more intuitive linguistic medium than any particular language.

Nevertheless, human expression being what it is, the greatest—or shall we say the most satisfying—literary artists, the Shakespeares and Heines, are those who have known subconsciously to fit or trim the deeper intuition to the provincial accents of their daily speech. In them there is no effect of strain. Their personal "intuition" appears as a completed synthesis of the absolute art of intuition and the innate, specialized art of the linguistic medium. With Heine, for instance, one is under the illusion that the universe speaks German. The material "disappears."

Every language is itself a collective art of expression. There is concealed in it a particular set of esthetic factors—phonetic, rhythmic, symbolic, morphological—which it does not completely share with any other language. These factors may either merge their potencies with those of that unknown, absolute language to which I have referred—this is the method of Shakespeare and Heine—or they may weave a private, technical art fabric of their own, the innate art of the language intensified or sublimated. The latter type, the more technically "literary" art of Swinburne and of hosts of delicate "minor" poets, is too fragile for endurance. It is built out of spiritualized material, not out of spirit. The successes of the Swinburnes are as valuable for diagnostic purposes as the semi-failures of the Brownings. They show to what extent literary art may lean on the collective art of the language itself. The more extreme technical practitioners may so over-individualize this collective art as to make it almost unendurable. One is not always thankful to have one's flesh and blood frozen to ivory.

An artist must utilize the native esthetic resources of his speech. He may be thankful if the given palette of colors is rich, if the springboard is light. But he deserves no special credit for felicities that are the language's own. We must take for granted this language with all its qualities of flexibility or rigidity and see the artist's work in relation to it. A cathedral on the lowlands is higher than a stick on Mont Blanc. In other words, we must not commit the folly of admiring a French sonnet because the vowels are more sonorous than our own or of condemning Nietzsche's prose because it harbors in its texture combinations of consonants that would affright on English soil. To so judge literature would be tantamount to loving *Tristan und Isolde* because one is fond of the timbre of horns. There are certain things that one language can do supremely well which it would be almost vain for another to attempt. Generally there are compensations. The vocalism of English is an inherently drabber thing than the vowel scale of French, yet English compensates for this drawback by its greater rhythmical alertness. It is even doubtful if the innate sonority of a phonetic system counts for as much, as esthetic determinant, as the relations between the sounds, the total gamut of their similarities and contrasts. As long as the artist has the wherewithal to lay out his sequences and rhythms, it matters little what are the sensuous qualities of the elements of his material.

The phonetic groundwork of a language, however, is only one of the features that give its literature a certain direction. Far more important are its morphological peculiarities. It makes a great deal of difference for the development of style if the language can or cannot create compound words, if its structure is synthetic or analytic, if the words of its sentences have considerable freedom of position or are compelled to fall into a rigidly determined sequence. The major characteristics of style, in so far as style is a technical matter of the building and placing of words, are given by the language itself, quite as inescapably, indeed, as the general acoustic effect of verse is given by the sounds and natural accents of the language. These necessary fundamentals of style are hardly felt by the artist to constrain his individuality of expression. They rather point the way to those stylistic developments that most suit the natural bent of the language. It is not in the least likely that a truly great style can seriously oppose itself to the basic form patterns of the language. It not only incorporates them, it builds on them. The merit of such a style as W. H. Hudson's or George Moore's [6] is that it does with ease and economy what the language is always trying to do. Carlylese, though individual and vigorous, is yet not style; it is a Teutonic mannerism. Nor is the prose of Milton and his contemporaries strictly English; it is semi-Latin done into magnificent English words.

It is strange how long it has taken the European literatures to learn that style is not an absolute, a something that is to be imposed on the language from Greek or Latin models, but merely the language itself, running in its natural grooves, and with enough of an individual accent to allow the artist's personality to be felt as a presence, not as an acrobat. We understand more clearly now that what is effective and beautiful in one language is a vice in another. Latin and Eskimo, with their highly inflected forms, lend themselves to an elaborately periodic structure that would be boring in English. English allows, even demands, a looseness that would be insipid in Chinese. And Chinese, with its unmodified words and rigid sequences, has a compactness of phrase, a terse parallelism, and a silent suggestiveness that would be too tart, too mathematical, for the English genius. While we cannot assimilate the luxurious periods of Latin nor the pointilliste style of the Chinese classics, we can enter sympathetically into the spirit of these alien techniques.

I believe that any English poet of to-day would be thankful for the concision that a Chinese poetaster attains without effort. Here is an example: [7]

> Wu-river [8] stream mouth evening sun sink,
> North look Liao-Tung,[9] not see home.
> Steam whistle several noise, sky-earth boundless,
> Float float one reed out Middle-Kingdom.

6. Aside from individual peculiarities of diction, the selection and evaluation of particular words as such.

7. Not by any means a great poem, merely a bit of occasional verse written by a young Chinese friend of mine when he left Shanghai for Canada.

8. The old name of the country about the mouth of the Yangtsze.

9. A province of Manchuria.

These twenty-eight syllables may be clumsily interpreted: "At the mouth of the Yangtsze River, as the sun is about to sink, I look north toward Liao-Tung but do not see my home. The steam-whistle shrills several times on the boundless expanse where meet sky and earth. The steamer, floating gently like a hollow reed, sails out of the Middle Kingdom." [10] But we must not envy Chinese its terseness unduly. Our more sprawling mode of expression is capable of its own beauties, and the more compact luxuriance of Latin style has its loveliness too. There are almost as many natural ideals of literary style as there are languages. Most of these are merely potential, awaiting the hand of artists who will never come. And yet in the recorded texts of primitive tradition and song there are many passages of unique vigor and beauty. The structure of the language often forces an assemblage of concepts that impresses us as a stylistic discovery. Single Algonkin words are like tiny imagist poems. We must be careful not to exaggerate a freshness of content that is at least half due to our freshness of approach, but the possibility is indicated none the less of utterly alien literary styles, each distinctive with its disclosure of the search of the human spirit for beautiful form.

Probably nothing better illustrates the formal dependence of literature on language than the prosodic aspect of poetry. Quantitative verse was entirely natural to the Greeks, not merely because poetry grew up in connection with the chant and the dance,[11] but because alternations of long and short syllables were keenly live facts in the daily economy of the language. The tonal accents, which were only secondarily stress phenomena, helped to give the syllable its quantitative individuality. When the Greek meters were carried over in Latin verse, there was comparatively little strain, for Latin too was characterized by an acute awareness of quantitative distinctions. However, the Latin accent was more markedly stressed than that of Greek. Probably, therefore, the purely quantitative meters modeled after the Greek were felt as a shade more artificial than in the language of their origin. The attempt to cast English verse into Latin and Greek molds has never been successful. The dynamic basis of English is not quan-

10. *I.e.*, China.
11. Poetry everywhere is inseparable in its origins from the singing voice and the measure of the dance. Yet accentual and syllabic types of verse, rather than quantitative verse, seem to be the prevailing norms.

tity,[12] but stress, the alternation of accented and unaccented syllables. This fact gives English verse an entirely different slant and has determined the development of its poetic forms, is still responsible for the evolution of new forms. Neither stress nor syllabic weight is a very keen psychologic factor in the dynamics of French. The syllable has great inherent sonority and does not fluctuate significantly as to quantity and stress. Quantitative or accentual metrics would be as artificial in French as stress metrics in classical Greek or quantitative or purely syllabic metrics in English. French prosody was compelled to develop on the basis of unit syllable-groups. Assonance, later rhyme, could not but prove a welcome, an all but necessary, means of articulating or sectioning the somewhat spineless flow of sonorous syllables. English was hospitable to the French suggestion of rhyme, but did not seriously need it in its rhythmic economy. Hence rhyme has always been strictly subordinated to stress as a somewhat decorative feature and has been frequently dispensed with. It is no psychologic accident that rhyme came later into English than in French and is leaving it sooner.[13] Chinese verse has developed along very much the same lines as French verse. The syllable is an even more integral and sonorous unit than in French, while quantity and stress are too uncertain to form the basis of a metric system. Syllable-groups—so and so many syllables per rhythmic unit —and rhyme are therefore two of the controlling factors in Chinese prosody. The third factor, the alternation of syllables with level tone and syllables with inflected (rising or falling) tone, is peculiar to Chinese.

To summarize, Latin and Greek verse depends on the principle of contrasting weights; English verse, on the principle of contrasting stresses; French verse, on the principles of number and echo; Chinese verse, on the principles of number, echo, and contrasting pitches. Each of these rhythmic systems proceeds from the unconscious dynamic habit of the language, falling from the lips of the folk. Study carefully the phonetic system of a language, above all its dynamic features, and you can tell what kind of a

12. Quantitative distinctions exist as an objective fact. They have not the same inner, psychological value that they had in Greek.

13. Verhaeren was no slave to the Alexandrine, yet he remarked to Symons, à propos of the translation of Les Aubes, that while he approved of the use of rhymeless verse in the English version, he found it "meaningless" in French.

verse it has developed—or, if history has played pranks with its phychology, what kind of verse it should have developed and some day will.

Whatever be the sounds, accents, and forms of a language, however these lay hands on the shape of its literature, there is a subtle law of compensations that gives the artist space. If he is squeezed a bit here, he can swing a free arm there. And generally he has rope enough to hang himself with, if he must. It is not strange that this should be so. Language is itself the collective art of expression, a summary of thousands upon thousands of individual intuitions. The individual goes lost in the collective creation, but his personal expression has left some trace in a certain give and flexibility that are inherent in all collective works of the human spirit. The language is ready, or can be quickly made ready, to define the artist's individuality. If no literary artist appears, it is not essentially because the language is too weak an instrument, it is because the culture of the people is not favorable to the growth of such personality as seeks a truly individual verbal expression.

SUMMARY

Though great literary art gives the illusion of complete freedom, the writer is bound by the limitations of his language, just as the sculptor is bound by the limitations of clay, bronze, or marble. But there are two levels of art: (1) a generalized non-linguistic level and (2) a specifically linguistical level. Scientific truths are non-linguistic and can be easily translated from language to language; some artists, whose spirits move in largely non-linguistic areas, seem to strain their language (Whitman, Browning). The most satisfying art combines the two levels (Shakespeare, Heine). Some artists move largely at the specifically linguistic level (Swinburne) and are all but untranslatable.

Languages provided the "material" for literary art, and languages vary in richness of resources; but art may not sensibly be judged solely by the richness of the material it works with. Great art suits its material.

Style is not absolute, but relative to language. Highly inflected languages make for periodic structures; analytic ones, for loose structures. Chinese allows for a terseness, Latin for a luxuriance which English cannot match.

In prosody one may see these generalizations illustrated. Quantity was natural to Greek and worked fairly well for Latin; English demands stress; French, having neither quantity nor stress, operates on syllable groupings and finds the echo of rhyme more useful than does

English; Chinese uses syllable-groupings, rhyme, and pitch contrasts.

Every language provides sufficient material and has sufficient leeway for artistic expression.

NOTES

A few notes, all over-simplified, perhaps, may help you understand some of the terms in the essay.

Stress in language refers to comparative loudness and softness of succeeding syllables. English illustrates this principle everywhere, as the following phrases show:

> I conTEST the conTest.
> I perMIT the PERmit.
> I adDRESS this to your ADDress.

Quantity in language is strange to us, for our ears are not sensitive to the *length* of syllables, as they are to syllable stress. But if we listen with care, we can hear that some syllables are longer in duration than others in our language: the second syllable in *repetition* (rep-e-ti-tion) is shorter than the others; likewise the second in *tantamount* (tant-a-mount) and in *beauty* (beau-ty), even if we say these words without changing the stress or accent from syllable to syllable. Speakers of a quantitative language have their ears tuned to differences in duration, quite as musicians have their ears trained to distinguish a quarter note from a half note (and both from a dotted quarter note) in terms of the *length* of the sound.

Rhyme, of course, is the echoing of a sound or set of sounds: *June* echoes *moon* and *tune* and *croon,* as we know from popular song lyrics.

Pitch contrasts are not foreign to English, though our language doesn't make use of them as Chinese does. An illustration of our various ways of saying "Oh" may help clarify this feature of language. Listen to the "tune" or pitch variations of "Oh" in the four following examples:

(1) "Johnny forgot his lunch money."
    "Oh?" [Is that so? I didn't know it.]
(2) "But he didn't know we were going."
    "Oh." [I see; that makes a difference.]
(3) "Stick 'em up, sister!"
    "Oh!" [Good Heavens! I'm being robbed!]
(4) "Johnny hurt his little finger."
    "Oh." [Poor little thing, I want to comfort him.]

The pitch of the "Oh" in (1) slides up: Oh $\nearrow$; the pitch in (2) slides down: Oh $\searrow$; the pitch in (3) stays high: Oh $\rightarrow$; the pitch in (4) stays low: Oh$_\rightarrow$.

Syllable-groupings may be understood, perhaps, if we consider them in some simple forms, such as college yells, which often use this pattern of 3, 3, 4, and 3 syllables:

Sis - boom - bah   (*3 syllables*)
Ha - ha - ha   (*3 syllables*)

Fee - Fie - Foe - Fum   (*4 syllables*)
Rah - Rah - Rah (*3 syllables*)

And some of you may have tried your hand at such syllabic forms as the Japanese *haiku,* which demands a pattern of 5, 7, and 5 syllables:

Rain is a drummer,   (*5 syllables*)
Beating on the earth in spring,   (*7 syllables*)
Exciting new life.   (*5 syllables*)   [by Joe Ivanko]

Periodic structures are sentences which do not become grammatically complete until the very end; *loose structures* are grammatically complete before they end, and typically various modifying structures are hung on to them. This is loose structure:

Mother stood at the head of the stairs, looking for all the world like a mad woman.

The same sentence, in periodic-structure pattern:

There at the head of the stairs, looking for all the world like a mad woman, *stood mother.*

SOME ENGLISH LYRICS

I

Let me not to the marriage of true minds
Admit impediments. Love is not love
Which alters when it alteration finds,
Or bends with the remover to remove:
O, no! it is an ever-fixèd mark
That looks on tempests, and is never shaken;
It is the star to every wandering bark,
Whose worth's unknown, although his height be taken.
Love's not Time's fool, though rosy lips and cheeks
Within his bending sickle's compass come;
Love alters not with his brief hours and weeks,
But bears it out even to the edge of doom:
     If this be error, and upon be proved,
     I never writ, nor no man ever loved.

—SHAKESPEARE

II

A child said *What is the grass?* fetching it to me with full hands;
How could I answer the child? I do not know what it is any more than he.

I guess it must be the flag of my disposition, out of hopeful green stuff woven.

Or I guess it is the handkerchief of the Lord,

A scented gift and remembrancer designedly dropped,

Bearing the owner's name someway in the corners, that we may see and
    remark, and say *Whose?*

Or I guess the grass is itself a child, the produced babe of the
    vegetation.

Or I guess it is a uniform hieroglyphic,
And it means, Sprouting alike in broad zones and narrow zones,
Growing among black folks as among white,
Kanuch, Tuckahoe, Congressman, Cuff, I give them the same, I receive
    the same.   —WHITMAN

III
At the midnight in the silence of the sleep-time,
    When you set your fancies free,
Will they pass to where—by death, fools think, imprisoned—
Low he lies who once so loved you, whom you loved so,
    —Pity me?

Oh to love so, be so loved, yet so mistaken!
    What had I on earth to do
With the slothful, with the mawkish, the unmanly?
Like the aimless, helpless, hopeless, did I drivel
    —Being—who?

One who never turned his back but marched breast forward,
    Never doubted clouds would break,
Never dreamed, though right were worsted, wrong would triumph,
Held we fall to rise, are baffled to fight better,
    Sleep to wake.

No, at noonday in the bustle of man's work-time
    Greet the unseen with a cheer!
Bid him forward, breast and back as either should be,
"Strive and thrive!" cry "Speed,—fight on, fare ever
    There as here!"   —BROWNING

IV
When the hounds of spring are on winter's traces,
    The mother of months in meadow or plain
Fills the shadows and windy places
    With lisp of leaves and ripple of rain;
And the brown bright nightingale amorous
Is half assuaged for Itylus,
For the Thracian ships and the foreign faces,
    The tongueless vigil, and all the pain.
Come with bows bent and with emptying of quivers,
    Maiden most perfect, lady of light,
With a noise of winds and many rivers,

> With a clamour of waters, and with might;
> Bind on thy sandals, O thou most fleet,
> Over the splendour and speed of thy feet;
> For the faint east quickens, the wan west shivers,
> Round the feet of the day and the feet of the night.
> —SWINBURNE

CLASSICAL METERS IN ENGLISH

[An attempt at classical hexameters]
Bluebeard spake to his wife in tones of tender affection:
"Barbara, take these keys; thine husband goes on a journey,
Such a necessity drives me to go: unwilling I leave thee;
Be thou keeper of all while Bluebeard mourns in his absence." . . .
Hearken, a noise in the hall, the strong portcullis ascending.
Bluebeard strode to his bride, and kissed his Barbara fiercely,
Thundering, "Where's my key?" but waiting long for an answer,
His blue beard grew dark and writhed in indigo blackness.
            —from *Bluebeard's Keys,* a nineteenth-century child's book

SOME ENGLISH PROSE

I

I deny not but that it is of greatest concernment in the Church and
Commonwealth, to have a vigilant eye how books demean themselves
as well as men; and thereafter to confine, imprison, and do sharpest
justice on them as malefactors. For books are not absolutely dead
things, but do contain a potency of life in them to be as active as that
soul was whose progeny they are; nay, they do preserve as in a vial the
purest efficacy and extraction of that living intellect that bred them. I
know they are as lively, and as vigorously productive, as those fabulous
dragon's teeth; and being sown up and down, may chance to spring up
armed men. And yet, on the other hand, unless wariness be used, as
good almost kill a man as kill a good book: who kills a man kills a
reasonable creature, God's image; but he who destroys a good book,
kills reason itself, kills the image of God, as it were, in the eye. Many a
man lives a burden to the earth; but a good book is the precious life-
blood of a master spirit, embalmed and treasured up on purpose to a
life beyond life.   —MILTON

II

Happiness of an approving Conscience! Did not Paul of Tarsus, whom
admiring men have since named Saint, feel that *he* was the "chief of
sinners"; and Nero of Rome, jocund in spirit (*wohlgemuth*), spend
much of his time in fiddling? Foolish Wordmonger and Motive-grinder,
who in thy Logic-mill hast an earthly mechanism for the Godlike itself,
and wouldst fain grind me out Virtue from the husks of Pleasure,—I
tell thee, Nay! To the unregenerate Prometheus Vinctus of a man, it is
ever the bitterest aggravation of his wretchedness that he is conscious

of Virtue, that he feels himself the victim not of suffering only, but of injustice. What then? Is the heroic inspiration we name Virtue but some Passion; some bubble of the blood, bubbling in the direction others *profit* by? I know not: only this I know, If what thou namest Happiness be our true aim, then are we all astray. With Stupidity and sound Digestion man may front much. But what, in these dull unimaginative days, are the terrors of Conscience to the diseases of the Liver!

—CARLYLE

III

The scientific mind in its questing after the truth reminds one of the stoat on the track of its quarry. Swift and elusive the quarry may be, besides having had a good start, but nothing will serve to turn aside or dishearten his pursuer, who follows steadily, patiently, without haste and without rest, with a deadly resolution and staying power which at last gets its reward. The difference is that the stoat makes no mistakes, and the seeker after truth makes many. And that is how it was with Herbert Spencer, when, after working out his theory of the origin of music to a triumphant conclusion, he set himself to find out and expound the function of music. On this second quest he goes off in the same temper, the same cold, deadly zeal, as on the first, and in the same way brings it to a victorious conclusion. Yet it was an imaginary scent he was following all the time, and an illusionary rabbit in which he set his teeth, and whose imagined heart he drains of blood to its last drop. There was no rabbit because there is no function.

—W. H. HUDSON *A Hind in Richmond Park* (New York: E. P. Dutton & Co., Inc., 1923), pp. 255–256. Reprinted by permission of the publisher.

Literature

CHARLES F. HOCKETT

Charles F. Hockett is professor of linguistics and anthropology at Cornell University. This selection from his Course in Modern Linguistics *(1958) suggests ways that linguistics may be applied to problems of literary analysis and criticism.*

[1] Literature is an art form, like painting, sculpture, music, drama, and the dance. Literature is distinguished from other art forms by the medium in which it works: language. Insofar as speech forms occur in other arts—sung words in music, speaking as well as action in drama—these other arts have literary aspects. The linguist is concerned with literature because it is his business to discover wherein literary discourse differs from everyday nonliterary discourse. So far, relatively few generalizations have been worked out along this line of investigation. In this section we merely report what little seems to be reasonably well established. If our remarks are seemingly trivial, it is because we must be more concerned with truth than with profundity.

Let us, in imagination, join a circle of Nootka Indians who are resting around the campfire after their day's work. One old man tells a story, which runs as follows in English translation [1]:

Kwatyat caught sight of two girls. "Whose daughters are you?" said Kwatyat to the two girls. The girls did not tell him who their father was. Many times did Kwatyat ask them who their father was, but they would not tell. At last the girls got angry. "The one whose children we are," said they, "is Sunbeam." For a long time the girls said this.

And then Kwatyat began to perspire because of the fact that their father was Sunbeam. Kwatyat began to perspire and he died. Now Kwatyat was perspiring and he swelled up like an inflated bladder, and

1. From Edward Sapir and Morris Swadesh, *Nootka Texts.* Linguistic Society of America, Philadelphia (1939).

it was because of the girls. Now Kwatyat warmed up and died. He was dead for quite a little while, and then he burst, making a loud noise as he burst. It was while he was dead that he heard how he burst with a noise.

The individual words and phrases of this story are mostly intelligible, but the narrative as a whole makes little sense to us—we might as well have heard it in the original Nootka. Yet as we look around the fire we note that the speaker is being followed with close attention and interest. The Nootka audience is getting something from the performance that we, as outsiders, cannot get. Furthermore, inquiry reveals that this same story has been told many times in the past; it is new to no one in the audience save ourselves.

Our own reaction to the story, be it bewilderment, boredom, disgust, or curiosity, is for our present purposes quite irrelevant. The point is that the participants in Nootka culture appreciate and value the story. Nor is it at all helpful for us to say, after recognizing this fact, that it is indicative of low or crude literary taste on the part of the Nootkas. This would simply be to resort, in a more indirect way, to our own personal responses. What we are after is at least the beginnings of an *objective* understanding of literature.

In every society known to history or anthropology, with one insignificant exception, there are some discourses, short or long, which the members of the society agree on evaluating positively and which they insist shall be repeated from time to time in essentially unchanged form. *These discourses constitute the literature of that society.*

The one insignificant exception to this generalization and definition is our own complex Western social order. For us, also, some discourses are highly valued and others are not; but, peculiarly—and unlike anything known in other societies—the discourses which the literary specialist values most highly tend to be most despised by the layman. One result of this strange situation is that Western society is a very bad point of departure if we want to understand the typical nature of literature. We are forced to look elsewhere at first, and only later turn to a self-examination.

Yet even when we do look closely enough at smaller and more homogeneous societies, we find inconsistencies and disagreements: the literary status of a discourse turns out to be a matter of degree rather than kind. One story may be repeated very often, another rarely. One story may be valued by a whole tribe, another only by some small segment. One story may retain its literary status for generations, while another may hold it only for a year or so.

Another question that immediately arises is: how changed can the form of a discourse be from one recounting to another, and still leave it "essentially" unchanged? There seems to be much variation in this; in general the degree of objective identity (that could be determined, for example, by carefully recording two successive recountings and listing the differences) seems to be irrelevant, and what is relevant is rather a feeling on the part of the members of the society that at a given time the discourse being told is one that has been told before.

COMMON FEATURES OF LITERARY DISCOURSE

[2] When the literature of a society has been collected, the analyst faces the problem of determining wherein it differs from ordinary non-literary discourse in the same society. This is not the problem of *definition*—we already know that the discourses in question are literary for the society in which they occur. Rather, it is the problem of *describing* or *characterizing* that which has already been defined.

For the most part this study has to be carried out separately for each society. But two general characteristics seem to be quite common, if not universal: *excellence of speech* and *special style*.

Excellence of Speech. Apparently in every society it is generally recognized that some individuals are more effective users of the machinery afforded by the society's language than are others. The Menomini Indians, for example, can name certain people who are unusually good speakers of Menomini, and others who are unusually poor. Some do very little hemming and hawing; others speak in badly disconnected spurts. The good speaker keeps his pronominal references and his concord, government, and cross-reference clear; the poor speaker gets lost in the emerging grammatical complexities of what he is trying to say. In other words, though the grammatical machinery is different, variations of effectiveness and fluency of control are much as they are with us.

Now it is very generally required, in an illiterate or a literate society, that literary discourse be characterized by excellence of speech. The story-teller must be a fluent and effective speaker; the writer in a literate society must write in such a way that reading can be fluent and effective. However, the converse of this generalization does not hold: not all excellent speech qualifies as literary.

It is easy to think one has found an exception when, in fact, one has not. For example, the Plains Cree have a favored manner of delivery for certain very familiar stories, in the form of a succession of short disconnected sentences which merely allude to the chief episodes. The hearers, knowing the details, are supposed to fill them in for themselves. This style seems like "poor speech" to us only because we do not have anything comparable. Actually, it calls for skill and judgment on the part of the narrator.

Special Style · The term "style" is not easy to define precisely. Roughly speaking, two utterances in the same language which convey approximately the same information, but which are different in their linguistic structure, can be said to differ in style: *He came too soon* and *He arrived prematurely,* or *Sir, I have the honor to inform you* and *Jeez, Boss, get a load of dis.* Stylistic variations within a single language are universal, and in many cases there are certain special styles which are felt to be peculiarly appropriate to certain circumstances. An Oneida chief, making a speech, begins with the style of pronunciation of everyday conversation, but gradually lapses into a special quavery sing-song. We all know the special style used by a minister at the pulpit, reciting the words of a hymn which is about to be sung, or intoning his share during responsive reading of a psalm. None of us would venture to use this style of speech in ordering groceries or in asking a girl for a date.

It is very common for literary discourse to differ from everyday speech in describable stylistic ways. In Fox, one recounts what happened to one in town yesterday using verb forms in the modes of the so-called independent order; but one tells a literary story using verb forms in the modes of the conjunct order. Conjunct order verbs in everyday speech mark dependent clauses; independent order verbs in literary narrative, on the other hand, mark direct quotations of things said by characters or else parenthetical

explanations addressed to the hearer. Sometimes, in other societies, the stylistic differences are much less prominent than this;
sometimes they are much more prominent. But where a clearly
literary narrative does not differ at all stylistically from everyday
speech, it seems that there is always something special about the
content. Everyday discourse about everyday content seems never
to qualify as literature.

Related to this is a customary use of a special manner of speech
whenever the words of some recurrent character or type of character are quoted. The customary recounting of *Goldilocks and
the Three Bears* incorporates such a device. We also use it, in
serious writing as well as in vaudeville jokes, when we quote the
prototypical Irishman, Scotsman, or Brooklynite. In Nootka mythological narratives the characters Deer and Mink regularly distort
the phonemic structure of words in one fashion (turning all occurrences of s c c'/ and š č č'/ into laterals /ł ƛ ƛ'), Raven in another,
and Kwatyat in a third. A story-teller who forgets to make the
proper changes may lose prestige.

Extensive use of figures of speech, or of one or another type of
figure of speech, can mark stylistic differences, and may serve to
distinguish literary from non-literary discourse, as well as the
literature of one community from that of another. The figures of
speech common in the literature of the aboriginal New World are
not the same as those most familiar to us: translations into English
of "classic" Indian speeches are apt to lose the native stylistic
values and replace them by those more familiar in our own literature. This shows up even in non-literary contexts. Such place-
names as *Father-of-Waters* (for the Mississippi) and *Cheop's
Temple* (for a butte in the Grand Canyon) are Old-World in style
and were invented by Europeans; the Fox Indian word/mešisi·
pi/, whence our *Mississippi*, means merely "big river," and the
Havasupai Indian word for the mountains which include Cheop's
Temple means merely "Buckskin mountains."

The stylistic examples given above are all on a low size-level—
that of words, phrases, sentences, or even that of phonemes
(Nootka phoneme-replacement in the speech of certain characters). Comparable phenomena at higher size-levels are not usually
classed as style by literary specialists, but as "structure." The relatively precise machinery of analysis which linguists have developed does not yet enable us to make effective statements about

stylistic or structural features of longer segments of discourse—conversations, narratives, "paragraphs," or whole stories. Literary scholars have a battery of terms, *plot, counterplot, introduction, climax, anticlimax, dénouement* with which they describe the larger-grained structure of certain types of literary discourse. A whole novel, we must assume, has some sort of a determinate IC-structure, its ICs in turn consisting of still smaller ones, and so on down until we reach individual morphemes. The terminological arsenal of the literary scholar applies, often very well, to the largest size-levels of this structure; that of the linguist applies equally well to the smallest size-levels; but there is at present a poorly explored terrain in between.

TYPES OF LITERATURE

[3]   The literature of a society may be anything but homogeneous. Usually there are two or more sharply different categories of literary discourse, occurring perhaps under different circumstances. Folklorists make use of various classificatory terms—"proverbs," "riddles," "folktales," "myths," "origin myths," and the like. But the use of such terms requires great care, for what we must always seek, in the first instance, is an indigenous classification—one overtly given by the participants of the society in question, or indicated by their differential behavior.

For example, the Plains Cree distinguish between an /a·tayo·hke·win/ or "sacred story," on the one hand, and an /a·cimo·win/ —any other sort of narrative—on the other. The former deals with events in an earlier stage of the history of the world, before things had settled into the familiar fixed patterns which now surround us: the characters are part animal, part human, and part spirit, and are prototypes of the actual animals and people of today. Any /a·tayo·hke·win/ under aboriginal conditions was by definition literary. An /a·cimo·win/, on the other hand, might or might not be, for the term is quite inclusive. The indigenous Cree classification may well be more complicated than just described, but of this two-way differentiation we are sure.

Whatever other sort of indigenous classification may appear in a society, the segregation of the sacred tale from all other kinds is very widespread; certainly it is found in many social groups within our own Western society.

PROSE AND POETRY

[4] Poetry is widespread, though not certainly known to exist in all societies. It is everywhere distinguished from prose in the same fundamental way, but the distinction is one of degree, not of kind.

Most poetry can be described as literature in the form of *verse.* Verse, in turn, can be defined as discourse in which the speaker binds himself in advance to follow certain more or less closely defined patterns of rhythm, regardless of the topic of the discourse. The rhythm is variously achieved in different languages: sometimes it is a spacing of stresses, lengths, or tones; sometimes it is a spaced recurrence of vowels or consonants or both (yielding *rhyme* and *assonance*). No matter how alien the pattern may be to our ears, the factor of controlled rhythm is present or the discourse cannot qualify as verse. The definition of verse obviously depends on phonological rather than grammatical properties of the discourse.

But not all poetry conforms neatly to the above description. Probably a better basic definition of poetic discourse is that in it as much as possible is made of the secondary associations of the shapes which represent morphemes, as a means of reinforcing the obvious literal meaning of the words. The emergence in poetry of rhythm, rhyme, and assonance then comes about as one formal means to the end. The works of Walt Whitman clearly count as English poetry under this basic definition, though they conform to no simple verse pattern. Contrariwise, discourse can be produced in the strictest verse pattern without being poetry—because it fails to qualify as literature.

It is clear that the exact grammatical and phonemic shape of a poem is important. Poetry under conditions of illiteracy tends to retain its shape from one recounting to another much more precisely than does prose literature, for obvious reasons. Even so, poetry passed down by word-of-mouth is subject to a remarkable amount of modification in course of time, as the most casual study of the folksongs of our own country will show.

THE IMPACT OF WRITING ON LITERATURE

[5] Most of our discussion so far has applied especially to the literature of illiterate societies. The development of writing in

relatively recent times (the last few thousand years, and only in certain parts of the world) has brought about certain transformations. We shall take these up under three headings: *the impact of writing style, the survival factor,* and *emphasis on authorship.*

The Impact of Writing Style · Orally transmitted literature is, of course, not cast in a writing style. This often proves embarrassing to the collector of folk-tales, who faces the task of producing a written record of what has not previously been written.

But if a literary artist lives in a community where his products will be cast in written form to begin with, the situation is different. The raw-materials of his trade are not simply the whole language, but rather the writing style of the language. This is not an uncompensated loss, for, although some elements of speech can be written only inaccurately, if at all, writing systems make up for this by developing devices which are independent of language and go beyond it. All of these devices are available to the writer in a literate community.

A few trivial examples must suffice. In the West there is an established special typographical convention for verse, by which certain rhythmic units are written in successive lines—and, because of this, are called "lines." Thus we have:

> The day is done, and the darkness
> Falls from the wings of Night,
> As a feather is wafted downward
> From an eagle in his flight.

The rhythmic organization of this poem is actually—save for the presence of rhyme—very similar to (though not identical with) that of *Evangeline:*

| The | dáy | is | dóne and the | dárkness | ‖ |
| | This is the | fórest | pri- | méval | ‖ |

| | fálls from the | wíngs | of | níght | |
| the | múrmuring | pínes and the | | hémlocks | |

(Remember that English has stress-timed rhythm, so that the number of stresses in a passage is the main determinant of its duration.) If Longfellow had followed the same orthographic convention here as he did for *Evangeline,* it would specifically seem like a major alteration, but we must conclude that the difference is not to any great extent linguistic.

A few writers have chosen to attain a special effect (we shall not venture to describe it) by printing their verses in solid paragraphs, like prose. Illustrating with the same poem, we should have:

The day is done, and the darkness falls from the wings of Night, as a feather is wafted downward from an eagle in his flight. I see the lights of the village gleam through the rain and the mist, . . .

There have been experiments with other typographical arrangements. George Herbert (early 17th century) wrote a poem called *The Altar* with long first and last lines, short and centered middle ones, so that the arrangement of print on the page forms a rough picture of an altar. Lewis Carroll's verse beginning *Fury said to a mouse* was originally printed so that the words formed a mouse's tail curling down the page.

One of the subjects studied by analysts and historians of literature is the stylistic peculiarities of different writers, the sources thereof, and the way in which one writer affects another along such lines. Individual styles are related to the general writing style of a language in that each of the former is some sort of specialization within the confines of the latter, just as the latter—save for the late-developed independent features of writing—is a specialization of the language as a whole.

The Survival Factor · In an illiterate society a story or other literary work will survive only as long as it continues to be learned by at least one person in each generation. If this process of transmission fails, either through changing taste or through accident, the story is gone.

With the introduction of writing the conditions for survival change. When a discourse is written down, it can be kept in essentially unchanged form much more easily; the exact degree of ease depends on the type of writing-materials, the ease with which copies are made (witness the tremendous impact of the invention of printing), and the extent to which it is the habit to make them.

There is no guarantee, however, that only discourse considered to have literary merit will be committed to writing. For example, the accidents of history have preserved for us a highly erratic collection of writings from the first few centuries of English-speaking Britain: *Beowulf*, parts of some other poems of various kinds, lives of the saints, laws, recipes for remedies, charms, historical chronicles, and so on. Specialists in Old English ignore no slightest scrap of this, but such specialists are not literary scholars in the narrow sense of the term; rather, they seek, through the sifting of all the available evidence, to determine as much as they can about the pattern of life in early England. Even for narrower literary purposes this background work is essential, for without it we cannot hope to find out which discourses or types of discourses, preserved or not, were actually literature for the Anglo-Saxons.

Literacy may preserve a discourse past the period in the history of a society during which it qualifies as literature. This, again, is unlikely or impossible in an illiterate society. Having thus survived, a discourse may be rediscovered by a later generation, and regain its literary status. This happened, in a way, to various of the works of classical Greek and Roman authors, which were nowhere read or appreciated during the earlier Middle Ages of Europe, but which are now once again treasured by a certain few elements of our society, if not by the man on the street.

Poetry, and literature which verges on the poetic, is sometimes valued primarily for reasons of style rather than content. But language constantly changes, and this means that the frame of reference for the rhythmic and associative features which constitute poetic style is also constantly changing. In an illiterate society the precise shape of a poem may gradually be modified, a word replaced here, a rhythm or rhyme brought up to date there, in such a way as to keep pace with the changing language. On this score the introduction of writing has some implications which might be called unfortunate. Once a poem is written down it is fixed: it has lost its ability to grow with the language. Sooner or later, the poem is left behind.

This has happened to Anglo-Saxon poetry in the last thousand years: it is meaningless to us unless we first study Old English as we would study French or Chinese, and no amount of labor can make it sound to us as it did to our ancestors. The poetry of Shakespeare, written only four-hundred-odd years ago, is still largely understandable, and was so extremely well contrived that it still moves many of us deeply. Yet nothing can prevent it from suffering, in the end, the same fate: its stylistic merits will in due time be lost forever to all but a handful of antiquarians.

Sufficiently strong motivation, such as that based in religious conviction, can fight a partially effective delaying action against this. The King James translation of the Bible is still with us, and preferred by many to the newer versions; the ritual discourses of the Church of England are even older. The ultimate outcome of this sort of delaying action appears in the use of a totally alien language for certain purposes: Latin in the Catholic Church, so-called Classical Arabic by Mohammedans. In extreme cases like these, the emotional attachment and positive valuation come first, and are by fiat, rather than because of the intrinsic properties of the discourses, associated with the latter.

Emphasis on Authorship. In an illiterate society the literary artist is the individual who recounts the traditional stories or recites the traditional poetry in a way which is pleasing and proper to his contemporaries. There is no distinction between creator and performer: the two are bound up in a single individual, whose discourse is largely that passed down to him from his predecessors, but who makes his own minor alterations, deletions, and additions, in keeping with the contemporary language of everyday affairs, current conditions of life, and his own personality. This does not mean, of course, that "folktales" are invented by the "folk" in any mystic sense. Every single element of a given folktale was invented by some specific artisan somewhere in the tale's past history.

We can find the same thing in the literature of literate communities. The Faust legend is much older than Marlowe; his was not the first treatment in written form, and his successors have included Goethe, librettists working for Gounod and for Boito, Thomas Mann, and many others. We could regard the legend itself as "the" literary unit, and think of all the writers and dramatists we have mentioned as passers-on of the legend, each adding his own modifications, just as in an illiterate society.

But there is a sharp difference. In the illiterate society no one is apt to be acquainted with more than two or three slightly differing manipulations of a single theme—one old man may put episode A before episode B, and another may reverse this order. In a literate society a single generation has access to many different treatments of a single theme, both those worked out by contemporaries and those inherited from earlier times. Thus we *have* Marlowe's play, and Goethe's, and Gounod's opera, and Boito's, and Thomas Mann's *Doktor Faustus,* and *The Devil and Daniel Webster,* to say nothing of rewrites of the same plot in one variety of contemporary pulp fiction. For the literary scholar this changes the emphasis. It is naturally worthy of note that a single legend threads through all these varied treatments; but of much greater interest are the differences: the creative artisanship of each writer, the ways in which he individually reflects—or repudiates—the temper of his own times and the pattern of his own language. Thus arises the *emphasis on authorship.*

This emphasis makes itself felt not alone in the work of the literary scholar or critic. It permeates the appreciation of literature by the layman, and, most important, invades the activity of the would-be literary artist and molds his work. The writer is forced by the nature of a literate literary tradition to drive towards individuality, towards the unique and different. This is no place to discuss the possible consequences, save to point out that such an orientation may well be directly antithetical to the original and fundamental nature of literature.

LANGUAGE, LITERATURE, AND LIFE

[6]   A common notion holds that great writers, such as Shakespeare and Milton, are the "architects of the English language"; that is, that individuals of special literary ability are those primarily responsible for the shape a language takes in the mouths of subsequent generations of ordinary speakers.

This theory is consonant with the emphasis on authorship of which we have just spoken, and is held with amazing tenacity by some scholars. Yet there is not a shred of evidence in its support. The scholars in question dip badly calibrated depth-gages into the river of language: they overestimate the extent and durability of the "surface froth" and underestimate the deeper more slowly flowing layers. Suppose, for example, that we examine Shakespeare's usage of English in comparison with our own. We find the following classes of forms and usages:

1. Numerous items shared by Shakespeare and ourselves, but inherited by Shakespeare from the everyday speakers who preceded him: the bulk of the grammatical pattern, most short idioms, and even slang phrases like *there's the rub.*

2. A few idioms invented by Shakespeare and now used, though only by some people and under rather special circumstances, because he used them (*allusions* and *quotations*); *to be or not to be, the most unkindest cut of all.* These are "surface froth."

3. Some passages which we cannot understand without help, because the words and phrases involved have since fallen into disuse:

> If I do prove her haggard,
> Though that her jesses were my dear heart-strings,
> I'd whistle her off, and let her down the wind,
> To prey at fortune.

The reference is to falconry, now largely a lost art.

Surprising as it may be, a comparable examination of, say, the King James Bible yields much the same results. The "architects" of our language are not literary artists, but the masses of people who use the language for everyday purposes. The greatness of a literary artist is not measured in terms of his stylistic novelty—if he does not operate within the body of shared conventions which constitute ordinary language, he can hope only for a short faddistic following—but by the extent to which he can develop freedom and variety of expression *within* the constraints imposed by the language. So far as language is concerned, the greatest of literary artists is infinitely more a recipient than a donor.

If we must thus conclude that the impact of literature on language is trivial, no comparable conclusion is justified about the impact of literature on the business of living. The existence of a stock of positively evaluated and oft-repeated discourses is a phenomenon made possible by language: it is patent that dogs and apes, having no language, also have no literature. One of the most important things about human language is that it serves as the medium for literature. The literary tradition of a community, in turn, is a vital mechanism in the training of the young in culturally approved attitudes and patterns of behavior; it serves to transmit the moral fiber of the community from one generation to the next. Speaking of Menomini sacred tales, Bloomfield wrote [2]:

[These stories deal] with a far-off time when the world as we know

2. From Leonard Bloomfield, *Menomini Texts*. Publications of the American Ethnological Society 12, New York (1928).

it was in process of formation. The spirit animals enter in human or semi-human form, and the powers of the sky still dwell on earth. These stories are considered as true; they are told to inform and instruct; they often explain the origin of things, especially of plants and animals, and of customs. Even the lovable ineptitudes of [the culture hero] indicate by contrast the correct human way of obtaining food and the like.

"Marginal men," their aboriginal heritage undermined by the intrusion of Western ways, lose their literature—if the stories are remembered, the evaluations are gone—and the cultural orientation which it provides. Perhaps this is not unrelated to the peculiar state of literature in Western society itself.

SUMMARY

[1]   Perhaps the linguist can best approach literature in illiterate societies. In all but our own culture literature seems to be those discourses which members of society agree upon in evaluation and insist be repeated in essentially unchanged form.

[2]   The common features of literature seem to be excellence of speech and special style.

[3]   Literary types must be determined by the society producing the literature; they cannot be imposed by outsiders. But the separation of sacred tales from other kinds is a widespread one.

[4]   Our poetry may be distinguished from prose in that it represents a discourse in which the speaker binds himself to more or less defined patterns of rhythm. But a better linguistic definition is that in poetry "as much as possible is made of the secondary associations of the shapes which represent morphemes, as a means of reinforcing the obvious literal meaning of the words."

[5]   Writing affects literature in that it provides devices not open to speech (lines, verse forms, etc.); it provides for survival of literature in exact form and serves as a conservative influence upon the language; and it throws emphasis upon authorship and hence individuality of the literature.

[6]   Contrary to popular belief, literary artists are not "architects of language"; they affect the language very little. But their impact upon life may be very great, and a society which loses its literature loses the cultural orientation which literature provides.

NOTES

Perhaps only one term in this essay needs an explanatory note. IC, mentioned at the end of section [2], stands for "immediate constituent." In linguistics, a "constituent" is any morpheme, word, or construction which enters into a larger construction. An "immediate constituent" is one of the two or more constituents which directly form a construction. So, in such a sentence as "The silly child has been singing hymns," each word is a constituent, but not an immediate constituent of the sentence. The immediate constituents of the sentence are the constructions "The silly child" and "has been singing hymns." The immediate constituents of "The silly child" are "The" and "silly child." The IC's of "silly child," of course, are "silly" and "child."

What Professor Hockett means by the IC structure of a novel is the linguistic structuring from the work as a whole down to words and morphemes. Literary critics have dealt generally with the work as a whole and its big divisions; linguists have worked with morphemes, words, and constructions up to sentence proportions. But between the sentence and the work as a whole, not much scholarly work has been done.

PART SEVEN   Of Various Vintages

Logic and Grammar

HENRY SWEET

Henry Sweet (1845–1912), world-famous English linguist, was a reader in phonetics at Oxford from 1901 until his death; he was never awarded an important chair at Oxford, to the amazement of scholars throughout the world. His New English Grammar, Logical and Historical *(1892, 1898), from which this selection is taken, is the most significant attempt to formulate a logical grammar of English.*

GRAMMATICAL AND LOGICAL CATEGORIES

[1]   A group of grammatical forms expressing the same meaning —having the same functions—constitutes a **grammatical category.** Thus the addition of *-s* in *trees,* of *-ren* in *children,* and the change of *a* into *e* in *men* together constitute—or help to constitute—the grammatical category "plural of nouns," which, again, falls under wider grammatical categories, such as "number" (singular and plural number), "inflection." So also the inflections in *I called, I held,* etc. constitute the grammatical category "preterite tense of verbs."

[2]   Every grammatical category is the expression of some general idea—some **logical category.** Thus the grammatical category "plural" expresses "more-than-oneness," and therefore falls under the wider logical categories of "number" and "quantity"; and the grammatical category "tense" corresponds to the logical category "time."

[3]   But in actual language—which is always an imperfect instrument of thought—the grammatical and logical categories do

not always exactly correspond to one another. Thus in the word-group *a ten pound note* compared with *ten pounds,* plurality is not expressed grammatically by any inflection of *pound,* but is left to be inferred from the meaning of *ten.* In such a word-group as *many a man,* the divergence between the grammatical and the corresponding logical category is still stronger; for the word *many* shows that "more than one" is meant, and yet the combination *a man* is the regular grammatical expression of "oneness" or the singular number.

[4] For this reason it will be advisable to get clear notions of the logical categories commonly expressed in language before dealing with the corresponding grammatical categories—that is, to learn to distinguish between *what* we say and *how* we say it. Under the head of logical categories we will learn to regard words solely from the logical point of view—to classify them entirely by the ideas they express, making, for instance, no distinction between *a man* in *many a man* and *men* in *many men,* but regarding them both as expressions of the idea of "more-than-oneness." Under the head of grammatical categories, on the other hand, we will regard *man,* not only in *one man* but also in *many a man,* as belonging to one and the same category of "singular number," although, of course, we shall point out such divergences between form and meaning, and try to explain the origin of them.

IDEAS EXPRESSED BY WORDS

SUBSTANCES AND THEIR ATTRIBUTES

[5] The ideas of which thoughts are made up are concerned mainly with **substances** (material things) and their **attributes.** Substances are known to us solely by their attributes, that is, the impressions these substances make on our senses. Thus the substance "gold" is known to us by its attributes of "hardness," "heaviness," "yellow colour," etc., which together make up our idea of the substance "gold." Such words as *gold, man, house* are, therefore, substance-words; such words as *hard, hardness, heavy, heavily, weight, yellow* are attribute-words.

[6] These last all express **permanent attributes.** There are also changing attributes or **phenomena.** Thus "man" is known to us not only by a number of permanent attributes—"shape," "size," etc.,— but also by the phenomena "movement," "speech," "thought," etc.

Hence we call *move, movement, motion, speak, speaking, speech, think, thought, thoughtful, thoughtfully,* etc., phenomenon-words.

[7]   For convenience, words denoting permanent attributes and those denoting changing attributes or phenomena, are included under the common name **abstract**. Every word which is not a substance-word must therefore be an abstract word. In grammar substance-words are generally called **concrete**. Thus *gold* is a concrete word.

"Concrete" and "abstract" also have a totally different logical meaning [16]. In this—which is the original—sense of the word, substance-words can be abstract as well as concrete.

[8]   It is evidently impossible to think of a substance without thinking of its attributes. But it is equally impossible to think of all these attributes at once. When we think of a substance, we are reminded only of some—perhaps only one—of its attributes; and under different circumstances different attributes become prominent in our minds. Thus in comparing "hair" to "gold," we think only of the colour of gold, not of its hardness or weight.

[9]   It is equally evident that the only way in which we can form an idea of any attribute, such as "yellow," is by thinking of a number of yellow substances, such as "gold," "buttercups," etc.

[10]   But it is easier to think of an attribute apart from substances than it is to think of a substance apart from its attributes. Phenomena are still more independent than permanent attributes. Thus, although we know that without something to burn—wood, coals, etc.—there can be no fire, and that what we call electricity can only show itself in connection with matter (substances), yet when we see a fire in the distance, a moving light, or a flash of lightning, we are inclined to consider these phenomena as independent objects. Among uncivilised races, indeed, such phenomena as fire and electricity are regarded as living beings, and are even worshipped as gods.

QUALIFIERS

[11]   When we distinguish between *a tall man* and *a short man, tall* and *short* are evidently attribute-words. But when we distinguish between *many men, all men,* and *some men* or *few men,* we cannot say that *many, all, some, few* are attribute-words; they are only **qualifiers**. When we say *some Englishmen are tall,* or *many*

Englishmen are tall, the majority of Englishmen are tall, English-
men are mostly tall, the words *some, many, majority, mostly* do
not give us any information about Englishmen: they merely
qualify, or limit, or define the idea expressed by *Englishmen.*
Englishmen are tall by itself might mean "all Englishmen," "many
Englishmen," "some Englishmen," or "only a few Englishmen"; so
we add the words *all, many, some, few,* etc., to qualify the idea
expressed by *Englishmen.* Attribute-words may be qualified as
well as substance-words. Thus *very* in *a very strong man* qualifies
the attribute-word *strong.* Qualifiers themselves may be qualified,
as in *very many Englishmen.*

It is easy to distinguish between an attribute-word and a qualifier by asking ourselves, Does this word, which at first sight looks
like an attribute-word, give us any direct information about the
word it is connected with? Thus it is easy to see that even in such
a statement as *we are seven,* the word *seven* does not really tell
us anything about the persons designated by *we,* at least not in
the same way as *we are young, we are English,* etc. would. In
many cases, indeed, a qualifier cannot be used to make a statement with at all. Thus from *these tall men* we can infer *these men
are tall,* but we cannot make *some Englishmen* into **Englishmen
are some,* or *half the island* into **the island was half.*

[12]   The qualifiers we have hitherto been considering are all
quantitative words. There is another important class of qualifiers
called **mark-words,** which, as it were, put a mark on the word they
are associated with, singling it out or pointing to it in various
ways. Thus *this* and *that, here* and *there,* as in *this house, the man
there,* are mark-words of place; *now, then* are mark-words of
time; while such mark-words as *the* point out an object in thought,
as in *give me the book,* meaning "the book you know of," "the
book we were speaking about." Some mark-words, instead of
merely qualifying a word, act as substitutes for it. Thus the mark-
word *he* may be used as a substitute for the words *John, the man,*
etc., and the mark-word *it* may be used as a substitute for *the
book.*

[13]   Attribute-words may be used as qualifiers. Thus when
we say *give me that red book, not the blue one,* although *red* and
blue give information about the two books, they are not used for
that purpose, but simply to distinguish between the two books:
red and *blue* are in fact here used as mark-words, though they still

preserve their full attributive meanings. When attribute-words are used in this way, we call them **qualifying attribute-words.**

GENERAL AND SPECIAL WORDS

[14] Some attributes are of more **general** application than others. Thus there are more things that we can call *red* than there are that we can call *dark red* or *yellowish red,* and *red* itself falls under the still more general attribute *colour.* So also the qualifiers *many, few, some* fall under the more general category of *quantity.* The same gradations are seen also in substance-words. Thus *cast iron* and *wrought iron* go under *iron; iron,* together with *gold, silver, lead,* etc. goes under *metal;* and *metal* itself goes under *mineral,* and so on.

[15] The more **special** a word is, the more meaning it has. Thus *iron* implies all the attributes implied by the more general word *metal,* and, in addition, all the attributes that distinguish iron from gold and the other metals.

[16] Even if we confine ourselves to a single word, we can make the same distinction. Thus the word *man* may suggest the idea either of "man in general," as in *man is mortal,* or of one particular man, as when we talk of *this man* or *the man.* We call the former the **generalizing** (abstract), the latter the **specializing** (concrete) use of the word *man.* The specializing use evidently puts more meaning into the word: *the man* not only implies all the attributes that men have in common, but also implies further attributes by which we distinguish "the man" from other men.

It must be observed that the logical and the grammatical meanings of the terms **abstract** and **concrete** are distinct and even contradictory. When we talk of "man in the abstract" we are using *abstract* in its logical sense, while in grammar *abstract* is a convenient means of including attributes and phenomena under a common name [7]. Hence in grammar it is best to restrict these words to their grammatical meaning, using *generalizing* and *specializing* to express their logical meaning.

COMBINATION OF WORDS TO EXPRESS THOUGHTS

ADJUNCT-WORDS AND HEAD-WORDS

[17] The most general relation between words in sentences from a logical point of view is that of **adjunct-word** and **head-**

word, or, as we may also express it, of **modifier** and **modified**. Thus in the sentences *tall men are not always strong, all men are not strong, tall, strong,* and *all* are adjunct-words modifying the meaning of the head-word *men*. So also *dark, quick, quickly* are adjunct-words in *dark red, he has a quick step, he walks quickly. Stone* is an adjunct-word in *stone wall, wall of stone,* because it modifies (defines) the meaning of *wall*. So also *book (books)* is an adjunct-word in *book-seller, bookselling, sale of books, he sells books, he sold his books,* the corresponding head-words being *seller, selling, sale, sells, sold.*

[18] The distinction between adjunct-word and head-word is only a relative one: the same word may be a head-word in one sentence or context, and an adjunct-word in another, and the same word may even be a head-word and an adjunct-word at the same time. Thus in *he is very strong, strong* is an adjunct-word to *he,* and at the same time head-word to the adjunct-word *very,* which, again, may itself be a head-word, as in *he is not very strong.*

SUBJECT AND PREDICATE

[19] As we have seen, such a thought as "the earth is round" is made up of the two ideas "the earth" and "round" or "roundness." All thoughts require at least two ideas: (*a*) what we think of, called the **subject**—in this case "the earth," and (*b*) what we think concerning it, called the **predicate**, namely that it is "round," or has the attribute of "roundness." Hence in such a sentence as *the earth is round,* we call *earth* a subject-word, *round* a predicate-word. In this example the predicate-word—or predicate, as we may call it for the sake of shortness—is an attribute-word; but the predicate may be also a qualifier, as in *he is here, we are seven.*

[20] Subject and predicate may be joined together in various ways. In the above example the connection between them is affirmed (stated as a fact)—such a sentence as *the earth is round* being therefore called an "affirmative" sentence; but it may also be stated doubtfully, as in *perhaps the earth is round,* or denied, as in *the earth is not flat,* and the relation between subject and predicate may be modified in various other ways.

ASSUMPTION

[21]   If instead of stating some attribute or qualification about
the subject, we take it for granted, as in—

> For so the whole round earth is every way
> bound by gold chains about the feet of God,
> —TENNYSON

the predicate becomes an **assumptive** (commonly called "attributive"), and the word *round*—as also *whole*—is said to be used
assumptively (attributively). From such a collocation as *the round
earth* we can infer the statement *the earth is round*. Thus assumption may be regarded as implied or latent predication, and predication itself may be regarded as strengthened or developed
assumption.

Assumption is generally called "attribution" in grammars; but
this term is objectionable because it is liable to cause confusion
with the logical term "attribute."

It is easy to see that every assumptive word must be an adjunct-
word as well as every predicate, just as every subject-word must
be a head-word. But every adjunct-word is not necessarily an assumptive, for in grammar we use this term in contrast with "predicative," so that when we call a word "assumptive," we generally
imply that it can be used also as a predicate. Thus *the* and *very*
in *the earth, very good* are adjunct-words, but there would be no
object in calling them assumptives. But in grammar such qualifying words as *whole, all, seven* are said to be used attributively
in such word-groups as *the whole earth, all men, seven men;*
for although we cannot make *all men* into the statement **men are
all*, we can make the statement *we are seven, there are seven of us,*
and, besides, we feel that *all men* is analogous to *good men,* etc.

SUBORDINATION AND COORDINATION

[22]   The relation of adjunct-word to head-word is one of
subordination. But ideas can also be connected together with little
or no subordination of one to the other—they can stand in a **coordinate** relation to one another. Thus in *you and I will be there
before the others*, we cannot say that either of the two words con-

nected by *and* is subordinated to the other: we do not necessarily think of "you" first and then join "I" on to it, but we think of the two simultaneously, just as we should do if we expressed the idea of "you and I" by the single word *we*. *You* and *I* in the above sentence are also coordinate through having the same predicate in common.

[23] Even in predication the subordination to the subject-word is often very slight, for although the subject is generally more prominent in our minds than the predicate, the union of subject and predicate in thought is instantaneous, and if the two are of nearly equal importance, it may sometimes be almost a matter of indifference which idea is regarded as subject, and which as predicate. Thus it does not matter much whether we say *the first day of the week is Sunday*, or *Sunday is the first day of the week*, just as in numbering the days of the week we might write either 1 *Sunday*, 2 *Monday*, etc., or *Sunday* 1, *Monday* 2, etc.

[24] So also there are degrees of subordination of assumptives to their head-words.

When an assumptive is, as it were, detached from its head-word —as in *Alfred, king of England,* compared with *king Alfred,* where *king* is entirely subordinate—it is said to be in apposition to it.   ✸ ✸ ✸

PARTS OF SPEECH

[25] As regards their function in the sentence, words fall under certain classes called **parts of speech,** all the members of each of these classes having certain formal characteristics in common which distinguish them from the members of the other classes. Each of these classes has a name of its own—noun, adjective, verb, etc.

[26] Thus, if we compare nouns, such as *snow, tree, man,* with adjectives, such as *big, white, green,* and verbs, such as *melt, grow, speak,* we shall find that all nouns whose meaning admits of it agree in having plural inflections—generally formed by adding *s* (*trees*); that adjectives have no plural inflections, but have degrees of comparison (*big, bigger, biggest*)—which nouns and verbs have not; that verbs have inflections of their own distinct from those of the other parts of speech (*I grow, he grows, grown*); that

each part of speech has special form-words associated with it (*a tree, the tree; to grow, is growing, has grown*); and that each part of speech has a more or less definite position in the sentence with regard to other parts of speech (*white snow, the snow melts, the green tree, the tree is green*).

[27]   If we examine the **functions** of these three classes, we see at once that all verbs are predicative words—that they state something about a subject-word, which is generally a noun (*the snow melts*); that adjectives are often used as assumptive words (*white snow*), and so on.

[28]   If we examine the **meanings** of the words belonging to the different parts of speech, we shall find that such nouns as *tree, snow, man,* are all substance-words, while the adjectives and verbs given above are all attribute-words, the adjectives expressing permanent attributes, the verbs changing attributes or phenomena. We can easily see that there is a natural connection between the functions and meanings of these parts of speech. We see that the most natural way of speaking of a substance is to imply or state some attribute about it (*white snow, the snow melts*); and that permanent attributes, such as "whiteness," can often be taken for granted, while phenomena, such as "melting," being often sudden and unexpected, require to be stated explicitly.

[29]   But this connection, though natural, is not necessary. In language it is often necessary to state, as well as imply, permanent attributes (*the tree is green*), and it is sometimes convenient to make statements about attributes as well as substances. Thus, instead of using the word *white* as a means of implying something about *snow* or any other substance, we may wish to state or imply something about the attribute itself, as when we say *whiteness is an attribute of snow,* or talk of *the dazzling whiteness of the snow.* It is easy to see that there is no difference of meaning between *whiteness is an attribute of snow* and *snow is white:* the difference between *white* and the noun *whiteness* is purely formal and functional—grammatical, not logical.

CLASSIFICATION OF THE PARTS OF SPEECH

[30]   The parts of speech in inflectional languages are divided into two main groups, **declinable,** that is, capable of inflection, and

indeclinable, that is, incapable of inflection.

[31] The declinable parts of speech fall under the three main divisions, **nouns, adjectives,** and **verbs,** which have been already described. **Pronouns** are a special class of nouns and adjectives, and are accordingly distinguished as **noun-pronouns,** such as *I, they,* and **adjective-pronouns,** such as *my* and *that* in *my book, that man.* **Numerals** are another special class of nouns and adjectives: *three* in *three of us* is a **noun-numeral,** in *three men* an **adjective-numeral.** **Verbals** are a class of words intermediate between verbs on the one hand and nouns and adjectives on the other: they do not express predication, but keep all the other meanings and grammatical functions of the verbs from which they are formed. Noun-verbals comprise **infinitives,** such as *go* in *I will go, I wish to go,* and **gerunds,** such as *going* in *I think of going.* Adjective-verbals comprise various **participles,** such as *melting* and *melted* in *melting snow, the snow is melted.*

[32] Indeclinable words or **particles** comprise adverbs, prepositions, conjunctions, and interjections. The main function of **adverbs,** such as *quickly* and *very,* is to serve as adjunct-words to verbs and to other particles as in *the snow melted quickly, very quickly.* **Prepositions,** such as *of,* are joined to nouns to make them into adjunct-words, as in *man of honour,* where *of honour* is equivalent to the adjective *honourable.* **Conjunctions,** such as *if,* are used mainly to show the connection between sentences, as in *if you do so, you will repent it.* **Interjections,** such as *ah! alas!,* are sentence-words expressing various emotions.

[33] For convenience we include nouns in the limited sense of the word, noun-pronouns, noun-numerals and gerunds under the common designation **noun-word.** So also we include adjectives, adjective-pronouns, adjective-numerals and participles under the common designation **adjective-word.**

The term "verb" is sometimes used to include the verbals, sometimes to exclude them. When necessary, the predicative forms of the verb as opposed to the verbals are included under the term **finite verb:** thus in *I think of going, think* is a finite verb as opposed to the verbal (gerund) *going,* although both are included under the term "verb" in its wider sense.

[34] The following is, then, our classification of the parts of speech in English:

declinable
{
noun-words: noun, noun-pronoun, noun-numeral, infinitive, gerund.
adjective-words: adjective, adjective-pronoun, adjective-numeral, participles.
verb: finite verb, verbals (infinitive, gerund, participles).
}
indeclinable (particles): adverb, preposition, conjunction, interjection.

The distinction between the two classes which for convenience we distinguish as declinable and indeclinable parts of speech is not entirely dependent on the presence or absence of inflection, but really goes deeper, corresponding, to some extent, to the distinction between head-word and adjunct-word. The great majority of the particles are used only as adjunct-words, many of them being only form-words, while the noun-words, adjective-words and verbs generally stand to the particles in the relation of head-words.

The Three Ranks

OTTO JESPERSEN

Many of Otto Jespersen's ideas on grammar have influenced all subsequent students of English, though he has not always been credited with the effect he has had. This selection from his Essentials of English Grammar *(1933) illustrates Jespersen's ability to combine his detailed knowledge of linguistics with interesting insights into the nature of language.*

[1]   While the assignation of a word to one of the classes dealt with in the preceding chapter concerns the word in itself—a substantive remains always a substantive in whatever surroundings it may be found, and can therefore be marked as such in a dictionary—we now come to another classification which is somewhat similar in nature, but differs from the former because it concerns the mutual relations of words in combinations only and is applicable not only to words, but also to groups of words as such.

Take the three words *terribly cold weather.* They are evidently not on the same footing, *weather* being, grammatically, most important, to which the two others are subordinate, and of these again *cold* is more important than *terribly. Weather* is determined or defined by *cold,* and *cold* in its turn similarly determined or defined by *terribly.* We have thus three ranks: "weather" is **Primary,** "cold" **Secondary,** and "terribly" **Tertiary** in this combination.

[2]   In this example we found a substantive as primary, an adjective as secondary, and a particle (an adverb) as tertiary; and there is so far a certain correspondence between the three ranks and the three word-classes mentioned, as substantives, adjectives and adverbs habitually stand in this relation to one another. But,

From Otto Jespersen, *Essentials of English Grammar* (New York, 1933). Reprinted by permission of George Allen & Unwin, Ltd.

as we shall soon see, the correspondence is far from complete, and the two things, word-classes and ranks, really move in two different spheres. In some combinations a substantive may be secondary or tertiary, an adjective may be a primary, etc.

[3] If we compare the two expressions *this furiously barking dog* and *this dog barks furiously,* it is easy to see that while *dog* is primary, *this* secondary, and *furiously* tertiary in both, the verb *bark* is found in two different forms *barking* and *barks;* but in both forms it must be said to be subordinated to *dog* and superior in rank to *furiously;* thus both *barking* and *barks* are here secondaries. There is, however, an evident difference between the two word-groups, of which the latter can stand alone as a communication in itself, while the former makes us expect a continuation (*e.g.* this furiously barking dog belongs to the butcher).

It is true that a tertiary may in some cases be further determined by a word that is subordinated to it, and this again by a fifth word, as in *a not very cleverly worded remark;* but this has no grammatical importance, and we therefore speak here of three degrees only, reckoning *not* and *very* in this example as tertiaries in the same way as *cleverly.*

[4] As adjectives are generally secondaries, and adverbs tertiaries, we see shiftings like the following, in which the adverbs have the ending *-ly:*

absolute novelty	absolutely novel
utter darkness	utterly dark
awful fun	awfully funny
perfect stranger	perfectly strange
adj.+sb.	adv+adj.
II+I	III+II

and similarly with verbs:

accurate description	describes accurately
frequent visits	visits frequently
severe judge	judges severely
careful reader	reads carefully
adj.+sb.	vb.+adv.
II+I	II+III

But in *an early riser* and *he rises early* there is no formal difference between the adjective and the adverb.

We shall now go through a considerable number of examples of words and word-groups employed in the three ranks, but it will not be necessary to give examples of the most normal cases, substantives as primaries, adjectives as secondaries, and adverbs as tertiaries. In some cases the rank is indicated in the form of the word concerned, but that is not always the case.

Grammatical Forms

LEONARD BLOOMFIELD

*Leonard Bloomfield (1887–1949) taught German philology and
linguistics at Illinois, Ohio State, Chicago, and Yale, and many
distinguished contemporary linguists were his students. His book*
Language *(1933) is a seminal text in modern linguistic study; this
selection is from that great book.*

[1]   Our discussion so far has shown us that every language consists of a number of signals, *linguistic forms*. Each linguistic form
is a fixed combination of signaling-units, the *phonemes*. In every
language the number of phonemes and the number of actually
occurring combinations of phonemes, is strictly limited. By utter-
ing a linguistic form, a speaker prompts his hearers to respond to
a situation; this situation and the responses to it, are the *linguistic
meaning* of the form. We assume that each linguistic form has a
constant and definite meaning, different from the meaning of any
other linguistic form in the same language. Thus, hearing several
utterances of some one linguistic form, such as *I'm hungry*, we
assume (1) that the differences in sound are irrelevant (unphonetic), (2) that the situations of the several speakers contain some
common features and that the differences between these situations are irrelevant (unsemantic), and (3) that this linguistic
meaning is different from that of any other form in the language.
We have seen that this assumption cannot be verified, since the
speaker's situations and the hearer's responses may involve almost anything in the whole world, and, in particular, depend
largely upon the momentary state of their nervous systems. Moreover, when we deal with the historical change of language, we
shall be concerned with facts for which our assumption does not
hold good. In the rough, however, our assumption is justified by

---

Pp. 158–169 from Leonard Bloomfield, *Language* (New York: Holt, Rinehart and Winston, Inc., 1933). Reprinted by permission of the publisher.

the mere fact that speakers co-operate in a very refined way by means of language-signals. In describing a language, we are concerned primarily with the working of this co-operation at any one time in any one community, and not with its occasional failures or with its changes in the course of history. Accordingly, the descriptive phase of linguistics consists in a somewhat rigid analysis of speech-forms, on the assumption that these speech-forms have constant and definable meanings.

Our basic assumption does have to be modified, however, right at the outset, in a different way. When we have recorded a fair number of forms in a language, we always discover a feature which we have so far ignored in our discussion: the *partial* resemblance of linguistic forms. Suppose we hear a speaker say

John ran

and a little later hear him or some other speaker say

John fell.

We recognize at once that these two forms, *John ran* and *John fell*, are in part phonetically alike, since both of them contain an element *John* [jɑn], and our practical knowledge tells us that the meanings show a corresponding resemblance: whenever a form contains the phonetic element [jɑn], the meaning involves a certain man or boy in the community. In fact, if we are lucky, we may hear someone utter the form

John!

all by itself, without any accompaniment.

After observing a number of such cases, we shall be constrained to modify the basic assumption of linguistics to read: In a speech-community some utterances are alike *or partly alike* in sound and meaning.

The common part of partly like utterances (in our example, *John*) consists of a phonetic form with a constant meaning: it answers, therefore, to the definition of a linguistic form. The parts which are not common to the partly-like utterances (in our example, *ran* in the one utterance, and *fell* in the other) may, in the same way, turn out to be linguistic forms. Having heard the form *John ran*, we may later hear the form *Bill ran*, and perhaps even (say, in answer to a question) an isolated *Ran*. The same will happen with the component *fell* in *John fell:* we may hear a form like *Dan fell* or even an isolated *Fell.*

In other cases, we may wait in vain for the isolated form. Knowing the forms *John, Bill,* and *Dan,* we may hear the forms, *Johnny, Billy,* and *Danny* and hope to hear now an isolated *-y* [-ij] with some such meaning as "little," but in this instance we shall be disappointed. In the same way, familiar with the forms *play* and *dance,* we may hear the forms *playing* and *dancing,* and then hope, in vain, to hear an isolated *-ing* [iŋ], which might reassure us as to the somewhat vague meaning of this syllable. In spite of the fact that some components do not occur alone, but only as parts of larger forms, we nevertheless call these components linguistic forms, since they are phonetic forms, such as [ij] or [iŋ], with constant meanings. A linguistic form which is never spoken alone is a *bound* form; all others (as, for instance, *John ran* or *John* or *run* or *running*) are *free* forms.

In other cases we wait in vain for the occurrence of a form even as part of some other form. For instance, having heard the form *cranberry,* we soon recognize the component *berry* in other forms, such as *blackberry,* and may even hear it spoken alone, but with the other component of *cranberry* we shall have no such luck. Not only do we wait in vain to hear an isolated **cran,* but, listen as we may, we never hear this element outside the one combination *cranberry,* and we cannot elicit from the speakers any other form which will contain this element *cran-.* As a practical matter, observing languages in the field, we soon learn that it is unwise to try to elicit such forms; our questions confuse the speakers, and they may get rid of us by some false admission, such as, "Oh, yes, I guess *cran* means red." If we avoid this pitfall, we shall come to the conclusion that the element *cran-* occurs only in the combination *cranberry.* However, since it has a constant phonetic form, and since its meaning is constant, in so far as a *cranberry* is a definite kind of *berry,* different from all other kinds, we say that *cran-,* too, is a linguistic form. Experience shows that we do well to generalize this instance: *unique elements,* which occur only in a single combination, are linguistic forms.

Sometimes we may be unable to decide whether phonetically like forms are identical in meaning. The *straw-* in *strawberry* is phonetically the same as the *straw-* in *strawflower* and as the isolated *straw,* but whether the meanings are "the same," we cannot say. If we ask the speakers, they will answer sometimes one way, sometimes another; they are no more able to tell than we. This difficulty is part of the universal difficulty of semantics: the practical world is not a world of clear-cut distinctions.

[2] We see, then, that some linguistic forms bear partial phonetic-semantic resemblances to other forms; examples are, *John ran, John fell, Bill ran, Bill fell; Johnny, Billy; playing, dancing; blackberry, cranberry; strawberry, strawflower.* A linguistic form which bears a partial phonetic-semantic resemblance to some other linguistic form, is a *complex form.*

The common part of any (two or more) complex forms is a linguistic form; it is a *constituent* (or *component*) of these complex forms. The constituent is said to be *contained in* (or to be *included in* or to *enter into*) the complex forms. If a complex form, beside the common part, contains a remainder, such as the *cran* in *cranberry,* which does not occur in any other complex form, this remainder also is a linguistic form; it is a *unique constituent* of the complex form. The constituent forms in our examples above are: *John, ran, Bill, fell, play, dance, black, berry, straw, flower, cran-* (unique constituent in *cranberry*), *-y* (bound-form constituent in *Johnny, Billy*), *-ing* (bound-form constituent in *playing, dancing*). In any complex form, each constituent is said to *accompany* the other constituents.

A linguistic form which bears no partial phonetic-semantic resemblance to any other form, is a *simple* form or *morpheme.* Thus, *bird, play, dance, cran-, -y, -ing* are morphemes. Morphemes may show partial phonetic resemblances, as do, for instance, *bird* and *burr,* or even homonymy as do *pear, pair, pare,* but this resemblance is purely phonetic and is not paralleled by the meanings.

From all this it appears that every complex form is entirely made up, so far as its phonetically definable constituents are concerned, of morphemes. The number of these *ultimate constituents* may run very high. The form *Poor John ran away* contains five morphemes: *poor, John, ran, a-* (a bound form recurring, for instance, in *aground, ashore, aloft, around*), and *way.* However, the structure of complex forms is by no means as simple as this; we could not understand the forms of a language if we merely reduced all the complex forms to their ultimate constituents. Any English-speaking person who concerns himself with this matter, is sure to tell us that the *immediate constituents* of *Poor John ran away* are the two forms *poor John* and *ran away;* that each of these is, in turn, a complex form; that the immediate constituents of *ran away* are *ran,* a morpheme, and *away,* a complex form, whose constituents are the morphemes *a-* and *way;* and that the constituents of *poor John* are the morphemes *poor* and *John.* Only in this way will a proper analysis (that is, one which takes account of the meanings) lead to the ultimately constituent morphemes. The reasons for this will occupy us later.

[3] A morpheme can be described phonetically, since it consists of one or more phonemes, but its meaning cannot be analyzed within the scope of our science. For instance, we have seen that the morpheme *pin* bears a phonetic resemblance to other morphemes, such as *pig, pen, tin, ten,* and, on the basis of these resemblances, can be analyzed and described in terms of three phonemes, but, since these resemblances are not connected with resemblances of meaning, we cannot attribute any meaning to the phonemes and cannot, within the scope of our science, analyze the meaning of the morpheme. The meaning of a morpheme is a *sememe.* The linguist assumes that each sememe is a constant and definite unit of meaning, different from all the other meanings, including all other sememes, in the language, but he cannot go beyond this. There is nothing in the structure of morphemes like *wolf, fox,* and *dog* to tell us the relation between their meanings; this is a problem for the zoölogist. The zoölogist's definition of these meanings is welcome to us as a practical help, but it cannot be confirmed or rejected on the basis of our science.

A workable system of signals, such as a language, can contain only a small number of signaling-units, but the things signaled about—in our case, the entire content of the practical world—may be infinitely varied. Accordingly, the signals (linguistic forms, with morphemes as the smallest signals) consist of different combinations of the signaling-units (phonemes), and each such combination is arbitrarily assigned to some feature of the practical world (sememe). The signals can be analyzed, but not the things signaled about.

This re-enforces the principle that linguistic study must always start from the phonetic form and not from the meaning. Phonetic forms—let us say, for instance, the entire stock of morphemes in a language—can be described in terms of phonemes and their succession, and, on this basis, can be classified or listed in some convenient order, as, for example, alphabetically; the meanings —in our example, the sememes of a language—could be analyzed or systematically listed only by a well-nigh omniscient observer.

[4] Since every complex form is made up entirely of morphemes, a complete list of morphemes would account for all the phonetic forms of a language. The total stock of morphemes in a language is its *lexicon*. However, if we knew the lexicon of a language, and had a reasonably accurate knowledge of each sememe, we might still fail to understand the forms of this language. Every utterance contains some significant features that are not accounted for by the lexicon. We saw, for instance, that the five morphemes, *John, poor, ran, way, a-* which make up the form *Poor John ran away*, do not fully account for the meaning of this utterance. Part of this meaning depends upon the arrangement— for example, upon the order of succession—in which these morphemes appear in the complex form. Every language shows part of its meanings by the *arrangement* of its forms. Thus, in English, *John hit Bill* and *Bill hit John* differ in meaning by virtue of the two different orders in which the morphemes are uttered.

The meaningful arrangements of forms in a language constitute its *grammar*. In general, there seem to be four ways of arranging linguistic forms.

(1) *Order* is the succession in which the constituents of a complex form are spoken. The significance of order appears strikingly in contrasts such as *John hit Bill* versus *Bill hit John*. On the other hand, **Bill John hit* is not an English form, because our language does not arrange these constituents in this order; similarly, *playing* is a form, but **ing-play* is not. Sometimes differences of order have connotative values; thus, *Away ran John* is livelier than *John ran away*.

(2) *Modulation* is the use of secondary phonemes. Secondary phonemes, we recall, are phonemes which do not appear in any morpheme, but only in grammatical arrangements of morphemes. A morpheme like *John* [jɑn] or *run* [rɔn] is really an abstraction, because in any actual utterance the morpheme is accompanied by some secondary phoneme which conveys a grammatical meaning. in English, if the morpheme is spoken alone, it is accompanied by some secondary phoneme of pitch: it is either *John!* or *John?* or *John* [.]—this last with falling final-pitch, as, in answer to a question—and there is no indifferent or abstract form in which the

morpheme is not accompanied by any final-pitch. In English complex forms, some of the constituents are always accompanied by secondary phonemes of stress; thus, the difference in the place of stress distinguishes the noun *convict* from the verb *convict.*

(3) *Phonetic modification* is a change in the primary phonemes of a form. For instance, when the forms *do* [duw] and *not* [nɑt] are combined into a complex form, the [uw] of *do* is ordinarily replaced by [ow], and, whenever this happens, the *not* loses its vowel, so that the combined form is *don't* [dow nt]. In this example the modification is optional, and we have also the unmodified forms in *do not,* with a difference of connotation. In other cases we have no choice. Thus, the suffix *-ess* with the meaning "female," as in *count-ess,* is added also to *duke* [d(j)uwk], but in this combination the form *duke* is modified to *duch-* [doč-], for the word is *duchess* ['dočes].

Strictly speaking, we should say that the morpheme in such cases has two (or, sometimes, more) different phonetic forms, such as *not* [nɑt] and [nt], *do* [duw] and [dow], *duke* and *duch-,* and that each of these *alternants* appears under certain conditions. In our examples, however, one of the alternants has a much wider range than the other and, accordingly, is a *basic alternant.* In other cases, the alternants are more on a par. In *run* and *ran,* for instance, neither alternant is tied to the presence of any accompanying form, and we might hesitate as to the choice of a basic alternant. We find, however, that in cases like *keep: kep-t* the past-tense form contains an alternant (*kep-*) which occurs only with a certain accompanying form (*-t*); accordingly, to obtain as uniform as possible a statement, we take the infinitive form (*keep, run*) as basic, and describe the alternant which appears in the past tense (*kep-, ran*) as a phonetically modified form. We shall see other instances where the choice is more difficult; we try, of course, to make the selection of a basic alternant so as to get, in the long run the simplest description of the facts.

(4) *Selection* of forms contributes a factor of meaning because different forms in what is otherwise the same grammatical arrangement, will result in different meanings. For instance, some morphemes spoken with exclamatory final-pitch, are calls for a person's presence or attention (*John! Boy!*), while others, spoken in the same way, are commands (*Run! Jump!*), and this difference extends also to certain complex forms (*Mr. Smith! Teacher!* versus

infinitive forms are marked off as a form-class, has a grammatical meaning (an episememe) which we may call a *class-meaning* and roughly define as "action."

A tagmeme may consist of more than one taxeme. For instance, in forms like *John ran; poor John ran away; the boys are here; I know,* we find several taxemes. One constituent belongs to the form-class of nominative expressions (*John, poor John, the boys, I*). The other constituent belongs to the form-class of finite verb expressions (*ran, ran away, are here, know*). A further taxeme of selection assigns certain finite verb expressions to certain nominative expressions; thus, the constituents are not interchangeable in the three examples *I am, John is, you are.* A taxeme of order places the nominative expression before the finite verb expression: we do not say **ran John.* Further taxemes of order, in part reversing the basic one, appear in special cases like *did John run? away ran John; will John?* A taxeme of modulation appears only in special cases, when the nominative expression is unstressed, an in *I know* [aj 'now]. Taxemes of phonetic modification appear also in certain special cases, such as *John's here,* with [z] for *is,* or *I'd go,* with [d] for *would.* Now, none of these taxemes, taken by itself, has any meaning, but, taken all together, they make up a grammatical form, a tagmeme, whose meaning is this, that the one constituent (the nominative expression) "performs" the other constituent (the finite verb expression).

If we say *John ran!* with exclamatory pitch, we have a complex grammatical form, with three tagmemes. One of these is "strong stimulus," the second is "(object) performs (action)," and the third has the episememe of "complete and novel" utterance, and consists, formally, in the selective feature of using an actor-action phrase as a sentence.

[6]   Any utterance can be fully described in terms of lexical and grammatical forms; we must remember only that the meanings cannot be defined in terms of our science.

Any morpheme can be fully described (apart from its meaning) as a set of one or more phonemes in a certain arrangement. Thus, the morpheme *duke* consists of the phonemes, simple and compound, [d], [juw], [k], in this order; and the morpheme *-ess* consists of the phonemes [e], [s], in this order. Any complex form can be fully described (apart from its meaning) in terms of the immediate constituent forms and the grammatical features (taxemes) by which these constituent forms are arranged. Thus, the complex form *duchess* ['dočes] consists of the immediate constituents *duke* [djuwk] and *-ess* [es], arranged in the following way:

Selection. The constituent *duke* belongs to a special class of English forms which combine with the form *-ess*. This form-class includes, for instance, the forms *count, prince, lion, tiger, author, waiter,* but not the forms *man, boy, dog, singer;* it is a sub-class of a larger form-class of male personal nouns. The form *-ess* constitutes a little form-class of its own, by virtue of the fact that it (and it alone) combines with precisely the forms in the class just described. All these facts, taken together, may be viewed as a single taxeme of selection.

Order. The form *-ess* is spoken after the accompanying form.

Modulation. The form *-ess* is spoken unstressed; the accompanying form has a high stress.

Phonetic modification. The [juw] of *duke* is replaced by [o], and the [k] by [č].

Given the forms *duke* and *-ess*, the statement of these four grammatical features fully describes the complex form *duchess*.

Any actual utterance can be fully described in terms of the lexical form and the accompanying grammatical features. Thus, the utterance *Duchess!* consists of the lexical form *duchess* and the two taxemes of exclamatory final-pitch and selection of a substantive expression.

If some science furnished us with definitions of the meanings of the units here concerned, defining for us the meanings (sememes) of the two morphemes (*duke* and *-ess*) and the meanings (episememes) of the three tagmemes (arrangement of *duke* and *-ess;* use of exclamatory final-pitch; selection of a substantive expression), then the meaning of the utterance *Duchess!* would be fully analyzed and defined.

[7] The grammatical forms are no exception to the necessary principle—strictly speaking, we should call it an assumption—that a language can convey only such meanings as are attached to some formal feature: the speakers can signal only by means of signals. Many students of language have been misled in this matter by the fact that the formal features of grammar are not phonemes or combinations of phonemes which we can pronounce or transcribe, but merely *arrangements* of phonetic forms. For this our scholastic tradition may be largely to blame; if it were not for

this tradition, there would perhaps be nothing difficult about the fact, for instance, that in English, *John hit Bill* and *Bill hit John* signal two different situations, or that *convict* stressed on the first syllable differs in meaning from *convict* stressed on the second syllable, or that there is a difference of meaning between *John!* and *John?* and *John.*

A form like *John* or *run,* mentioned in the abstract, without, for instance, any specification as to final-pitch, is, properly speaking, not a real linguistic form, but only a lexical form; a linguistic form, as actually uttered, always contains a grammatical form. No matter how simple a form we take and how we utter it, we have already made some selection by virtue of which the utterance conveys a grammatical meaning in addition to its lexical content, and we have used some pitch-scheme which, in English at any rate, lends it a grammatical meaning such as "statement," "yes-or-no question," "supplement-question," or "exclamation."

The grammatical forms of a language can be grouped into three great classes:

(1) When a form is spoken alone (that is, not as a constituent of a larger form), it appears in some *sentence-type.* Thus, in English, the use of the secondary phoneme [!] gives us the sentence-type of exclamation, and the use of a substantive expression gives us the type of a call (*John!*).

(2) Whenever two (or, rarely, more) forms are spoken together, as constituents of a complex form, the grammatical features by which they are combined, make up a *construction.* Thus, the grammatical features by which *duke* and *-ess* combine in the form *duchess,* or the grammatical features by which *poor John* and *ran away* combine in the form *poor John ran away,* make up a construction.

(3) A third great class of grammatical forms must probably be set up for the cases where a form is spoken as the conventional substitute for any one of a whole class of other forms. Thus, the selective feature by which the form *he* in English is a conventional substitute for a whole class of other forms, such as *John, poor John, a policeman, the man I saw yesterday, whoever did this,* and so on (which forms, by virtue of this habit, constitute form-class of "singular male substantive expressions"), must doubtless be viewed as an example of a third class of grammatical forms, to which we may give the name of *substitutions.*

Revolution in Grammar

W. NELSON FRANCIS

W. Nelson Francis is professor of English and linguistics at Brown University. His Structure of American English *(1958) is a standard textbook on the subject. The following essay, which first appeared in* The Quarterly Journal of Speech, *has been widely reprinted. He is also the author of* The English Language: An Introduction, *an introductory textbook which combines a modern linguistic description of English with a history of the language.*

[1]   A long overdue revolution is at present taking place in the study of English grammar—a revolution as sweeping in its consequences as the Darwinian revolution in biology. It is the result of the application to English of methods of descriptive analysis originally developed for use with languages of primitive peoples. To anyone at all interested in language, it is challenging; to those concerned with the teaching of English (including parents), it presents the necessity of radically revising both the substance and the methods of their teaching.

A curious paradox exists in regard to grammar. On the one hand it is felt to be the dullest and driest of academic subjects, fit only for those in whose veins the red blood of life has long since turned to ink. On the other, it is a subject upon which people who would scorn to be professional grammarians hold very dogmatic opinions, which they will defend with considerable emotion. Much of this prejudice stems from the usual sources of prejudice—ignorance and confusion. Even highly educated people seldom have a clear idea of what grammarians do, and there is an unfortunate confusion about the meaning of the term "grammar" itself.

Hence it would be well to begin with definitions. What do people mean when they use the word "grammar"? Actually the word is used to refer to three different things, and much of the

Reprinted from *The Quarterly Journal of Speech* (October 1954) with the permission of the Speech Association of America and the author.

emotional thinking about matters grammatical arises from confusion among these different meanings.

✗ The first thing we mean by "grammar" is "the set of formal patterns in which the words of a language are arranged in order to convey larger meanings." It is not necessary that we be able to discuss these patterns self-consciously in order to be able to use them. In fact, all speakers of a language above the age of five or six know how to use its complex forms of organization with considerable skill; in this sense of the word—call it "Grammar 1"—they are thoroughly familiar with its grammar.

✓ The second meaning of "grammar"—call it "Grammar 2"—is "the branch of linguistic science which is concerned with the description, analysis, and formulization of formal language patterns." Just as gravity was in full operation before Newton's apple fell, so grammar in the first sense was in full operation before anyone formulated the first rule that began the history of grammar as a study.

✓ The third sense in which people use the word "grammar" is "linguistic etiquette." This we may call "Grammar 3." The word in this sense is often coupled with a derogatory adjective: we say that the expression "he ain't here" is "bad grammar." What we mean is that such an expression is bad linguistic manners in certain circles. From the point of view of "Grammar 1" it is faultless; it conforms just as completely to the structural patterns of English as does "he isn't here." The trouble with it is like the trouble with Prince Hal in Shakespeare's play—it is "bad," not in itself, but in the company it keeps.

As has already been suggested, much confusion arises from mixing these meanings. One hears a good deal of criticism of teachers of English couched in such terms as "they don't teach grammar any more." Criticism of this sort is based on the wholly unproved assumption that teaching Grammar 2 will increase the student's proficiency in Grammar 1 or improve his manners in Grammar 3. Actually, the form of Grammar 2 which is usually taught is a very inaccurate and misleading analysis of the facts of Grammar 1; and it therefore is of highly questionable value in improving a person's ability to handle the structural patterns of his language. It is hardly reasonable to expect that teaching a person some inaccurate grammatical analysis will either improve the effectiveness of his assertions or teach him what expressions are acceptable to use in a given social context.

These, then, are the three meanings of "grammar": Grammar 1, a form of behavior; Grammar 2, a field of study, a science; and Grammar 3, a branch of etiquette.

[2]   Grammarians have arrived at some basic principles of their science, three of which are fundamental to this discussion. The first is that a language constitutes a set of behavior patterns common to the members of a given community. It is a part of what the anthropologists call the culture of the community. Actually it has complex and intimate relationships with other phases of culture such as myth and ritual. But for purposes of study it may be dealt with as a separate set of phenomena that can be objectively described and analyzed like any other universe of facts. Specifically, its phenomena can be observed, recorded, classified, and compared; and general laws of their behavior can be made by the same inductive process that is used to produce the "laws" of physics, chemistry, and the other sciences.

A second important principle of linguistic science is that each language or dialect has its own unique system of behavior patterns. Parts of this system may show similarities to parts of the systems of other languages, particularly if those languages are genetically related. But different languages solve the problems of expression and communication in different ways, just as the problems of movement through water are solved in different ways by lobsters, fish, seals, and penguins. A couple of corollaries of this principle are important. The first is that there is no such thing as "universal grammar," or at least if there is, it is so general and abstract as to be of little use. The second corollary is that the grammar of each language must be made up on the basis of a study of that particular language—a study that is free from preconceived notions of what a language should contain and how it should operate. The marine biologist does not criticize the octopus for using jet-propulsion to get him through the water instead of the methods of a self-respecting fish. Neither does the linguistic scientist express alarm or distress when he finds a language that seems to get along quite well without any words that correspond to what in English we call verbs.

A third principle on which linguistic science is based is that the analysis and description of a given language must conform to the requirements laid down for any satisfactory scientific theory.

These are (1) simplicity, (2) consistency, (3) completeness, and (4) usefulness for predicting the behavior of phenomena not brought under immediate observation when the theory was formed. Linguistic scientists who have recently turned their attention to English have found that, judged by these criteria, the traditional grammar of English is unsatisfactory. It falls down badly on the first two requirements, being unduly complex and glaringly inconsistent within itself. It can be made to work, just as the Ptolemaic earth-centered astronomy can be, but at the cost of great elaboration and complication. The new grammar, like the Copernican sun-centered astronomy, solves the same problems with greater elegance, which is the scientist's word for the simplicity, compactness, and tidiness that characterize a satisfactory theory.

[3]   A brief look at the history of the traditional grammar of English will make apparent the reasons for its inadequacy. The study of English grammar is actually an outgrowth of the linguistic interest of the Renaissance. It was during the later Middle Ages and early Renaissance that the various vernacular languages of Europe came into their own. They began to be used for many kinds of writing which had previously always been done in Latin. As the vernaculars, in the hands of great writers like Dante and Chaucer, came of age as members of the linguistic family, a concomitant interest in their grammars arose. The earliest important English grammar was written by Shakespeare's contemporary, Ben Jonson.

It is important to observe that not only Ben Jonson himself but also those who followed him in the study of English grammar were men deeply learned in Latin and sometimes in Greek. For all their interest in English, they were conditioned from earliest school days to conceive of the classical languages as superior to the vernaculars. We still sometimes call the elementary school the "grammar school"; historically the term means the school where Latin grammar was taught. By the time the Renaissance or eighteenth-century scholar took his university degree, he was accustomed to use Latin as the normal means of communication with his fellow scholars. Dr. Samuel Johnson, for instance, who had only three years at the university and did not take a degree, wrote poetry in both Latin and Greek. Hence it was natural for these men to take Latin grammar as the norm, and to analyze English in terms of Latin. The grammarians of the seventeenth and eighteenth centuries who formulated the traditional grammar of English looked for the devices and distinctions of Latin grammar in English, and where they did not actually find them they imagined or created them. Of course, since English is a member of the Indo-European family of languages, to which Latin and Greek also belong, it did have many grammatical elements in common with them. But many of these had been obscured or wholly lost as a result of the extensive changes that had taken place in English—changes that the early grammarians inevitably conceived of as degeneration. They felt that it was their function to resist further change, if not to repair the damage already done. So preoccupied were they with the grammar of Latin as the ideal that they overlooked in large part the exceedingly complex and delicate system that English had substituted for the Indo-European grammar it had abandoned. Instead they stretched unhappy English on the Procrustean bed of Latin. It is no wonder that we commonly hear people say, "I didn't really understand grammar until I began to study Latin." This is eloquent testimony to the fact that the grammar "rules" of our present-day textbooks are largely an inheritance from the Latin-based grammar of the eighteenth century.

Meanwhile the extension of linguistic study beyond the Indo-European and Semitic families began to reveal that there are many different ways in which linguistic phenomena are organized —in other words, many different kinds of grammar. The tone-languages of the Orient and of North America, and the complex agglutinative languages of Africa, among others, forced grammarians to abandon the idea of a universal or ideal grammar and to direct their attention more closely to the individual systems employed by the multifarious languages of mankind. With the growth and refinement of the scientific method and its application to the field of anthropology, language came under more rigorous scientific scrutiny. As with anthropology in general, linguistic science at first concerned itself with the primitive. Finally, again following the lead of anthropology, linguistics began to apply its techniques to the old familiar tongues, among them English. Accelerated by the practical need during World War II of teaching languages, including English, to large numbers in a short time, research into the nature of English grammar has moved rapidly in the last fifteen years. The definitive grammar of English is yet to be written, but the results so far achieved are spectacular. It is now as unrealistic to teach "traditional" grammar of English as it is to teach "traditional" (i.e. pre-Darwinian) biology or "traditional" (i.e. four-element) chemistry. Yet nearly all certified teachers of English on all levels are doing so. Here is a cultural lag of major proportions.

[4] Before we can proceed to a sketch of what the new grammar of English looks like, we must take account of a few more of the premises of linguistic science. They must be understood and accepted by anyone who wishes to understand the new grammar. First, the spoken language is primary, at least for the original study of a language. In many of the primitive languages,[1] of course, where writing is unknown, the spoken language is the *only* form. This is in many ways an advantage to the linguist, because the written language may use conventions that obscure its basic structure. The reason for the primary importance of the spoken language is that language originates as speech, and most of the changes and innovations that occur in the history of a given language begin in the spoken tongue.

Secondly, we must take account of the concept of dialect. I suppose most laymen would define a dialect as "a corrupt form of a language spoken in a given region by people who don't know any better." This introduces moral judgments which are repulsive to the linguistic scholar. Let us approach the definition of a dialect from the more objective end, through the notion of a speech community. A speech community is merely a group of people who are in pretty constant intercommunication. There are various types of speech communities: local ones, like "the people who live in Tidewater Virginia"; class ones, like "the white-collar class"; occupational ones, like "doctors, nurses, and other people who work in hospitals"; social ones, like "clubwomen." In a sense, each of these has its own dialect. Each family may be said to have its own dialect; in fact, in so far as each of us has his own vocabulary and particular quirks of speech, each individual has his own dialect. Also, of course, in so far as he is a member of many speech com-

---

1. "Primitive languages" here is really an abbreviated statement for "languages used by peoples of relatively primitive culture"; it is not to be taken as implying anything simple or rudimentary about the languages themselves. Many languages included under the term, such as native languages of African and Mexico, exhibit grammatical complexities unknown to more "civilized" languages.

munities, each individual is more or less master of many dialects and shifts easily and almost unconsciously from one to another as he shifts from one social environment to another.

In the light of this concept of dialects, a language can be defined as a group of dialects which have enough of their sound-system, vocabulary, and grammar (Grammar 1, that is) in common to permit their speakers to be mutually intelligible in the ordinary affairs of life. It usually happens that one of the many dialects that make up a language comes to have more prestige than the others; in modern times it has usually been the dialect of the middle-class residents of the capital, like Parisian French and London English, which is so distinguished. This comes to be thought of as the standard dialect; in fact, its speakers become snobbish and succeed in establishing the belief that it is not a dialect at all, but the only proper form of the language. This causes the speakers of other dialects to become self-conscious and ashamed of their speech, or else aggressive and jingoistic about it —either of which is an acknowledgment of their feelings of inferiority. Thus one of the duties of the educational system comes to be that of teaching the standard dialect to all so as to relieve them of feelings of inferiority, and thus relieve society of linguistic neurotics. This is where Grammar 3, linguistic etiquette, comes into the picture.

A third premise arising from the two just discussed is that the difference between the way educated people talk and the way they write is a dialectal difference. The spread between these two dialects may be very narrow, as in present-day America, or very wide, as in Norway, where people often speak local Norwegian dialects but write in the Dano-Norwegian *Riksmaal*. The extreme is the use by writers of an entirely different language, or at least an ancient and no longer spoken form of the language—like Sanskrit in northern India or Latin in western Europe during the later Middle Ages. A corollary of this premise is that anyone setting out to write a grammar must know and make clear whether he is dealing with the spoken or the written dialect. Virtually all current English grammars deal with the written language only; evidence for this is that their rules for the plurals of nouns, for instance, are really spelling rules, which say nothing about pronunciation.

This is not the place to go into any sort of detail about the methods of analysis the linguistic scientist uses. Suffice it to say that he begins by breaking up the flow of speech into minimum sound-units, or phones, which he then groups into families called phonemes, the minimum significant sound-units. Most languages have from twenty to sixty of these. American English has forty-one: nine vowels, twenty-four consonants, four degrees of stress, and four levels of pitch. These phonemes group themselves into minimum meaningful units, called morphemes. These fall into two groups: free morphemes, those that can enter freely into many combinations with other free morphemes to make phrases and sentences; and bound morphemes, which are always found tied in a close and often indissoluble relationship with other bound or free morphemes. An example of a free morpheme is "dog"; an example of a bound morpheme is "un-" or "ex-". The linguist usually avoids talking about "words" because the term is very inexact. Is "instead of," for instance, to be considered one, two, or three words? This is purely a matter of opinion; but it is a matter of fact that it is made up of three morphemes.

In any case, our analysis has now brought the linguist to the point where he has some notion of the word-stock (he would call it the "lexicon") of his language. He must then go into the question of how the morphemes are grouped into meaningful utterances, which is the field of grammar proper. At this point in the analysis of English, as of many other languages, it becomes apparent that there are three bases upon which classification and analysis may be built: form, function, and meaning. For illustration let us take the word "boys" in the utterance "the boys are here." From the point of view of form, "boys" is a noun with the plural ending "s" (pronounced like "z"), preceded by the noun-determiner "the," and tied by concord to the verb "are," which it precedes. From the point of view of function, "boys" is the subject of the verb "are" and of the sentence. From the point of view of meaning, "boys" points out or names more than one of the male young of the human species, about whom an assertion is being made.

Of these three bases of classification, the one most amenable to objective description and analysis of a rigorously scientific sort is form. In fact, many conclusions about form can be drawn by a person unable to understand or speak the language. Next comes function. But except as it is revealed by form, function is dependent on knowing the meaning. In a telegraphic sentence like "ship sails today" [2] no one can say whether "ship" is the subject of "sails" or an imperative verb with "sails" as its object until he knows what the sentence means. Most shaky of all bases for grammatical analysis is meaning. Attempts have been made to reduce the phenomena of meaning to objective description, but so far they have not succeeded very well. Meaning is such a subjective quality that it is usually omitted entirely from scientific description. The botanist can describe the forms of plants and the functions of their various parts, but he refuses to concern himself with their meaning. It is left to the poet to find symbolic meaning in roses, violets, and lilies.

At this point it is interesting to note that the traditional grammar of English bases some of its key concepts and definitions on this very subjective and shaky foundation of meaning. A recent English grammar defines a sentence as "a group of words which expresses a complete thought through the use of a verb, called its predicate, and a subject, consisting of a noun or pronoun about which the verb has something to say." [3] But what is a complete thought? Actually we do not identify sentences this way at all. If someone says, "I don't know what to do," dropping his voice at the end, and pauses, the hearer will know that it is quite safe for him to make a comment without running the risk of interrupting an unfinished sentence. But if the speaker says the same words and maintains a level pitch at the end, the polite listener will wait for him to finish his sentence. The words are the same, the meaning is the same; the only difference is a slight one in the pitch of the final syllable—a purely formal distinction, which signals that the first utterance is complete, a sentence, while the second is incomplete. In writing we would translate these signals into punctuation: a period or exclamation point at the end of the first, a comma or dash at the end of the second. It is the form of the utterance, not the completeness of the thought, that tells us whether it is a whole sentence or only part of one.

Another favorite definition of the traditional grammar, also based on meaning, is that of "noun" as "the name of a person, place, or thing"; or, as the grammar just quoted has it, "the name of anybody or anything, with or without life, and with or without

2. This example is taken from C. C. Fries, *The Structure of English* (New York, 1952), p. 62. This important book will be discussed below.
3. Ralph B. Allen, *English Grammar* (New York, 1950), p. 187.

substance or form." [4] Yet we identify nouns, not by asking if they name something, but by their positions in expressions and by the formal marks they carry. In the sentence, "The slithy toves did gyre and gimble in the wabe," any speaker of English knows that "toves" and "wabe" are nouns, though he cannot tell what they name, if indeed they name anything. How does he know? Actually because they have certain formal marks, like their position in relation to "the" as well as the whole arrangement of the sentence. We know from our practical knowledge of English grammar (Grammar 1), which we have had since before we went to school, that if we were to put meaningful words into this sentence, we would have to put nouns in place of "toves" and "wabe," giving something like "The slithy snakes did gyre and gimble in the wood." The pattern of the sentence simply will not allow us to say "The slithy arounds did gyre and gimble in the wooden."

One trouble with the traditional grammar, then, is that it relies heavily on the most subjective element in language, meaning. Another is that it shifts the ground of its classification and produces the elementary logical error of cross-division. A zoologist who divided animals into invertebrates, mammals, and beasts of burden would not get very far before running into trouble. Yet the traditional grammar is guilty of the same error when it defines three parts of speech on the basis of meaning (noun, verb, and interjection), four more on the basis of function (adjective, adverb, pronoun, conjunction), and one partly on function and partly on form (preposition). The result is that in such an expression as "a dog's life" there can be endless futile argument about whether "dog's" is a noun or an adjective. It is, of course, a noun from the point of view of form and an adjective from the point of view of function, and hence falls into both classes, just as a horse is both a mammal and a beast of burden. No wonder students are bewildered in their attempts to master the traditional grammar. Their natural clearness of mind tells them that it is a crazy patchwork violating the elementary principles of logical thought.

[5] If the traditional grammar is so bad, what does the new grammar offer in its place?

x It offers a description, analysis, and set of definitions and formu-

4. *Ibid.*, p. 1.

las—rules, if you will—based firmly and consistently on the easiest, or at least the most objective, aspect of language, form. Experts can quibble over whether "dog's" in "a dog's life" is a noun or an adjective, but anyone can see that it is spelled with " 's" and hear that it ends with a "z" sound; likewise anyone can tell that it comes in the middle between "a" and "life." Furthermore he can tell that something important has happened if the expression is changed to "the dog's alive," "the live dogs," or "the dogs lived," even if he doesn't know what the words mean and has never heard of such functions as modifier, subject, or attributive genitive. He cannot, of course, get very far into his analysis without either a knowledge of the language or access to someone with such knowledge. He will also need a minimum technical vocabulary describing grammatical functions. Just so the anatomist is better off for knowing physiology. But the grammarian, like the anatomist, must beware of allowing his preconceived notions to lead him into the error of interpreting before he describes—an error which often results in his finding only what he is looking for.

When the grammarian looks at English objectively, he finds that it conveys its meanings by two broad devices: the denotations and connotations of words separately considered, which the linguist calls "lexical meaning," and the significance of word-forms, word-groups, and arrangements apart from the lexical meanings of the words, which the linguist calls "structural meaning." The first of these is the domain of the lexicographer and the semanticist, and hence is not our present concern. The second, the structural meaning, is the business of the structural linguist, or grammarian. The importance of this second kind of meaning must be emphasized because it is often overlooked. The man in the street tends to think of the meaning of a sentence as being the aggregate of the dictionary meanings of the words that make it up; hence the widespread fallacy of literal translation—the feeling that if you take a French sentence and a French-English dictionary and write down the English equivalent of each French word you will come out with an intelligible English sentence. How ludicrous the results can be, anyone knows who is familiar with Mark Twain's retranslation from the French of his jumping frog story. One sentence reads, "Eh bien! I no saw not that that frog has nothing of better than each frog." Upon which Mark's comment is, "if that isn't grammar gone to seed, then I count myself no judge." [5]

The second point brought out by a formal analysis of English is that it uses four principal devices of form to signal structural meanings:

1. Word order—the sequence in which words and word-groups are arranged.

2. Function-words—words devoid of lexical meaning which indicate relationships among the meaningful words with which they appear.

3. Inflections—alterations in the forms of words themselves to signal changes in meaning and relationship.

4. Formal contrasts—contrasts in the forms of words signaling greater differences in function and meaning. These could also be considered inflections, but it is more convenient for both the lexicographer and the grammarian to consider them separately.

Usually several of these are present in any utterance, but they can be separately illustrated by means of contrasting expressions involving minimum variation—the kind of controlled experiment used in the scientific laboratory.

To illustrate the structural meaning of word order, let us compare the two sentences "man bites dog" and "dog bites man." The words are identical in lexical meaning and in form; the only difference is in sequence. It is interesting to note that Latin expresses the difference between these two by changes in the form of the words, without necessarily altering the order: "homo canem mordet" or "hominem canis mordet." Latin grammar is worse than useless in understand this point of English grammar.

Next, compare the sentences "the dog is the friend of man" and "any dog is a friend of that man." Here the words having lexical meaning are "dog," "is," "friend," and "man," which appear in the same form and the same order in both sentences. The formal differences between them are in the substitution of "any" and "a" for "the," and in the insertion of "that." These little words are function-words; they make quite a difference in the meanings of the two sentences, though it is virtually impossible to say what they mean in isolation.

5. Mark Twain, "The Jumping Frog; the Original story in English; the Retranslation Clawed Back from the French, into a Civilized Language Once More, by Patient and Unremunerated Toil," *1601 . . . and Sketches Old and New* (n.p., 1933), p. 50.

Third, compare the sentences "the dog loves the man" and "the dogs loved the men." Here the words are the same, in the same order, with the same function-words in the same positions. But the forms of the three words having lexical meaning have been changed: "dog" to "dogs," "loves" to "loved," and "man" to "men." These changes are inflections. English has very few of them as compared with Greek, Latin, Russian, or even German. But it still uses them; about one word in four in an ordinary English sentence is inflected.

Fourth, consider the difference between "the dog's friend arrived" and "the dog's friendly arrival." Here the difference lies in the change of "friend" to "friendly," a formal alteration signaling a change of function from subject to modifier, and the change of "arrived" to "arrival," signaling a change of function from predicate to head-word in a noun-modifier group. These changes are of the same formal nature as inflections, but because they produce words of different lexical meaning, classifiable as different parts of speech, it is better to call them formal contrasts than inflections. In other words, it is logically quite defensible to consider "love," "loves," "loving," and "loved" as the same word in differing aspects and to consider "friend," "friendly," "friendliness," "friendship," and "befriend" as different words related by formal and semantic similarities. But this is only a matter of convenience of analysis, which permits a more accurate description of English structure. In another language we might find that this kind of distinction is unnecessary but that some other distinction, unnecessary in English, is required. The categories of grammatical description are not sacrosanct; they are as much a part of man's organization of his observations as they are of the nature of things.

If we are considering the spoken variety of English, we must add a fifth device for indicating structural meaning—the various musical and rhythmic patterns which the linguist classifies under juncture, stress, and intonation. Consider the following pair of sentences:

> Alfred, the alligator is sick!
> Alfred the alligator is sick.

These are identical in the four respects discussed above—word order, function-words, inflections, and word-form. Yet they have markedly different meanings, as would be revealed by the intonation if they were spoken aloud. These differences in intonation are to a certain extent indicated in the written language by punctuation—that is, in fact, the primary function of punctuation.

[6] The examples so far given were chosen to illustrate in isolation the various kinds of structural devices in English grammar. Much more commonly the structural meaning of a given sentence is indicated by a combination of two or more of these devices: a sort of margin of safety which permits some of the devices to be missed or done away with without obscuring the structural meaning of the sentence, as indeed anyone knows who has ever written a telegram or a newspaper headline. On the other hand, sentences which do not have enough of these formal devices are inevitably ambiguous. Take the example already given, Fries's "ship sails today." This is ambiguous because there is nothing to indicate which of the first two words is performing a noun function and which a verb function. If we mark the noun by putting the noun-determining function-word "the" in front of it, the ambiguity disappears; we have either "the ship sails today" or "ship the sails today." The ambiguity could just as well be resolved by using other devices: consider "ship sailed today," "ship to sail today," "ship sail today," "shipping sails today," "shipment of sails today," and so on. It is simply a question of having enough formal devices in the sentence to indicate its structural meaning clearly.

How powerful the structural meanings of English are is illustrated by so-called "nonsense." In English, nonsense as a literary form often consists of utterances that have a clear structural meaning but use words that either have no lexical meaning, or whose lexical meanings are inconsistent one with another. This will become apparent if we subject a rather famous bit of English nonsense to formal grammatical analysis:

All mimsy were the borogoves
And the mome raths outgrabe.

This passage consists of ten words, five of them words that should have lexical meaning but don't, one standard verb, and four function-words. In so far as it is possible to indicate its abstract structure, it would be this:

All .... y were the .... s
And the ...   ... s   ....

Although this is a relatively simple formal organization, it signals some rather complicated meanings. The first thing we observe is that the first line presents a conflict: word order seems to signal one thing, and inflections and function-words something else. Specifically, "mimsy" is in the position normally occupied by the subject, but we know that it is not the subject and that "borogoves" is. We know this because there is an inflectional tie between the form "were" and the "s" ending of "borogoves," because there is the noun determiner "the" before it, and because the alternative candidate for subject, "mimsy," lacks both of these. It is true that "mimsy" does have the function-word "all" before it, which may indicate a noun; but when it does, the noun is either plural (in which case "mimsy" would most likely end in "s"), or else the noun is what grammarians call a mass-word (like "sugar," "coal," "snow"), in which case the verb would have to be "was," not "were." All these formal considerations are sufficient to counteract the effect of word order and show that the sentence is of the type that may be represented thus:

All gloomy were the Democrats.

Actually there is one other possibility. If "mimsy" belongs to the small group of nouns which don't use "s" to make the plural, and if "borogoves" has been so implied (but not specifically mentioned) in the context as to justify its appearing with the determiner "the," the sentence would then belong to the following type:

[In the campaign for funds] all alumni were the canvassers.
[In the drought last summer] all cattle were the sufferers.

But the odds are so much against this that most of us would be prepared to fight for our belief that "borogoves" are things that can be named, and that at the time referred to they were in a complete state of "mimsyness."

Moving on to the second line, "And the mome raths outgrabe," the first thing we note is that the "And" signals another parallel assertion to follow. We are thus prepared to recognize from the noun-determiner "the," the plural inflection "s," and the particular positions of "mome" and "outgrabe," as well as the continuing influence of the "were" of the preceding line, that we are dealing with a sentence of this pattern:

And the lone rats agreed.

The influence of the "were" is particularly important here; it guides us in selecting among several interpretations of the sentence. Specifically, it requires us to identify "outgrabe" as a verb in the past tense, and thus a "strong" or "irregular" verb, since it lacks the characteristic past-tense ending "d" or "ed." We do this in spite of the fact that there is another strong candidate for the position of verb: that is, "raths," which bears a regular verb inflection and could be tied with "mome" as its subject in the normal noun-verb relationship. In such a case we should have to recognize "outgrabe" as either an adverb of the kind not marked by the form-contrast ending "ly," an adjective, or the past participle of a strong verb. The sentence would then belong to one of the following types:

And the moon shines above.
And the man stays aloof.
And the fool seems outdone.

But we reject all of these—probably they don't even occur to us —because they all have verbs in the present tense, whereas the "were" of the first line combines with the "And" at the beginning of the second to set the whole in the past.

We might recognize one further possibility for the structural meaning of this second line, particularly in the verse context, since we are used to certain patterns in verse that do not often appear in speech or prose. The "were" of the first line could be understood as doing double duty, its ghost or echo appearing between "raths" and "outgrabe." Then we would have something like this:

All gloomy were the Democrats
And the home folks outraged.

But again the odds are pretty heavy against this. I for one am so sure that "outgrabe" is the past tense of a strong verb that I can give its present. In my dialect, at least, it is "outgribe."

The reader may not realize it, but in the last four paragraphs I have been discussing grammar from a purely formal point of view. I have not once called a word a noun because it names something (that is, I have not once resorted to meaning), nor have I called any word an adjective because it modifies a noun (that is, resorted to function). Instead I have been working in the opposite direction, from form toward function and meaning. I have used only criteria which are objectively observable, and I have assumed only a working knowledge of certain structural patterns and devices known to all speakers of English over the age of six. I did use some technical terms like "noun," "verb," and "tense," but only to save time; I could have got along without them.

If one clears his mind of the inconsistencies of the traditional grammar (not so easy a process as it might be), he can proceed with a similarly rigorous formal analysis of a sufficient number of representative utterances in English and come out with a descriptive grammar. This is just what Professor Fries did in gathering and studying the material for the analysis he presents in the remarkable book to which I have already referred, *The Structure of English.* What he actually did was to put a tape recorder into action and record about fifty hours of telephone conversation among the good citizens of Ann Arbor, Michigan. When this material was transcribed, it constituted about a quarter of a million words of perfectly natural speech by educated middle-class Americans. The details of his conclusions cannot be presented here, but they are sufficiently different from the usual grammar to be revolutionary. For instance, he recognizes only four parts of speech among the words with lexical meaning, roughly corresponding to what the traditional grammar calls substantives, verbs, adjectives, and adverbs, though to avoid preconceived notions from the traditional grammar Fries calls them Class 1, Class 2, Class 3, and Class 4 words. To these he adds a relatively small group of function-words, 154 in his materials, which he divides into fifteen groups. These must be memorized by anyone learning the language; they are not subject to the same kind of general rules that govern the four parts of speech. Undoubtedly his conclusions will be developed and modified by himself and by other linguistic scholars, but for the present his book remains the most complete treatment extant of English grammar from the point of view of linguistic science.

[7]   Two vital questions are raised by this revolution in grammar. The first is, "What is the value of this new system?" In the minds of many who ask it, the implication of this question is, "We have been getting along all these years with traditional grammar, so it can't be so very bad. Why should we go through the painful

process of unlearning and relearning grammar just because linguistic scientists have concocted some new theories?"

The first answer to this question is the bravest and most honest. It is that the superseding of vague and sloppy thinking by clear and precise thinking is an exciting experience in and for itself. To acquire insight into the workings of a language, and to recognize the infinitely delicate system of relationship, balance, and interplay that constitutes its grammar, is to become closely acquainted with one of man's most miraculous creations, not unworthy to be set beside the equally beautiful organization of the physical universe. And to find that its most complex effects are produced by the multi-layered organization of relatively simple materials is to bring our thinking about language into accord with modern thought in other fields, which is more and more coming to emphasize the importance of organization—the fact that an organized whole is truly greater than the sum of all its parts.

There are other answers, more practical if less philosophically valid. It is too early to tell, but it seems probable that a realistic, scientific grammar should vastly facilitate the teaching of English, especially as a foreign language. Already results are showing here; it has been found that if intonation contours and other structural patterns are taught quite early, the student has a confidence that allows him to attempt to speak the language much sooner than he otherwise would.

The new grammar can also be of use in improving the native speaker's proficiency in handling the structural devices of his own language. In other words, Grammar 2, if it is accurate and consistent, *can* be of use in improving skill in Grammar 1. An illustration is that famous bugaboo, the dangling participle. Consider a specific instance of it, which once appeared on a college freshman's theme, to the mingled delight and despair of the instructor:

Having eaten our lunch, the steamboat departed.

What is the trouble with this sentence? Clearly there must be something wrong with it, because it makes people laugh, although it was not the intent of the writer to make them laugh. In other words, it produces a completely wrong response, resulting in total breakdown of communication. It is, in fact, "bad grammar" in a much more serious way than are mere dialectal divergences like "he ain't here" or "he never seen none," which produce social reactions but communicate effectively. In the light of the new grammar, the trouble with our dangling participle is that the form, instead of leading to the meaning, is in conflict with it. Into the position which, in this pattern, is reserved for the word naming the eater of the lunch, the writer has inserted the word "steamboat." The resulting tug-of-war between form and meaning is only momentary; meaning quickly wins out, simply because our common sense tells us that steamboats don't eat lunches. But if the pull of the lexical meaning is not given a good deal of help from common sense, the form will conquer the meaning, or the two will remain in ambiguous equilibrium—as, for instance, in "Having eaten our lunch, the passengers boarded the steamboat." Writers will find it easier to avoid such troubles if they know about the forms of English and are taught to use the form to convey the meaning, instead of setting up tensions between form and meaning. This, of course, is what English teachers are already trying to do. The new grammar should be a better weapon in their arsenal than the traditional grammar, since it is based on a clear understanding of the realities.

The second and more difficult question is, "How can the change from one grammar to the other be effected?" Here we face obstacles of a formidable nature. When we remember the controversies attending on revolutionary changes in biology and astronomy, we realize what a tenacious hold the race can maintain on anything it has once learned, and the resistance it can offer to new ideas. And remember that neither astronomy nor biology was taught in the elementary schools. They were, in fact, rather specialized subjects in advanced education. How then change grammar, which is taught to everybody, from the fifth grade up through college? The vested interest represented by thousands upon thousands of English and Speech teachers who have learned the traditional grammar and taught it for many years is a conservative force comparable to those which keep us still using the chaotic system of English spelling and the unwieldy measuring system of inches and feet, pounds and ounces, quarts, bushels, and acres. Moreover, this army is constantly receiving new recruits. It is possible in my state to become certified to teach English in high school if one has had eighteen credit hours of college English—let us say two semesters of freshman composition (almost all of which is taught by people unfamiliar with the new grammar), two semesters of a survey course in English literature, one semester of Shakespeare, and one semester of the contemporary novel. And since hard-pressed school administrators feel that anyone who can speak English can in a pinch teach it, the result is that many people are called upon to teach grammar whose knowledge of the subject is totally inadequate.

There is, in other words, a battle ahead of the new grammar. It will have to fight not only the apathy of the general public but the ignorance and inertia of those who count themselves competent in the field of grammar. The battle is already on, in fact. Those who try to get the concepts of the new grammar introduced into the curriculum are tagged as "liberal" grammarians—the implication being, I suppose, that one has a free choice between "liberal" and "conservative" grammar, and that the liberals are a bit dangerous, perhaps even a touch subversive. They are accused of undermining standards, of holding that "any way of saying something is just as good as any other," of not teaching the fundamentals of good English. I trust that the readers of this article will see how unfounded these charges are. But the smear campaign is on. So far as I know, neither religion nor patriotism has yet been brought into it. When they are, Professor Fries will have to say to Socrates, Galileo, Darwin, Freud, and the other members of the honorable fraternity of the misunderstood, "Move over, gentlemen, and make room for me."

A Brief Bibliography

GRAMMARS

Lowth, Robert. *A Short Introduction to English Grammar*. London, 1762. This is the granddaddy of English "school" grammars. A Latin grammar Englished, with a good bit of prescriptive usage based on Latin and "logic" thrown in, it has been openly and covertly scissored-and-paste-potted for nearly two centuries—often, alas, in ignorance.

Sweet, Henry. *A New English Grammar*. 2 vols. Oxford, Clarendon Press, 1892, 1898. Of first importance, this is a logical and historical grammar; it is the bravest attempt at a logical grammar of English ever made, though Sweet abandons the logical approach. His logical basis is Lockean psychology and Newtonian physics.

Curme, George O. *Syntax*. New York, Heath, 1931. *Parts of Speech and Accidence*. Boston, Heath, 1935. A well-packed grammar, from an old-fashioned functional point of view, this is probably the best known of American grammars worthy of the name.

Jespersen, Otto. *Essentials of English Grammar*. New York, Holt, Rinehart and Winston, 1933. A one-volume abridgment of Jespersen's big grammar, this presents what is now considered old-fashioned formalism.

Aiken, Janet Rankin. *A New Plan of English Grammar*. New York, Holt, Rinehart and Winston, 1933. Now out of print and difficult to find, this is a remarkably simplified and coherent functional approach; but functional concepts are extremely hard to define, and this otherwise fine book glosses over that hard fact.

Fries, Charles Carpenter. *American English Grammar*. New York, Appleton-Century, 1940. The first "scientific" study of American English, a significant mark in the study of English grammar, and of great influence upon all subsequent American grammars of consequence, this is indispensable reading for all teachers of English, along with Fries's *The Structure of English*, New York, Harcourt, Brace and World, 1952. A study of spoken English (the former book studies written English), with radically new terminology, this is the most influential and perhaps best written "structural" grammar.

Roberts, Paul. *Understanding Grammar*. New York, Harper and Row, 1954. A transitional grammar, this best explains and reconciles logical, functional, and formal points of view. By the time the book appeared, Roberts had "gone structural": his *Patterns of English*, New York, Harcourt, Brace and World, 1957, is a structural grammar for high school use; and his *Understanding English*, New York, Harper and Row, 1958, is a handbook for freshman English in college with structural approach. His *English Sentences*, New York, Harcourt, Brace and World, 1961, introduces transformational ideas at the high school level. All are beautifully written.

Myers, L. M. *American English*. Englewood Cliffs, N. J., Prentice-Hall, 1952. Written with admirable lucidity and charm, this grammar approaches the language from the point of view of form.

Whitehall, Harold. *Structural Essentials of English.* New York, Harcourt, Brace and World, 1956. A structural approach to written English, with new and to some extent individual terminology, this is a short and exciting book, but not entirely consistent: Whitehall's treatment of connectives, for instance, is logical.

Lloyd, Donald J. and Harry R. Warfel. *American English in its Cultural Setting.* New York, Knopf, 1956. A treatment of the language from the structural point of view, this, as its title suggests, ranges rather farther into backgrounds than other books of its type.

Zandvoort, Robert. *A Handbook of English Grammar.* London, Longmans, Green, 1957. A traditional book, but, like Sweet and Curme, rich in details.

Brown, Dona Worrall, Wallace C. Brown, and Dudley Bailey. *Form in Modern English.* New York, Oxford, 1958. An introductory grammar with structural approach but traditional terminology, this is simply written and usable at high school as well as college level.

Sledd, James. *A Short Introduction to English Grammar.* Chicago, Scott, Foresman, 1959. A structural approach, with, for the most part, traditional terminology, this covers phonology, morphology, and syntax and has a fine chapter on applied grammar—a discussion of problems of English prose style.

Ives, Sumner. *A New Handbook for Writers.* New York, Knopf, 1960. A handbook for freshman English in college, this text has structural approach but largely traditional terminology.

Long, Ralph B. *The Sentence and Its Parts.* Chicago, University of Chicago, 1961. Remarkably rich in details, in the tradition of Jespersen and Curme, this is a sophisticated functional grammar which makes use of recent linguistic findings.

THE BIG ENGLISH GRAMMARS

Jespersen, Otto. *A Modern English Grammar.* 6 vols. Heidelberg, C. Winter, 1901–1941. The most comprehensive of English grammars, this great work is on the one hand imaginative and detailed but on the other hand ridden, like all of Jespersen's work, by curious inconsistencies.

Poutsma, H. *Grammar of Late Modern English.* 5 vols. Groningen, Noordhoff, 1914–1929. A massive collection of grammatical details, but not of interest for new ideas or theories.

Kruisinga, Etsko. *A Handbook of Present Day English.* 4 vols. Groningen, Noordhoff, 5th Edition, 1931. Like Poutsma, and in the same sense inferior to the work of Jespersen.

THE BIG DICTIONARIES

New English Dictionary (also known as the *Oxford English Dictionary;* also known as *Murray's English Dictionary*). 12 vols. and Supplement. Oxford, Clarendon Press, 1884–1928, 1933. Easily the greatest of English dictionaries, though already in need of revision, this is known as the *NED* or *OED.* Ignorance of it is unforgivable.

Century Dictionary and Cyclopedia. New York, Century, 1891 (and many later editions). 6 to 10 vols., depending on edition. Though somewhat dated, this is the greatest of American dictionaries.

Dictionary of American English. 4 vols. Chicago University Press, 1936–1944. A supplement to the NED, concentrating upon American English. Called the *DAE.*

Webster's New International Dictionary, 3rd ed. Springfield, Mass., Merriam, 1961. The "unabridged" dictionary, this has probably more entries than any other (excepting its predecessor, the 2nd edition), but by no means the wealth of information to be found in the *NED, DAE,* or Century.

HISTORIES OF THE ENGLISH LANGUAGE

Baugh, Albert C. *History of the English Language,* 2nd ed. New York, Appleton-Century-Crofts, 1957. Usually regarded as the standard book on the subject, this is well complemented by both Robertson and Schlauch.

Robertson, Stuart. *The Development of Modern English,* 2nd ed. Revised by Frederic Cassidy. Englewood Cliffs, N. J., Prentice-Hall, 1954. This is especially strong on word formation, changes of meanings and values of words, and modern English.

Schlauch, Margaret. *The English Language in Modern Times.* Warsaw, Panstwowe Wydawnictwo Naulowe, 1959 (distributed outside Poland by Oxford University Press). A description of English since the fourteenth century, less rich than Baugh or Robertson-Cassidy on vocabulary, more succinct on phonology and morphology, and especially strong on syntax; includes suggestive comment on English prose style in each century since Chaucer.

Marckwardt, Albert H. *Introduction to the English Language.* New York, Oxford, 1942. Truly an introduction, this text works from modern English back to Old English and presents a series of inductive exercises for students. Not so full as Baugh or Robertson-Cassidy, but in ways rather more exciting.

Jespersen, Otto. *The Growth and Structure of the English Language,* 8th ed. Leipsig, Tuebner, 1935. (Reprinted in paperback, Doubleday Anchor Books, 1955.) This has the usual charm of the "great Dane," but is neither so full nor so accurate as Baugh or Robertson-Cassidy.

AMERICAN ENGLISH

Krapp, George P. *The English Language in America.* 2 vols. New York, Appleton-Century-Crofts, 1925. The standard book, full and accurate (but now dated), but by no means so excitingly written as Mencken.

Mencken, H. L. *The American Language,* 4th ed. New York, Knopf, 1936. A lively book, written brilliantly, this is subject to an overdose of Anglophobia.

Marckwardt, Albert H. *American English.* New York, Oxford, 1958. A running story of the development of American English, with emphasis upon the cultural factors which influenced its development.

SEMANTICS

Hayakawa, S. I. *Language in Action.* New York, Harcourt, Brace and World, 1949. An easy introduction to "semantics," or the study of the problems of meaning in language, this is fast and fascinating reading.

USAGE

Fowler, H. W. *A Dictionary of Modern English Usage.* Oxford, Clarendon, 1926. For a full generation *the* authority on English usage, this, usually abbreviated *MEU*, is one of the juiciest books ever compiled.

Nicholson, Margaret. *A Dictionary of American-English Usage.* New York, Oxford, 1957. Based on Fowler, much of whose best stuff is retained, this is a much more conservative and on the whole less satisfactory authority than

Evans, Bergen, and Cornelia Evans. *Dictionary of Contemporary American Usage.* New York, Random House, 1957. Reflecting a liberal linguistic viewpoint, this is an accurate authority on present American usage.

Perrin, Porter G. *Index to English.* Chicago, Scott, Foresman, 1939. (With Perrin's *Writer's Guide,* 1942; revised 1950.) For nearly twenty years, the best American dictionary of usage, and still quite good, but now pretty much replaced by the fuller dictionaries of Nicholson and the Evanses, this book had immense effect on college teaching of English.

Hook, J. N., and E. G. Mathews. *Modern American Grammar and Usage.* New York, Ronald, 1956. As its title suggests, this is more than a dictionary of usage. It has a good bit of carefully established information on current American usage, as well as really fine chapters on the backgrounds of present study and on the major questions involved in such study.

LINGUISTICS

Bloomfield, Leonard. *Language.* New York, Holt, Rinehart and Winston, 1933. Quite difficult reading, but probably the most important book on language in the past century.

Sturtevant, Edgar H. *An Introduction to Linguistic Science.* New Haven, Conn., Yale University, 1947. A reliable and readable introduction.

Hall, Robert A. *Leave Your Language Alone.* Ithaca, N. Y., Linguistica, 1950. A fresh statement of the modern linguist's view about language study.

Gleason, Henry A., Jr. *An Introduction to Descriptive Linguistics,* rev. ed. New York, Holt, Rinehart and Winston, 1961. Probably the most satisfactory introductory text on the subject.

Bloch, Bernard, and George L. Trager. *Outline of Linguistic Analysis.* Baltimore, Linguistic Society of America, 1942. Along with Trager and Henry Lee Smith, Jr., *An Outline of English Structure,* Norman, Okla., Battenburg Press, 1951, basic summaries of American linguistic principles.

Francis, W. Nelson. *The Structure of American English.* New York, Ronald, 1958. The most readable full treatment of the language from a structural linguistic point of view.

Hockett, Charles F. *A Course in Modern Linguistics*. New York, Macmillan, 1958. More difficult than Gleason or Francis; but three good chapters at the end.

Hill, Archibald A. *Introduction to Linguistic Structures*. New York, Harcourt, Brace and World, 1958. Rather difficult; but interesting appendices on Eskimo and Latin.

Chomsky, Noam. *Syntactic Structures*. The Hague, Mouton, 1957. A criticism of the structural linguists which offers a partial summary of the "transformational" or "generative" approach to language study. Difficult reading, but it has had tremendous effect upon American linguists.